IRIDOLOGY

How to discover your own
pattern of health and well-being
through the eye

Dorothy Hall

PIATKUS

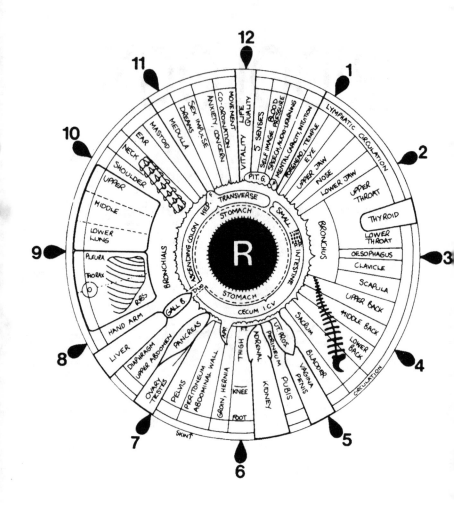

The Iris Map, right eye
(*looking at another person's right eye*)

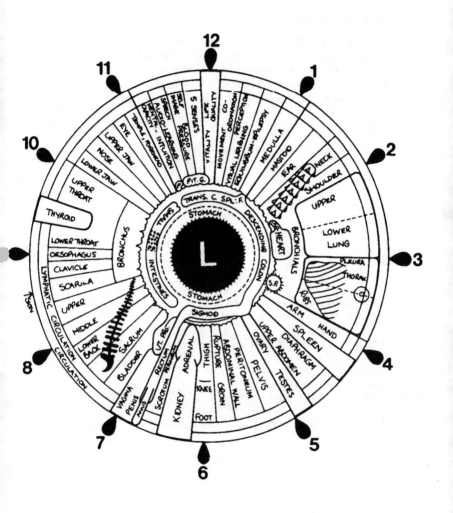

The Iris Map, left eye
(*looking at another person's right eye*)

About the Author

Dorothy Hall is the teaching principal of her own herbal medicine college at which iridology is taught as a diagnostic tool. She is a naturopath and herbalist and has written nine books including best-sellers *The Book of Herbs* and *The Natural Health Book*.

First published in Great Britain in 1994 by
Judy Piatkus (Publishers) Ltd of
5 Windmill Street, London W1P 1HF

First paperback edition 1994

First published by Thomas Nelson,
Australia, 1980 and Penguin
Books, Australia Limited, 1989

A catalogue record for this book is
available from the British Library

ISBN 0-7499-1343-6
      0-7499-1343-6 (pbk)

Illustrated by Richard Gregory
Cover design by Ron Hampton

Set in Linotron Baskerville by
Professional Data Bureau, London SW17
Printed & bound in Great Britain by
Bookcraft Ltd, Midsomer Norton, Avon

Contents

1

INTRODUCTION

Don't you wish you could know a person through from outside to inside at first meeting? Assess strengths and weaknesses; likes and dislikes; compatibility with you; understand what they're all about—before signing a lease, entering a relationship, or launching a business?

When you meet someone new, look objectively at his eyes as an indicator of the whole person. What colour are they? is that colour clear and bright or muddy-looking? Do you get a good feeling from looking directly at him? Is he getting the same feeling from looking at you? Why are you both looking at each other's *eyes*, anyway: not hands or hair or other more or less obvious personal characteristics?

Try a simple experiment. Go through a magazine or newspaper and black out only the eyes of people in the photographs. Do you now find it much more difficult to assess their ages, their sex even, their character, and their *life* quality? You can't tell whether they're animated or lethargic, happy or sad, can you?

Black out the sparkles in the eyes of Al Pacino and he becomes just an oval-faced man with dark hair and regular features. Similarly, black out the cautious eyes of Prince Charles and he loses his dignity.

1

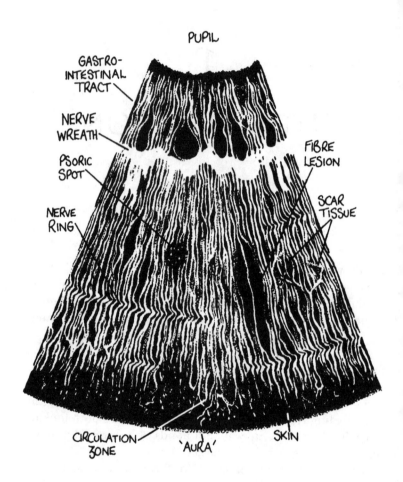

Iris Features

INTRODUCTION

One lovely man of my acquaintance complains that women shut their eyes in bed, while men don't. Ladies, keep your eyes open and enjoy the difference!

How many descriptions of emotional states refer to eyes? Eyes 'glazed with fear', 'blazing with anger'; 'starry-eyed with love', 'pop-eyed with surprise', 'cold-eyed and calculating'. Does someone talk to you but gaze over the top of your head and around the room? Forget him or her. Does another look deeply into your eyes, and instinctively you trust and feel secure? 'Eyeball to eyeball' contact is a primal recognition system available to humans. How to interpret what you can see can be a simple process of feeling or a complicated one of analysis. Scientific study of what is visible in eyes has begun again: the Chinese used it in antiquity, and it was reintroduced by Dr Ignats von Peczeley, a German doctor, late last century.

In my own practice as a naturopath and herbalist I listen to symptoms and case histories and make a general assessment of the patient. The eyes then provide me with the 'fine-tuning' analysis of biochemistry and of emotional and circumstantial factors hard to determine by any other method. Illnesses past and present can still be visible, recorded in the iris; and measures can be taken to treat the present ones and prevent recurrence. I enjoy working with children, for often a lifetime's potential ill-health pattern can be spotted before it begins and nutritional, emotional, or circumstantial correction or prevention can be undertaken. Looking at eyes can save taxpayers' money!

As with any system, skills must be acquired to make accurate assessment. Therapeutic analysis from the eye is a delicate art/science needing years of training; but anyone can learn some basic indications. Examples and photographs in this book should give you general competence: but don't suddenly inform your girlfriend that her right kidney is failing as you gaze into her eyes over the praline and cherry brandy!

If more accuracy in assessing people can be gained, better and more positive communication can be established with them. As a tool for people-analysis there's more in eyes than meets the eye!

Before we begin to explore the intricate personal map of the iris, its shapes, colours, and patterns, it is necessary to learn a few simple skills in using an iris torch to give some increase in light and magnification.

Please study these instructions well before you attempt to look at *any* eyes, even your own.

HOW TO INSPECT AN IRIS

I have used many types of equipment for iris observation, and still feel that the best instrument for the layman is a hand-held magnifying lens of the type used in looking at stamps. These are available from optical instrument retailers and sometimes from optometrists and electrical and hardware stores. The one I prefer is the Peake Light Lupe, 10x magnification, which is a simple torch, battery-powered, with a circular lens-piece fitting which can be placed up close to the eye as you bend your head down to sight through its eye-piece.

I prefer to look at a patient's iris *from the side*. A face-to-face confrontation only a few millimetres apart is off-putting to many people. Stand at their side, gently lift the top eyelid with your index finger, and keep your own head and body at the least point of contact with the person's face. There is nothing more disconcerting than a fascinated would-be iridologist breathing his garlic lunch all over you as he mutters and exclaims a millimetre away from your cheekbone!

Children and animals, even some people, are instinctively wary of what they allow close to an eye. The sideways approach *slowly* is reassuring. I often get small children to look through the torch first at a parent's eye, to look at the big black 'hole' and the blue colour, and even to look for a pixie in there, or a rainbow, as hard as they can. I then reverse the torch and look at the wide-open iris as fast as possible.

Many adults shrink backwards as the light, torch, and iridologist's head approach them. Leaning the person's head on the back of a chair, or against a wall, gets over this one. Have the patient face directly ahead and look as straight forward and as *still* in gaze as possible. Give him a point to stare at, if necessary, to place the iris as centrally to the torch as possible. An eye looking all about, and a head turned sideways towards you, make an accurate reading impossible.

O Never Leave A Torch On Too Long Over The Eye

This is *the* most important rule for a layman iridologist. Remember how sensitive is that apparatus in there, and expose the eye to light for no more than about ten seconds at a time. Move away, write something down, let the eye relax, then come back again. This is why I don't like the torch-and-magnifying-glass type of equipment. The intensified light can be used in a clinical situation; but damage to the eye is a possibility if it is used at home. The medical headpiece of magnifying glass and optical beam is a specialised tool and certainly not for amateurs.

Don't make the mistake of asking for 'a thing to look at eyes with', and being sold an ophthalmoscope. It's a thing to look at *irises* with (an iris torch) that you need.

There is a safer way to take your time and inspect an iris— your own or someone else's. Have a photograph taken with a specialised iris camera and project the transparency onto your living-room wall. Please remember, though, that it's not a parlour-game. You may learn a little or you may learn much from it; but it's as close as you'll get to the soul of the person in there, so tread lightly, and with understanding.

My own iris camera, a magnificently accurate piece of German engineering, has provided the photographs for this book. Many changes in irises are recorded as treatment progresses, and I often take photographs of unusual, or typical, or 'unexplainable', iris indications in order to teach my students. The camera photograph eliminates movement and makes placement of the zones and boundaries more accurate than observation from the iris itself allows. Keep a record of your health year to year. A different birthday present for the person who has everything!

Ask many questions as you look at irises. Patient feedback is not only helpful but absolutely necessary. How else will you decide whether that white flare at the 'lower jaw' is an infected tooth, a mouth ulcer, an old fracture, or suppressed emotion? The patient must contribute towards the puzzle putting-together.

Let me inspire you with the feelings I experience every time I look at an iris: awe at the complexity; astonishment at the simplicity; and a humble, awareness of the proud individuality of each one of us. There is nothing so personally your own as your irises and the story they tell.

2

AROUND
THE CLOCK

*The Circles, Segments And
Zones Of The Eye*

Identification of structural types and biochemical variables
can be made from a general view of the iris; but how can it
be determined whether it's your liver, your pancreas, or your
stomach, that's the prime cause of your indigestion problems? Is it an infected kidney that's producing the recurrent
cystitis attacks, or is it just an over-acid and inflamed
bladder? Does your migraine stem from vascular congestion
under tension and stress, or is it hormonally triggered by
your endocrine glands? A more detailed system of analysis
is needed to pinpoint *causes*; to identify body systems and
organs which may not be functioning at their optimum peak.
From experience, a method has evolved of classifying these
zones.

   If we think of both irises as circular 'clock-faces', segments
can be marked off radially at '1 o'clock', '2 o'clock', and so
on, to divide the iris into twelve basic zones. It's simpler to
talk about 'a brown flare at ten past two, right iris' than to
say 'in the tonsil zone'; for the latter method needs constant
reference to an iris chart to recall where the tonsil zone is.
Looking at the eyes of another person, read each iris round
clockwise, from 12 o'clock at the top. Looking at your own

irises in a mirror, you must, of course, reverse the whole clock-face.

READING THE CIRCLES

Let's assume that you are looking at the irises of a friend, using a low magnification iris torch (see p. 4). In his otherwise clear blue irises, you find some yellowish-white foggy 'blobs', and you imagine the clock-face numerals superimposed. These patches of discoloration fall between 9 o'clock and 10 o'clock in the right iris. A quick reference to your iris chart, and you see this sector of the circle allotted to bronchial tree and right lung. Which is it? Or is it both? Or do you need yet another system of division to decide? As well as the radial sections of the clock face, a second system of concentric circles helps to make an analysis even more accurately based.

It always astounds me that simplicity is regarded as too plain and direct to be 'scientific'. To be *recognised*, by more orthodox medicine, a system seems required to be complex and therefore impossible for a mere layman to understand. Happily, the iris and its implications are mostly free of such complexity. Its geometric logic, and the few circles, segments, and zones, of iridology take no more understanding than common sense can provide.

○ The Three Inner Circles

Commencing from the pupil outwards, try to visualise the iris as a direct diagram, representational of the body and its *layers*. The most obvious innermost circle around the pupillary margin represents the inner 'pipe' of the body, centrally placed: the digestive tract of stomach and small and large intestines. The structure and biochemical function of this body system is of prime importance, and, as we shall see later, problems originating in this circular zone can spill out into the next circular section: the *organs* area lying adjacent to its outside rim.

Between these two circles—the digestive tract and bowel and organs area—lies another fine circle, often visible without any magnification or close observation as being *different* from the rest of the iris. To find its significance in analysis we must learn some simple anatomy and physiology.

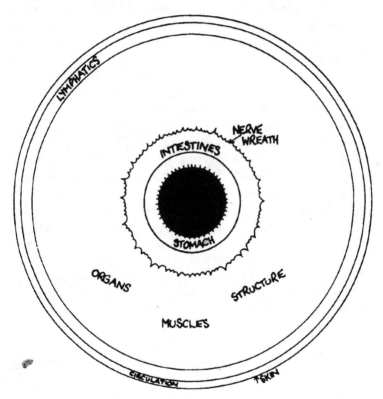

Iris Zones

I call it 'the spinal nerve wreath', but it represents the autonomic nervous system—the self-regulating control system which monitors body functions without the need for

conscious command. Our breathing; the peristaltic movement of the bowel; the nerve supply to various organs; even
our ability to stand up without falling over—are all jobs for
this system. Although we can 'interfere' with our conscious
mind and redirect many of its functions (put off having a
bowel movement until we get home from work; stiffen up a
sagging spine mid-afternoon by some yoga postures; issue an
'adrenal command' to muscles exhausted from athletic effort
to give just that extra spurt of strength to win), our
autonomic nervous system can keep going at its own speed
and in some sort of balance without conscious direction at
all. It jogs along at lower revs while we are asleep; but at no
time does it close down even some of its functions unless it
is damaged by illness of physical origin.

This part of the nervous system has little to do with the
type of illness one of my patients so simply described: 'I've
got nerves,' he said apologetically and miserably. 'So have
I,' I answered; 'but what you are suffering from is *emotions*,
not nerves.' Emotional causes of nervous overload can
certainly contribute to *imbalance* between the 'unconscious'
and conscious nervous systems; but each is separate in
function. It is true that if you are an 'uptight' person your
bowel may also be uptight and chronic constipation may be
your lot. This is what I mean by an imbalance between the
two systems. Your bowel should function regularly and
automatically without being interfered with by your head's
unnecessary meddling.

So this thin circle representing autonomic nerves can show
whether you are letting your body 'do its own thing' or
whether you are interfering with what should be automatic
processes. The 'nerve wreath' also shows the boundary
between those functions which are automatically controlled
and those which can be more consciously directed. *Inside* the
nerve wreath are the stomach, and small and large intestine
areas; outside are those functions and structures more under
the control of direct will.

Theoretically, the nerve wreath should be visible about
one-third of the way out from pupil to iris margin. Many

people show this average good balance between the sympathetic and parasympathetic systems of control, but others have a nerve wreath so closely contracted towards the pupil as to be barely visible. These are the ones with uptight conscious control—over-strong 'meddlers' in their body's automatic processes.

If the nerve wreath is farther out than one-third the distance from the pupil to the iris edge, this person is much more at the mercy of body demands. The body rules here, sending all sorts of requests and signals which the conscious control has little hope of denying. More about the nerve wreath is on pp. 189-93.

○ The Next, Wider Circle

The organs and glands, as body units (distinct from their food and control systems), are represented in the next, wider circular area. The bones and general body structure are also found in this wide zone. Simplicity applies here, too. As we progress out from the centre of the iris we move out to less central body areas. In this zone we find the liver and the spleen and the kidneys, and glands like the adrenals and the pancreas and the thyroid also show their condition. Body 'spaces' also show here: abdominal cavity, pleural cavities hollow pipes, like bronchial tree and oesophagus; hollow organs like uterus and bladder. Within this broad general zone are moving parts of various body systems, showing their structure and function. A quick look at our basic charts at the front and back of the book will show some of these organs in radiating sections right from the autonomic circle to the outer rim of the iris.

Let's take as an example the spleen (4.15-4.30, left iris). It is quite a large organ physically, so it merits a large iris area. But say you find a small congested brownish spot right up close to the nerve circle in one person's iris, and a similar congestion spot close to the outer rim of the iris in another's. How do you interpret the difference? To do this we must progress through yet another circle, lying around the outer periphery of the iris: the circulation zone. This rather narrow area shows circulation to and from the organs and body parts adjacent to each section of it.

○ Circulation Zones

Some iridologists, particularly the Germans and French, place a secondary circulation area close in against the nerve wreath, representing *deep* circulation and major arteries and veins. Though sometimes this second zone is disturbed in function and structure in the same way as the outer circulation circle is, for our purposes, the outer circulation zone is accurate enough.

Let's go back to our spleen example. The congestion patch lying closer to the nerve wreath, or nerve circle, could be expected to be caused by poor or impeded *nerve* supply to the organ; the congestion lying farther out towards the circulation zone could be assessed as poor or impeded blood supply to that organ. If a third person showed such a discoloured patch in the spleen centrally placed between the other two, this would indicate congestion of the spleen itself.

You can see how such accuracy of diagnosis can help a therapist in deciding whether to treat the nervous system, the circulatory system, or the organ itself—or even all three if the condition shows as affecting all three together.

This narrowing of diagnostic possibilities is one of the most valuable uses of iris analysis in clinical practice. As an example, I remember a patient who came to me with an illness classified by his medical practitioner as 'gout' in the left foot. He was a heavy drinker and showed all the text-book symptoms of gout: swollen, hot red foot and toes, extreme pain and pressure, irritability, and the gaining of some relief with the foot elevated above the horizontal. A look at his iris, however, showed a different story. Circulation of blood and lymphatic fluid to and from the left foot was blocked around a lymph gland just above the ankle, causing all the symptoms. Gravity helped, when the foot was elevated, to drain the blockage somewhat; but the iris indication explained why the medical treatment for gout had not produced the desired relief: it was not gout! Treatment with herbs to clear the lymphatic circulation blockage removed the symptoms within twenty-four hours, and they have never returned—in spite of continued heavy drinking. Excess uric acid, built up into crystals causing the pain and irritability of true gout, was just not the problem that time.

I have mentioned lymphatic circulation. This one of the nine body systems also registers in the circulation zone of the iris. You can allot a simple function to lymph glands if you think of them as members of the overall 'rubbish-removal' team of the body; and they do their work in collecting rubbish from cells and bloodstream. You could liken the bowels to the outside 'garbage can', having its accumulated and decomposing contents removed every so often. The kidneys do work similarly to a plastic garbage-bag full of liquid empties. The lungs have the effect of opening all the house windows to let out stale air and the unwanted smells of yesterday's cooking and cigarette-butts, since they excrete the metabolic remains of carbonic acid wastes, carbon dioxide. The lymph glands are like the kitchen garbage pail, removing day-to-day metabolic refuse from individual cells all over the body, and holding it in lymphatic ducts and storage/collection spots until it can be re-cycled through and out, via either the kidneys or bowels, or by another major excretory area, the skin. If you don't sweat when you should sweat, in heat and after exertion, your lymph glands may need a boost. The kitchen garbage-pail is overflowing, even though the outside garbage-can may have been recently emptied! (If your sweat is strong-smelling and over copious, your lymph glands may be subsidising slow or inefficient bowels and kidneys.) You can see then why the lymphatics show in the general circulation zone at the outer rim of the iris, approaching the outer physical 'envelope' of the body, the skin. Just *how* they show inefficiency and loss of function is mentioned in the chapter 'Special Signs'.

O Peripheral Margin—The Skin

Just as the skin 'contains' all of the physical body, the peripheral margin of the iris can indicate what sort of package you are in. Does your skin glow with a healthy colour and shine, or is it dull, greyish, or—worse—greenish and covered in blemishes? The *colour* of the extreme outer rim of the iris can show an observer whether this enormous 'organ' (its square footage is surprising) is functioning efficiently as the packaging on which the outside world may assess you. I don't know about the 'skin-deep' beauties, but I know that I have never yet found a healthy skin without a healthy person inside it. This enormous body unit should show in the iris as clear-coloured (blue or brown) without greyish or yellowish tones.

A last zone outwards, circularly placed where the iris and the sclera (the white of the eye) meet, I find one of the most fascinating of all. Strictly speaking, it is outside the iris itself, but it shows the *interaction* of the person with the outside world. Have you an extra sensitive skin? Do you sniffle and snuffle in a room full of tobacco smoke? Are you hyper-reactive to 'bad vibes' from the people around you or the situations you find yourself in? The line where iris and sclera meet can be like a 'fringe', an open interaction with circumstances and people, showing that you may be too vulnerable, too 'damaged' by them. A harder, definite demarcation edge between iris and sclera can indicate a better-defended ego: 'slings and arrows' of any type do not affect your moods or your reactions to outside stimuli so much. A really insensitive person, over well-defended, not touched by anyone or anything except signals from his or her own ego centre, can show a hard edge, clearly defined, between iris colour and white sclera. Not much affects this person; but not much interaction takes place either.

One of the most fascinating irises I have ever seen was owned by a man who had all his life had an extreme sensitivity to all sorts of common contact stimuli on the skin. The wrong shirt material would make him cringe; new bed sheets had to be washed umpteen times before he could lie on them, an adhesive plaster on the skin could start up massive impetigo and red, angry inflammation. His iris showed one of the most sensitive 'fringe' borders I have ever seen; but it had been surrounded by a yellow intellectual 'control' of his reactions to people and their emotional impingement on him. His strong will had filtered away the damaging effect of other people's 'vibes', but the sensitive skin 'fringe' remained. I would also add that a *loving* touch of his skin was one of the happiest things he ever experienced. Watch this outer border of the iris for the non-physical, auric envelope of the person.

○ Muscle Indications In All Areas

In all this walking around the body, we have apparently ignored one major body system, the muscles. Muscle tone and function can be observed from several areas of the iris. First, we look for it in the big general 'moving parts' circle, but it can also show in the nerve wreath and again in the basic fibres radiating out from the pupil (the inherited structure). Muscles come in many layers of the body: the visceral deep layers around organs; the stronger middle layers around joints and articular parts of the skeleton; and surface muscles which can keep skin from sagging in folds around chin and abdomen and maintain a youthful resilience in that outside 'envelope'. So you could expect to find muscle indications in all these areas.

The straight, closely aligned fibres of a Silk-type iris indicate muscle strength as well as physical endurance due partly to such inherited patterns. But the *developed* muscle (from sporting training), or the overtight muscle group (the typist, working under deadline stress, with her copy always to her left side so that her trapezius and deltoid shoulder and neck muscles pull tighter and tighter as the deadline approaches), can often cause sharp *retractions* of the nerve-wreath circle back towards the pupil at that body segment.

It looks like, and is, a stressful *nerve* supply, pulling one muscle group tighter than the rest to meet the pressure. Many such *retractions* of the nerve wreath towards the pupil, in a sharp inwards-pointing V-shape, show up under various job stresses. Conversely, a relaxing outwards of the nerve wreath, away from the pupil, can indicate slack muscle-tone and function at that point.

Some asthmatics at the onset of the illness pattern, show sharp *retraction* of the nerve wreath at bronchial zones (over-tight diaphragm and chest muscles producing spasms under stress), then over-relaxed muscles and sagging outward of the nerve wreath as the illness becomes a chronic one (tired muscles, not relaxing after the spasms, but over-strained constantly and poor in tone always).

A very small pupil in relation to the rest of the iris can also indicate good or over-good muscle tone and function. Such a person needs regular and testing physical exercise to use up energy and allow muscles to relax.

The patient with 'nerves', mentioned previously, was not exhibiting any abnormal signs in the nerve-wreath circle, but much evidence to show that his *emotions* were producing disturbances and imbalance between his consciously and unconsciously controlled nervous systems, the sympathetic and the parasympathetic.

Let us go right back again to the inside border of the iris, up against the pupil. In some people, this border circle shows a pattern of reddish-brown 'cog-wheel' indentations. It is not the stomach zone we are talking of, but that border between it and the inner iris rim. Just as the outer rim of the iris shows one's interaction with the outside world, so does the inner rim show one's harmony, or otherwise, with one's deeper inner world. A person showing this brownish cog-wheel circle here will be most prone to illness as inner emotions produce turmoil that lowers energy and resistance to disease. This circle is often called the 'neurasthenic ring'. Such people can walk around hale and hearty in the middle of winter when flu has reduced all the rest of us to non-starters—*while they are emotionally harmonious.* But a sudden

16

emotional slump can produce an active flu virus within hours. They are over-reactive to their *inner* climate, as sensitive as those who get hay-fever when the nights get cold or the pollen flies about in spring breezes: but prey to attacks from within rather than without. Control of their own emotional climate should be a skill to be developed. An inner toughening-up is required, plus a turning away from what may be an obsession with their own mood fluctuations.

This innermost circle is, as you would expect, the central core of all the circular zones. Try once more to think of the iris as a 'map' of the body, and you will begin to see, after looking at many eyes, how the more particular zones, circles, and segments, refer to the anatomical arrangement of us all.

Please note:
The iris map (front endpaper) applies to viewing another person's eyes with a torch.

If looking at one's own eyes, the mirror image is seen and must be transposed, e.g. 10 o'clock is 2 o'clock, 4 o'clock is 8 o'clock and so on. Remember to allow for this. An iris map showing one's own eyes through a mirror can be found in the back endpaper.

RIGHT AND LEFT IRIS

If you are right-handed, the right side of your body is going to get more wear and tear physically than the left side; so you would expect to see more evidence of physical problems in the right iris. With a left-handed person, similar assumptions can be made, except that I have always found, from experience in my practice, that a left-handed person, even as a child, has some tendency towards limited right-hand usage. Truly ambidextrous people (and there are many more of them around than are ever classified) show both irises with almost identical configuration. My own extremely similar irises had always puzzled me, since I had from childhood been aggressively right-handed, having no inclination to use my left hand or left side at all. After a sailing accident to my right elbow, which immobilised it for six weeks, I was astounded at the ease with which my left hand started ironing, cooking, and lifting two small children—even signing my name to the satisfaction of my bank manager: skills I never knew it possessed. I now use either hand to do almost anything. Check your irises, and if one is hardly distinguishable from the other start developing your latent skills.

The majority of people show much more departure from 'normal' structure and function in one iris than in the other. This circumstance keeps chiropractors in business, because such constant over-use of one side in a potentially two-sided organism brings about much misalignment of bones constantly pulled out of anatomical balance by muscles and ligaments. Theoretically, and in practice, bones move around all day (and all night whilst you are asleep) as the muscles and ligaments pull them; but just as theoretically they should flop back into anatomical balance position as the muscles and ligaments let go again. In practice this does not often happen properly. Since muscles get more use on one side than the other they develop unevenly, and an anatomical imbalance is produced. The best sports and relaxation methods for humans are those that use both sides of the body, rhythmically and in proportion. Swimming, walking, jogging, running, bicycling, canoeing, horse riding, sailing: all such forms of exercise *balance* the body. Tennis, squash, golf, pole-vaulting and shot-putting are anatomical hazards.

This body balance shows, too, in the placement of segments 'around the clock' in each iris. The right and left irises are a true mirror-image pair. As you would expect from an anatomically paired body from side to side, the general layout of each iris is also anatomically paired with the other. Organs and structural parts which have their balance unit on the opposite side of the body show in both irises. The right kidney shows in the right iris, the left kidney is mirrored around the clock in the left iris. The same happens with every unit where the body is symmetrically divided. The thyroid has a left and right lobe; the pituitary likewise. The spine is (or should be) symmetrically visible in its right and left vertebral arms, and in each iris. The two hands and two arms, the legs, eyes, ears and tonsils—all show in opposite pairing in both irises. But what do we do with *one* liver, *one* heart and *one* spleen? The obvious thing is to place them again anatomically in the iris on the side where they are physically situated: the liver in the right hand iris, the spleen in the left; the heart and aorta also in the left iris, since it is in the body towards the left side. In a female, the larger part of the uterus is towards the right side in the pelvic cavity, while the rectum and anus are more to the left; so that is how placement in the iris 'map' has been made—from many years of finding, over and over, that iris signs confirm the case histories of patients.

From all the previous anatomical and biochemical logic, you would also expect to find that the top end of the body— the head and all it's structure and function—would be found represented in the top portion of the iris; and the feet, knees and legs should theoretically be found indicating their structure and function at the bottom (6 o'clock) iris seg- ment—as, in fact, they are. Such beautiful 'divine plan' symmetry has been confirmed again and again in the clinical practice of iris diagnosis when physiological and traumatic symptoms are obvious in the body. The rest of the body is spread neatly between, with anatomically central portions observable at the 3 o'clock and 9 o'clock segments.

The general logic of iris analysis is so simple: From the inside out; from the top to the bottom; from the structure to the function; from one half to the other half. Just as the body *is*, so it shows itself represented.

○ 'Cross Over' Iris Signs

Just to keep you on your diagnostic toes, Nature flips in one of her unexpected catches. Some people 'cross over' their iris signs from the neck upwards, so that sometimes it's the left side recorded in the right iris and vice versa, As yet, there seems to be no way of determining who is going to record it straight and who is crossing the pathways of the optic nerve to show signs in the iris opposite to where the real problem is.

It is wise to ask, and not tell, the person about the problem if it's above the fourth cervical vertebra (roughly anything that is happening *above* lower-jaw level in the body). The tooth that needs attention may record its near-abscessed state in the *left* lower jaw area; but it may actually be in the *right* lower jaw. Ask again. 'Do you have pain or soreness in the lower left jaw?' If the patient says, 'No', then ask about the same symptoms on the right side. If the answer is 'Yes' this time, check the right iris, and if *no* abnormal signs are found in that area, you have probably got a 'cross-over' person.

Don't worry unduly about this rather rare pattern; but be aware of it as a possibility if you ask someone about an earache on the left side and they answer, 'No, but my right ear is always a problem.' Check the right iris, and if no abnormality is found in the ear zone, it can confirm the 'diagonal' recording above the neck for this patient.

True 'cross-over' signs are found registered in the iris only for this part of the body, and they are rare.

3

STRUCTURE

What Your Ancestors Have Bequeathed To You

From our generalisations so far, can you begin to see how the computer/camera/filter/monitor of the iris records in minature your autobiographical details day by day as well as your initial programming from birth? As to that genetic programme, the limitations and strengths are next to impossible to change wholly; but knowledge of your basic type and its inherent limits can help you get the very best out of what you are stuck with. *Knowing* that your muscles are stronger than normal and can be trained to do almost anatomically impossible tasks can get you into the circus or the weight-lifting event and out from behind a car-wheel or office desk, where your built-in bonus may never be developed or even discovered.

It is so rewarding in my practice to be able to point out where such strengths are obvious from an iris. The patient may otherwise go through life not only in a wrong pattern for all-round health and happiness, but also in ignorance of the full extent of talents and latent skills. What a waste of living time!

Such strengths and weaknesses can begin to be seen registered in the iris from somewhere between six weeks and six months of age. The new-born child usually has clear blue or brown irises beautiful to see, but totally innocent as yet of any of life's experience ('innocent' in the sense of not perceiving, or seeing yet). As impressions accumulate—the recognition of comfort and warmth, discomfort and frustration, noises pleasant and unpleasant, hunger, pain—the iris begins its pattern of change that continues all through life. I have seen the eyes of the very old and those close to death become again like the clear eyes of little children as they realise life can no longer touch them: they are left as they began—whole and 'innocent'.

PATTERNS

Such observations prove to me over and over again that no subsequent pattern is fixed, unless we accept it, no experience change is impossible. Life, as observed from irises, really is what we *make* it, what we accept and reject by the use of the will and the instincts in balance. And there are our irises, jotting down all the events and possibilities in coloured shorthand to help us 'see' the right choices for us.

If your grandparents lived to their nineties, with hardly a day's illness between them, you have probably inherited what I call a 'Scottish constitution', the type of *structural* strength which will stand rock-like against internal and external stresses. If grandparents, and probably parents, too, were obliged to think constantly of their health as illness after illness befell them, then it is more than probable that you will also have to take more conscious steps to achieve and maintain a good health pattern. It is mostly a physical, *structural* genetic inheritance that repeats itself in this way. Selective breeding of animals passes structural characteristics down the Mendelian line much more predictably than functional, intellectual, or emotional patterns. The length of bones, the hardness of teeth, the growth-rate of hair, and the type of skin, are all 'fixed' genetically. The other variables (emotions and functions) can be changed by choice (accepting or not accepting) right through life; but it is impossible 'by taking thought' to add one cubit to the stature.

The most obvious initial impression, from an eye one is looking at, is this basic structural-type classification. Under even the small magnification of a simple iris torch (6x to 10x), it is very easy to see a general pattern of radiating 'fibres' or threads extending from the pupillary margin to the outer rim of the iris. These filaments look like a skein of wool spread out, threads lying close together or farther apart, straight or crossed, crimped, zig-zagged. They are much more clearly visible in the blue iris and its variations; not so visible at all in genetic brown eyes. Mostly the filaments show as a whitish, raised pattern spread right around the iris. They indicate the *structural type* only; anatomically they represent the consciously controlled nervous system.

It is certainly true that disturbance of the basic pattern of these fibres can be observed in illnesses causing structural breakdown of a body area. A broken leg; any surgery (deep or more superficial); atrophy of an organ when cells die off and structural replacement is not made fast enough; chronic infection with later structural breakdown; postural stresses (one leg shorter than the other): all illnesses involving the body as a collection of moving parts, taking stresses and strains, show variations in these fibre filaments *different* from the overall fibre pattern.

O Fibre Lesions

Often such changes register equally fast in the iris as they happen circumstantially. A broken wrist can show a crossing of several fibres around the arm/hand zone in the iris even a few hours afterwards. As the injury heals, the fibres return to their normal position. However, if the healing is slow, or incomplete, there may be continuing fibre disturbance showing in the iris for months or years afterwards. Such a sign—temporary or more permanent—is called a 'fibre lesion' in iridology.

23

Although an 'echo' lesion, as a faint record of past damage, may register for long periods, such a parting and separation of the fibres is eventually filled in with what looks like 'darning', as healing takes place. A criss-cross hatched-in pattern of fibres indicates that good major repair work has been done, new cells have replaced damaged ones; and the repaired 'patch' may be now even stronger than the surrounding tissue—much as darning an old sock with new wool gives better strength than before the hole appeared.

A slightly better indication of lesion-healing is where the 'hole' or disturbance in fibres heals up to be just the *same* as it was before. This means that the filaments radiate again, do not criss-cross; so that there is none of the over-strengthening (like scar-tissue growth) that could eventually pull the darned patch away from the sock altogether. Scar-tissue formation can show as just what it is: a thickening of the fibres in that area. Adhesions after internal surgery, keratosed skin after burns heal, bones that bump out in thickened sections after fractures: all are signs of over-compensation for damage, a kind of insurance against further trauma—and they may register in the iris as broader white fibre threads at that point (the darned hole appearance).

○ Surgical Signs

Just after any surgery, a black, diamond-shaped hole appears in the iris at the point where the tissue has been severely damaged or removed. As expected, the iris registers what has just happened: Part of the structure has been cut away, so the fibres look as if they have been neatly sliced through and removed to show the black hole underneath. Such a 'surgical sign' can fade within hours or a few days, or it may remain longer in slow healers.

Shortly after explaining surgical signs to a group of my students, one was rushed off to hospital with a dangerously inflamed appendix, which was removed the next morning.

STRUCTURE

She came out of the anaesthetic hollering for 'an iris torch to look at the black hole'—which nurses put down to the usual garbled nonsense anaesthesia may produce. When she did get her husband to bring in her torch the same evening, nurses and medicos stopped laughing as she showed them the black, diamond-shaped sign in her right iris at the appendix area. Within a few days it had faded away as the healing process began to take effect.

Extraction of wisdom teeth especially, but teeth in general, can leave a deep 'black hole' in the iris for quite some time. Such tissue removal is major, and the gap left remains until other teeth slide along the jaw-bone slowly to balance the mouth again. A class of rather hard-to-convince doctors proved this one. As I spoke of wisdom teeth and other black-hole phenomena, one smiled smugly and pulled a large triple-rooted tooth from his shirt pocket. 'It was removed two days ago,' he challenged. 'There had better be a black hole showing.' I insisted every member of that class take a close look to prove it to themselves. What's more, the following week he had a second wisdom tooth extracted and I was able to tell him that there was much less difficulty and pain with this one, since the surgical sign was much smaller and almost gone a few days later. Sheepishly, he confirmed the iris recording as accurate.

If the *contents* of organs and body cavities are removed without the removing of surrounding tissue, no surgical sign may show. If you pass a large kidney stone, with great pain and stress, but there is no tearing of tissue or part of the kidney removed (as is sometimes the case with surgical excision), no black hole should be visible, although the body has itself removed some of its tissue. The same happens in childbirth, when part of an associated 'structure' removes itself from the body: no black surgical sign. But if the birth is very difficult and tissues are torn and broken a small surgical sign may show.

One bright spark in my regular class of students always pipes up, 'What about when you have your hair cut short? Do you show black surgical signs all round the head area?'

After the class hilarity has died down, I reply that in trimming the hair cells are removed which have lived past their usefulness, and new cells farther back along each hair are waiting to replace them. (On the other hand, if your *head* is cut off, a black hole would probably show!) The same applies to trimming of finger-nails and toenails, and the shedding of skin cells every twenty-five days or so as they die. Removal of dead or dying structures does not show any surgical sign unless surrounding live tissue is also damaged. Black holes show only when *living* tissue is removed, especially if it is *suddenly* removed. The shock to the body registers in the iris.

The picture builds so logically. When part of the live body is removed, the appropriate section of the iris records the change. As healing processes begin in the body, so does the iris mirror the gradual return to normal function.

STRUCTURAL TYPES

How can we simply classify structural types by their fibre patterns in the iris? Some iridologists use wood grains as analogy (hardwood, oak, maple, pine). As the fibres lying close together in hardwoods result in a strong, dense, heavy structure, so an iris in which fibres lie close, straight, and tightly aligned together shows a tougher physical type. The open, knotty grain of pine gives less strength and weight. This timber corresponds in the iris to the more open fibres of a less inherently strong physical type—a person who must take more care of the building he lives in.

Other practitioners and teachers look at the iris as material weave types; fine silk, linen, cheesecloth, hessian, net. Again the structure strength of each cloth type is analogous to its physical human equivalent. The 'Silk' eye is at the top end with almost invisible fibres because of their fineness and closeness together. A silky patina is apparent on these rarely found, almost-perfect-physically type irises. The open mesh of coarse net, at the other end of the scale, shows a much duller iris surface.

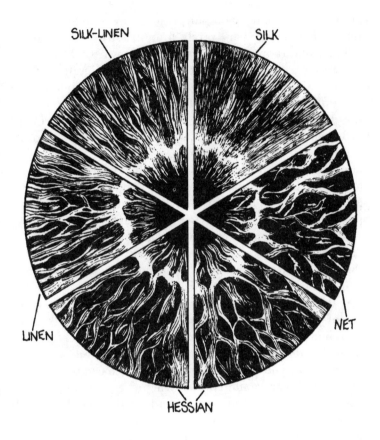

Iris Structure

You can number the iris types 1 to 5 for even more simplicity, but I feel some association with well-known substances, like wood or cloth, makes classification more easily memorable.

O The Silk Iris

It is a sad commentary on our present way of living that the Silk iris is not only very rarely found, but usually is found in folk from about fifty years of age onwards. My grandmother had a clear blue fine-textured iris which reflected not only her simple homegrown nutrition but also her direct, uncomplicated outlook on life, and her healthy ancestry. One did one's best. One did not hurt others. One worked hard, wept when sad, laughed when happy. Food was grown in the back yard beside the hens and ducks, milk was delivered warm from the cow three blocks down the street, and a large family was reared on love and discipline in equal parts. All this was done not in idyllic country surroundings, but as the general way of living in an inner Sydney suburb. I find now that many of my elderly patients, who remind me of her, have Silk irises. I have not seen any young people with a Silk iris, with the exception of new-born babies who may have Silk irises at the very beginning.

As the nutritional habits, the environment, the stresses of present-day life, take their toll, such potentially Silk irises often begin to acquire the *colour* changes that can limit physical endowments. Even so, an underlying Silk constitution can give you a head start in several basic ways.

Have you ever wondered why, when you are being so good about your carbohydrate intake and jogging painfully each morning, your friend next door who drinks like a fish and lives on pies and chips is really much healthier—and happier—than you are? Odds on, your friend was born with a Silk potential—even if it's now rather dirty silk, with some biochemical and metabolic stains showing in the iris. It's the *structure*, remember? Such a person can dance all night, drink and eat too much, bound out of bed after a log-like sleep without a hangover or indigestion, and work with vitality and enthusiasm all through the day. You hate them, don't you? They seem to be able to throw off tiredness and stress, stay calm and simple, and work with prodigious effort but no tension. They really are the lucky ones genetically, as were their grandparents and parents before them. Silk irises breed more Silk irises, even though the degree of Silk structure may decrease marginally or deteriorate biochemically. Praise God if you were so endowed! Your physical strength is your greatest blessing. However, if you *live with* a Silk type, you may feel that you have good cause to complain to the Almighty.

It is quite difficult for a Silk person to comprehend the ordinary physical limitations of the less lucky majority. Since their physical structure is so *easily* strong, they tend to believe you are slacking or just plain lazy if you can't keep up with them in endurance and energy.

I have an example in a Dutch friend of mine, without whose impossible strength I would have died when lost in the Snowy Mountains in New South Wales, some years ago. After scrambling through rain-forest jungles for nine hours at a time each day, trying to find enough open space to get an accurate bearing on our direction, I had to rely on him to lift me by the hands up vertical precipices and down waterfalls, and his rate of progress ahead of me through this nightmare country was not as surprising as I should have found it had I not been an iridologist. I have a 'Silk/Linen' iris myself, but his fine-silk-texture, clear blue eyes were amongst the best I have ever seen. He lives on fruit, physical exercise, and his work energy-input as a chiropractor. He had no idea why I became so tired as each day of our six-day ordeal dragged on.

A second drawback for anyone associated with a Silk person is that this enormous physical strength is balanced by a weakness in other areas. As well as lacking understanding of others' apparent physical weaknesses, the Silk people can lack *emotional* understanding. For them, life is simple and direct; in a straight line from beginning to end. Their will-power and control, their blinkered application to 'task doing', are often frightening. They certainly need to use this strength of theirs to avoid illness and frustration, but their emotions can be phlegmatic (to use the least unkind word). The emotional storms of others can be viewed with an insensitivity verging on bland astonishment at such loss of control.

You'll do better with your Silk man if you take a course in upholstery or car maintenance rather than meet him at the door in hysterics after a wet day at home with the kids. If you are blessed with a Silk Mum or Grandma you'll admire and love and respect her, but you won't want to confess, in tears, your emotional inadequacy in your new relationship, or your insecurity under your new job stress. You'll get a calm, puzzled look from those clear eyes and: 'What nonsense! Have a cup of tea and you'll feel better.' Emotional empathy can be totally absent, although simple kindness can replace it. You'll get practical help putting up a fence, learning to ski. You'll be carried up three flights of stairs if you break your ankle; but you won't get sympathy for the pain, or understanding of your extra distress because the accident happened two days before a date with a fascinating new man. 'Grin and bear it,' your Silk friend will say. 'That's life!'

These people are work-oriented. While physical work for them is more congenial, they can get by very contentedly with sedentary jobs if a physically challenging sport is available in leisure time (although 'leisure', for them, often means just a change of task). Get your Silk folk stimulated to greater and greater challenge, physical or circumstantial. Like the horse from *Animal Farm*, they will be out there in the thunderstorm (or at the board-meeting, or on the construction-site) long after everyone else has given up from sheer exhaustion. Their sport will be tackled in the same way, as a challenging task to be completed.

Invincible yet vulnerable

A Silk type can turn all this fantastic energy into metabolic efficiency, too, and get away with nutritional murder and circumstantial mayhem, refusing to accept the results of his sinning. He just doesn't get high cholesterol or bad blood pressure or liver damage. One of my patients is the most incredibly indestructible man who commits every sin in the book from one week to the next. He can drink a whole flagon of red wine at lunch and stay cold sober for the fastest game of squash you ever saw at 5 p.m. He will then chair a Rotary meeting and finish off the evening with six or eight pints of beer and a pie. He's likely to paint the ceiling until 3 a.m. when he gets home. A recent car accident catapulted him head-on into a concrete kerbing through the open car door. The ambulance man pronounced him dead, but on the way to hospital he sat up asking questions. They couldn't find any anaesthetic that would knock him out while they put thirty-two stitches in his scalp. One week later he was back at work. Truly a man who tests his structure to its full limits!

This type, although they live long and usually healthy, vital lives, should still be aware of their limitations. They have fewer structural problems than any other type, so they tend to believe they are totally indestructible in every way, not only physically. They may never consciously feel tired or overloaded, but in that very unawareness lies their vulnerability. It is quite impossible to stop a Silk type tipping the scales farther and farther towards humanly impossible tasks until the 'last straw' situation is reached, under which even their enormous structural strength has to collapse. Then comes a heart attack, or arterial hardening or arthritic degeneration of one type or another—to bring such Goliaths back to humanity and its limitations. Their *surprise* when this happens can be a heavy experience. The restrictions imposed by weakness, even if temporary, *may* turn Silk people into slightly more understanding friends or relatives. But when they are able to they are quite likely to get up and do the whole thing over again in exactly the same way.

You can see why it's maybe easier to *be* a Silk person than to be *around* one! Hard on themselves, these people demand great efforts from those around them, too. Heaven help you if you have a Silk boss. He won't appreciate sub-perfect work for any reason whatsoever, nor will he accept your excuse—'I'm just having a bad day today.' 'Make it a better one, then,' he'll say as he works twice as hard to make up for your 'slackness'.

The straight fine fibres visible radiating outwards in a Silk iris indicate the straight-line thinking of this type of person. Able to handle enormous work-loads, they will still show 'one thing at a time' concentration. Tasks will be carried out from the beginning to the end, and their intense concentration and energy direction will be obvious. Hard to side-track, they can become 'workaholics' if too many tasks are lined up in front of them.

Selective 'filtering' of experiences can screen out many external conditions in a Silk iris. This is not the same as the instinctive 'Net' type filter system to be discussed later. Silk types sort out which impressions they will or will not accept (and record in the iris) by narrowing their paths and *ignoring* or refusing to 'see' certain distracting or disturbing circumstances. This can lead to insensitivity in its negative aspect; but it can also mean that these people are not easily upset. They can be insensitive to conditions that would have a weaker mortal screaming or crying or shouting under the stress. It is therefore a good idea to place them in positions and jobs in which a high physical or mental or intellectual work-load must be shouldered without emotional disturbance. Don't give them positions that require a high degree of emotional sensitivity. Don't expect them to be tactful or diplomatic with clients (although their kindness is often obvious). But whatever they do, you'll find them working longer hours and getting more mileage/result than any other staff member.

We mentioned their inability to feel tired and their 'last-straw' collapse. Ill-health in these people is usually fought off with the same energy as they give to every other part of their lives; and this shrugging off of difficult conditions can mean that an ill-health pattern gets a long, strong hold before it is even recognised, let alone talked about. These are the people who can bleed from the bowel for years without telling anyone and even without noticing it much themselves. They may ache with stiff joints every morning of their lives and be unaware that rheumatoid arthritis has gained a hold. When a friend or relative finally insists on their seeking treatment, they can be stubborn and even stupid: not following the physician's advice, ignoring warnings, and forgetting to take medicine. You will need Silk strength yourself to cope with your Silk patient. Many of them die in total astonishment that their body has let them down.

Don't rush to classify too many irises as Silk type: they are rare. They were more common two generations ago, when the Empire-builders had them and so did the pioneer women and the Antarctic explorers: simple people with direct aims and the physical structure to put them into practice.

○ The Silk/Linen Iris

Most of the very strong middle-aged people of the current generation are a kind of failed-Silk type. If they could have lived in better environmental and nutritional and emotional circumstances, as their parents did, they may have retained their birthright—a Silk iris.

The surface of this Silk/Linen iris is not so shiny and the fibres are slightly thicker, spread maybe a little wider apart, with a few tiny lesions even. This iris type is still usually blue, and fairly clear and bright. Most Silk/Linen irises had Silk parents or grandparents. The 'perfect' inheritance genetically has started to deteriorate under more complex living conditions, and especially, I believe, under more *crowded* living conditions. Just as fish in an aquarium tank will lose colour, become aggressive, or sulk behind rocks, and have little or no success in breeding, so, I believe, do human animals tend to produce rather inferior stock physically as individual 'space' becomes smaller.

Where have you been to lately where there was no one else but you? A favourite secluded tiny beach? There were three boatloads of weekend trippers there before you clambered down the path to it. A mountain walking track? The Boy Scouts beat you! A quiet fishing spot on the rocks below a sandstone cliff? The hang-gliders swoop over you and the other forty-nine people fishing from the same rocks all seem to have a better spot than you've established as your 'territory'. When was the last time you've been the sole passenger in the railway carriage; the only one on the bus? Your 'territory' is getting smaller: genetically your *structure* is being undermined by all these other structures competing for living room.

I have seen Silk irises in the over-fifties often; I have seen them in infants; but I have *never* seen them in older children, teenagers, or young adults. Even silk/Linen irises are rare. My patients come from all over Australia, city and country. Some eat good simple food and live theoretically simple lives; others commit every dietary sin and live a totally 'civilised' existence. It doesn't make any difference: that *structure* is less strong than in our parents and grandparents.

The cause for this I find quite obvious. Little demand is made on physical strength and endurance in present-day living and (genes being what they are: a selective mechanism of breeding to suit circumstances) when a faculty is not needed and used it slowly breeds out of the species. Sportsmen and women, circus performers, fitness fanatics: all can *train* their bodies in a particular direction, but they are not necessarily born that way and their irises may show a remarkable overlay of head control upon what may have been initially a weak physical structure. The true Silk and the Silk/Linen iris can be found more amongst the blue-collar people—the municipal gardeners and the tug-boat crews and the house-painters; people who work, eat and sleep, love their families and pay their taxes. One of my colleagues accuses me of being a peasant because I talk a lot about the pleasures of work. He's right, too! I have a Silk/Linen iris and enjoy the peasant satisfaction in achievement of physical tasks.

Why problems arise

Problems with Silk/Linen irises (and some real Silk ones, too) mainly occur when biochemical function from day to day is less than the strong basic structure requires. When more than work and eating and sleeping is required of them, such iris types find the demands more difficult to handle *functionally* than more emotionally reactive, more complex, personalities do. Many *colour* abnormalities, spread around in such a basic good-structure iris, indicate that day-to-day function for that person involves now much more than working, eating, sleeping, and direct thinking. The civilising process has clouded the clear iris colours; the basic simplicity has gone, and the children and children's children will go lower down the iris structure scale.

I also believe that physical structures are now not endurance-tested in the young. The Spartan exposure of a new-born child to the elements is a little extreme for 'civilisation'; but we have gone to the other extreme in driving children a half-mile to school and sitting them in front of a television set for three or four or more hours when they come home. The structure, even if inherently good, will not stay strong unless it is used.

A Dutch friend of mine, now over seventy, keeps me enthralled with tales of challenges to his strength as a young man—riding, running, mad contests involving endurance, so that he found the strength of his structure by constantly testing it. He fixes me with his clear Silk-type brilliant blue eyes, while he tells the story. At the age of fifty he broke his back in two places falling from a horse and was told he would never ride again. 'Rubbish!' was his comment. A matter of weeks later he was lifted onto a horse; several months later he was competition-riding again. He knew his endurance level and this time tested it to the full. It was as strong as ever. His efficient body processes had repaired the scaffolding of his spine to make it like new.

I should like to see more challenges to children and youths, both male and female, in the area of stamina: not necessarily group or individual competition against others, but competition *against oneself.* The satisfaction, the sense of achievement, the pride and self-confidence gained, are like several coats of rust-preventing paint on their scaffolding. The anxieties and achievement-doubts that now fill psychiatrists' notebooks might not occur later in life if confidence in one's own strength had been established by *using* it. A whole generation of Silk-type irises could arise again, healthily self-reliant.

Useful comparisons

For the moment, however, we must content ourselves with the silk/Linen iris as the top of average. If you own an eye like this, your illnesses should be few and are most likely to be produced by emotional disturbance, accidental damage, or functional disorders. You are wearing a light chain-mail armour inside and out—bones, muscles and ligaments, even skin. (A Silk iris, of course, is in full battle armour, visor down as well—so that he does not always *see* as clearly as he might, and may see only in one direction at a time, full speed ahead.)

If you think about both these pictures, do you come up with the words 'heavy' and 'stiff'? You're right; because both types are not so invulnerable as to escape being slightly human. Built into their strong, metal-like structures is the possibility of an opposite, negative side of the balance Nature always provides—corroding rigidity. In later life, a Silk or Silk/Linen type has a high probability of becoming an osteo-arthritic, forming stones in organs like kidneys and gall-bladder, becoming stiff with rheumatism, or spondylitis, unless the strength is continually used and that mighty structure kept flexible.

Sitting down and meditating should not be the relaxation for such people. Let them get out and chop wood, or swim down the Nile; but they must not *sit still!* They will start to rust, and those extra-strong muscles and ligaments will pull the bones together like a vice, nipping nerves and contracting blood vessels until the body aches and becomes numb here and there. The doctor will tell these people it's all tension, and he's right: the body is held tight all over by steel cables of connective tissue. These types not only enjoy physical exercise but also need it to escape diseases of tightness, hardness, rigidity, inherent in their genetic pattern.

One Silk-type man I know tears about all day doing his

stamina-things of managing a very large company's sales division. After he stops and 'relaxes' (for ten minutes or so) he then leaps up from his chair, or the floor, or his bed, with, 'Well, it's time for me to *move!*' He knows. If he stays there longer he's at risk.

Both Silk and Silk/Linen types usually sleep well if hard physical exercise is undertaken often. They often eat very little by average standards, but enjoy what they eat when they do. If they are *positive* examples of their type and in their right circumstantial pattern, they will be simple, instinctive eaters, if allowed to be. Most of their vitality comes from a high adrenal stimulus and good mineral balance, so their food intake can be light on quantity if the quality is high. Home-grown goodies from the garden and raw whole foods like nuts and seeds and grains suit these people—as long as their *liquid* intake is high, to move all those heavy minerals around the body, not leaving them to settle in tissues where insidious residue build-up can make them solidify into rock-like mineral deposits and calcification. A positive Silk or Silk/Linen person is often thirsty naturally. To stay in peak condition, it is better for him or her to increase fluid intake and decrease the size of solid-food meals.

Movement of one sort or another is always essential: flexing of the structure; physical going from place to place, leisure involving change of scene and type of activity; movement of fluids around that heavy body to ensure mineral waste leaves the system faster than it can accumulate.

Such people can tend towards constipation, even though their physical health may otherwise be good. There is so much tightness in partially contracted muscles and liga-ments—even in visceral muscles—that the bowel's peristaltic signals, which should normally indicate its need for evacu-ation, may not get through. These people can also be guilty of 'not going', even as children, if something interesting is happening or they are concentrating on finishing a job. Their will-power makes the body do what the head tells it, and habits so formed may set just as rigidly for them as any other rigidity pattern. In fact, habit, developed and incorporated into 'armour' units, is often indicative of Silk and Silk/Linen people, without the added evidence of their irises.

Do your Silk and Silk/Linen friends a good turn and point out that their *output* channels (bowels, kidneys, skin, lungs) should also *move*. High fluid intake should keep the positive ones urinating and perspiring freely, but a negative person of this type—rigid, tight, stiff, aching and corroding in mineral deposition with not enough fluids to move the accumulation out of the body efficiently—can gradually resemble a stalactite or the battery of your car when the terminals are covered with greenish mineral build-up. Even the skin of the face should probably move a little more than it does, to give expression. Make your Silk great-uncle of ninety *laugh*; and even after his third heart attack that small amount of movement of the muscles and skin can be beneficial.

The lungs are also an organ of excretion, and positive Silk and Silk/Linen types often have large chest measurements and large hearts and lungs to *move* a goodly amount of oxygen around the body and carbon dioxide out again. Beware of a Silk or Silk/Linen person who sighs a lot. The oxygen-carrying ability is falling behind because the chest is not expanding sufficiently. Tightness is setting in again. The big sigh should be the signal to get up and *move* again, even if it's only to the window for some breaths of fresh air.

So you see it's not a *carte blanche* gift of the Gods to be stronger physically than average. Understanding of the balancing weakness tendencies can make it a lot easier to be a *positive* Silk/Linen, Silk or any other type of iris, and to avoid suffering, unaware, the pitfalls of its possible disadvantages or negativity.

I have not mentioned these positive and negative aspects of the same type in as much detail as they warrant individually, because only the general characteristics of the types can be broadly covered. But let me point out that a totally *negative* Silk is infinitely worse off than a positive 'Net'-type iris person (the weakest structurally of the lot). By negative, I mean a person who has done or is doing all the wrong things for his iris type and genetic pattern. A rock-like, stolid, slow, arthritic Silk with heart disease, constipation and cholesterol build-up is just as much a disaster as a negative person of any other iris type—in fact, more so. He is not used to illness and handles it badly; he becomes frustrated and rude, and gives everyone else a pain in the same nether regions where he is suffering his haemorrhoids from chronic constipation. As the positive structural potential is higher, so is the negative aspect of the same thing more difficult to deal with.

Straight, clear advice

I give my Silk and Silk/Linen patients straight, clear advice and analysis, without too much consideration for their 'feelings'. They are practical people who wish to get better as soon as possible (wanting to have their arthritis removed by me overnight, or at least within a week); and the basic physical strength is certainly there for complete recovery if they will do what is necessary. But this is not often achieved, for they race back to work again half-fixed, impatient to be on the *move* once more. You'll have to talk horse-sense and talk it loudly to get through the habit/pattern of 'I'm invincible.' Until recently such people probably were.

Vitamins are not as necessary for such people as is the balancing of their mineral metabolism. Glandular function is usually hyper-normal, especially in the control organs of pituitary, thyroid, and adrenals. Watch that apparently slow, solid, imperturbable, positive Silk (Silk/Linen slightly less obviously) move like greased lightning under the challenge of a game of squash, an injured child on the soccer field, or an end-of-the-month deadline at the office. Out comes the adrenalin into the bloodstream, the pituitary slides up a few notches, and you've got that *movement* again. If your favourite Silk or Silk/Linen is sitting in a corner yawning, he's very seldom tired (he'd be asleep if he were—much more sensible); he's *bored*. Give him a challenge and he'll be off and running.

The emotional pitfalls for Silk and Silk/Linen people are less troublesome for them than for those emotionally or otherwise involved with them. Several of their emotional 'sins' lie in their apparent lack of sensitivity: over-responsibility for other people's weaknesses and problems or, at the other extreme, failure to realise that anyone around them has a problem at all. They can cheerfully take on the work-load of five when the office staff is decimated by flu, or they can astonish you with their assumption of everyone's self-sufficiency. (I can fix any of my problems; I expect you to fix all of yours yourself too!) Mostly, though, you'll get cheerful, practical help from them. Keep emotional displays and hysterical fireworks for someone else's shoulder; you'll go down in their estimation if you lose control. They don't; and if they don't then why should anyone else? This attitude of theirs can spur others to either furious sledgehammering (it won't get through) or inspirational determination ('All right, I'll try'). Silk and Silk/Linen types really do believe that it's all pretty easy if you really try. Many of them have a truly humble outlook on their own achievements which are often many and outstanding. 'If I can do it, then everyone else can, too. There's nothing out of the ordinary about me.' But there is—that structure, and all that goes with it.

○ The Linen Iris

I'll bet by now you have been to the mirror once or twice to check your own eyes, and have looked more closely at those folk around you, too. Are your own irises rather multi-coloured in patches and spots? If this is obvious just from a mirror, it is possible that fibre structure is not visible much between such patches. Get out your iris torch (p. 5) and have a closer look. Now you can see the underlying pattern a little more. It's irregular, there are lesions between the fibres perhaps; some are thicker 'threads' than others, a more tangled wool-skein pattern.

Join the club: you are an average human being! Most of

us fall into the middle area of being not too strong, not too weak, with spells of being a little stronger or a little weaker depending on the stars or the financial situation or the wife's moods. Our structure is less outstanding; we get tired and cross, we moan a little, then laugh and forget it; but some of the selective control mechanisms let us down when we need will-power, stamina, and what my father used to call 'stickability'.

Knowing when to stop

A Linen iris type will say, 'I'm exhausted, let's have a coffee-break', while the Silk and Silk/Linen plough doggedly on until the job's done before they allow themselves to feel hungry and thirsty. You don't have to feel inferior so often with the much more human Linen type. You can be ordinary and show your weaknesses and get tired feet and hangovers. You won't he criticised much by other Linens either. They'll have their own chilblains and weight to worry about. Comfortable people, they are, without too much moral fibre and able to feel with you and for you because you are as they are. The conversation covers a wider and less-censored range of topics than whether the job is or is not finished and whether it is time to get up or go to bed or eat.

Linen people are more vulnerable in structure; more prone to droop in the torso when tired, stand on one leg then the other, flop down in chairs when the pressure and stress levels rise. They therefore begin to have what the two former types lacked: consciousness of their own physical limits and a certain protective inability to pass them. Although they can, and do, work hard, they know when to stop. They get a headache or a leg-cramp or they are just plain tired, and they *stop*. Or if circumstances don't permit them to stop they complain, showing they are aware of their own body structure and its load tolerance. They don't often take on gargantuan tasks individually, as the former types do, but are very capable indeed of working with a group, each one using different strengths and skills to complement the others. For this reason alone, they make better employees, at least socially and co-operatively, than either of the previous types—unless the whole group happens to be flying to the moon or drilling for oil in the North Sea!

The Linen iris has a structure that has been affected by external circumstances, over generations maybe, but is still holding its own and *not necessarily weakly either*. Don't make the mistake of thinking the first two iris types are the best: they can have pretty severe problems unless understood. But here we are talking of *structure*, and undeniably the Linen structure is built of lighter-gauge scaffolding with less tensile strength. A Silk type may wrench your arm off at the elbow when shaking your hand, insensitive to the differences between your tensile patterns. A Linen person's handshake is more aware of the 'feel' of your hand, and is probably 'sensing' your qualities instinctively. This middling structural pattern gives more diversity; more awareness of and reaction to outside circumstances and other people; and Linen people have less need to keep moving. Adrenal flow is less, mineralisation is less heavy, and expressed emotions are more of tolerance and understanding of others. There is less obsession with doing and achieving, and a greater sensitivity to outside experiences. Since the iris is not filtering out so many sensations, sights, sounds, and other diversions are allowed to enter; so the straight-line thinking of the Silks grows broader and spreads over a wider range in the Linens.

Get a Linen type to take clients to lunch, smooth over an office faction fight, talk to the managing director's wife at dinner. A Linen mum will be less demanding of her children and her man than the former types, if occasional slides from grace occur or dirty socks are not put in the clothes-basket. There are probably some Mondays when she refuses to do the washing because she has a migraine or pre-menstrual tension.

Linen people have occasional ill-health and, when they do, they seek help and comfort and running repairs. It is sad that they may never experience the adrenal vitality of the stronger physical types. Often they come to my consulting room looking puzzled and apologetic: 'I'm not really sick,' they say, 'but I'm not as well as I feel I should be, either.' Much more therapeutic *advice* may need to be given to Linen types than to Silks. But often it is only a matter of replacing minor deficiencies, adjusting a few simple nutritional balances, and giving general *tonic* herbal remedies; and a week or so later the Linen patient will be ringing up ecstatically to say how marvellous is the feeling of *positive* health—health in reserve, so to speak, health in the bank. The Silks may still be doggedly removing their arthritic spurs years later, but a true Linen type responds well in structure to some general repair work at obvious stress points.

While a *minor* structural stress can be quickly thrown off, or ignored, by a Silk/Linen type, the same minor structural assault may make a Linen type feel really ill. A head cold may pass unnoticed by the Silks as they work away, sinuses jammed with mucus and running a slight temperature. They'll be over it in a day or two. The Linen type moans and sniffs inhalants and cancels appointments and goes to bed with a hot-water bottle and be damned to the washing-up! Even so, a troublesome cough may persist for weeks afterwards.

There is nothing remarkable about possessing average structure; and the acquired strength of a Linen type can be effectively greater than the in-built fortitude of a Silk who is not using his potential advantage. Faint not if your iris gets middle rating in structure: you can develop your energy and endurance, though it may take more effort to do so. You may need cough mixture for a month or so after that aforementioned cold; but there's no reason why you can't heal up again completely and strongly.

Linens are in the majority amongst iris types. Later, when we discuss iris colours, the biochemical function of Linens can be seen to be of greater importance to their general health and well-being than their structure.

○ The Hessian Iris

Now we come to the interesting combination of inherently weaker structure with greater awareness and sensitivity: a higher level of emotional response as opposed to physical 'doing'. 'Hessian' people certainly are not weaklings any more than 'Net' people are; but their life-emphasis is more on what they *feel* than on what they are doing. Such people may need more impetus from outside themselves, more encouragement and praise, a firmer kick to get started on physical work, than the preceding types. These are the people who can think about doing something, discuss it over a beer or two or a cup of tea: and several hours, days, or years later, they will still walk past the job saying, 'I must get around to doing that.' Their biochemical function and their glandular and hormonal balance control their moods and determine which way their feelings will swing back and forth.

Hessian people can probably describe to you a different 'feeling' for every hour of the day, and their physical activity is largely regulated by which feeling dominates while they are working at any task.

A Silk or even a Linen would tend to grab the materials for the job out of the hands of a Hessian type who is dreamily *not*-doing. Such people have less physical stamina, and therefore are not as robust in doing tasks demanding heavy use of their structure; but there is absolutely no reason why a little more head control cannot be achieved, and the job done by brain, not necessarily brawn. I suspect that many of our inventors of mechanical aids for mankind have been positive Hessian types, using their heads to find ways and means of lightening the physical burdens of work.

Silk types are individualists: if it can't be done using one's own strength, courage, and will-power, don't ask anyone else's help—take time and effort and learn the required skill the hard way. Hessian types, more likely to use their heads to save their bodies, may regard Silks and Linens as boorish and uncivilised, or even as stupid to work so hard without more rest and relaxation.

Nature provides such opposites to keep the system in balance: but why do they always marry each other? If both types are positive examples, not at the negative ends of their patterns, such a balance of opposites can produce real equilibrium in the partnership. The Silk man is glad to take the physical day-to-day load from his Hessian lady's shoulders; or the Silk woman can feed the kids, prepare the dinner, and smile unaffected by her Hessian husband's emotional catalogue of the day's happenings at the office. Trouble occurs only when one or both are at *negative* places in their pattern: the Silks take heavy unnecessary loads dropped by clever, lazy Hessians, the Hessians moan to friends and neighbours and the greengrocer that the Silk in their life is too busy looking after the team/job/friend/business and has no time or inclination to relax in their company.

Study the structure of the iris to find these basic type differences. You will never change one into the other, but an understanding of the strengths and weaknesses of each can produce a good positive combination.

Open structures, thicker fibres

Just as the weave of hessian is open and coarse, the fibres knotted and of irregular thickness, so does the Hessian iris show its fibre structure in loose, thicker, and broader arrangement. The pattern is heavier and more gross than in the fine, straight, often almost invisible fibres of a Silk iris, and to some extent a Silk/Linen iris, too. Twists and kinks and even crossing of fibres show that nerve messages are transmitted through the physical wires of the body with more haphazard connection than in that person-to-person (or person-to-job) directness of the Silks. Hessians can be side-tracked, re-routing messages, or can be subject to outside interference in signals between the brain control and the physical structure.

In terms of biochemical function, Hessian people are lower in magnesium phosphate, and probably calcium phosphate, too, than the more structurally blessed Silks. Calcium, phosphorus, and magnesium are always high when the iris fibres are very white, irrespective of the iris type; but an iris may still reflect an *imbalance* of such minerals in the body, producing abnormal or disease conditions. The Silk iris person can have these three minerals in perfect balance if he's doing all the right things for his pattern; the Hessian will need to take constant care to maintain whatever his balance is, especially in regard to the calcium supply available for the stomach and digestion. A look at his iris will show you the irregular open pattern of fibres around the stomach and intestines zones that produces a 'nervous stomach' under stress. Taken before bedtime, a cup of camomile tea, with its high natural calcium phosphate plus lesser amounts of magnesium and potassium phosphates, can turn a worried, tense, over-emotional Hessian into a sensitive, sympathetic, pleasantly relaxed human being ready for the next day's assaults on his structure.

Hessian types have another big thing going for them—their flexibility. If you've ever done upholstery work with hessian, you will know how the lack of rigidity in the material lets you pull it about and tack it without loss of strength. Hessians do not break, they bend. They ask for help when they feel it's needed and accept it when it's offered. They know their strength limits and accept them, too. 'Never say die,' shouts the Silk and conquers the mountain in a blizzard, flag in one hand. 'Let's sit down and have a glass of wine and look at it from a different angle,' says the Hessian. 'Why don't we have a picnic instead down here in the foothills? It's so pleasant and the sun is so warm for this time of the year. We can discuss our next attempt in a civilised manner.' Hessians live to fight another day. If negative, they can moan and kick and dramatise small happenings, while the Silks grit their teeth and get on with it (maybe stiffening as they go).

Hessian people are much more aware of structural changes in the short term as the day's stresses come and go. They slump. They yawn and stretch and get up and walk about to shift structural demands from one part of the body to another. Ask a Hessian, 'How are you?' and you'll be told. They *know* how they are and their work and social life reflect the changing picture. Ask a Silk the same question. 'Fine!' will come the reply, irrespective of whether he or she has the flu, arthritic aches and pains in every joint, or terminal cancer.

Observe the basic structure in assessing a prospective employee, a new emotional partner, or a landlord. Analysing types from the iris can save you expecting genetically impossible reactions or achievements. Square pegs in square holes result from accurate assessment of structure.

◯ The Net Iris

Logically, you would expect a Net person to be shot full of holes and able to be scrunched up into almost any shape under stress: but think of the strength of a trawler's net, full of fish, allowing some things to get through (like water and small fish) while retaining the important part of the catch. What about a spider's web or net? It lets the wind through and flexes on the branches that support its structure—but it catches the fly. Nets can be filmy and tear at a touch, or be as strong as steel cables. The difference between the two is in the structural strength of each strand of the net itself.

Net people show a typical Net pattern in the iris: whitish fibres 'blown' out from the pupillary margin into a criss-cross web pattern, fibres interfaced and appearing as quite raised above the general iris plane. Characteristically, Net people can filter out some experiences and retain others. They do not generally moan or complain about their lot; they don't intellectualise much either; and their strength can be as variable as a situation demands. They seem to be people who live right up to their load limits, but when these limits are in danger of being passed they don't stop or complain or put off or carry on; they *filter*.

Lateral thinking survivors

Some Net people just go away under stress. Yell at them and they've gone before you get to the punch-line; try to get them to do something and their *instincts* will decide whether the job's acceptable, rather than their heads or their hearts or their sense of duty. I call them the 'Moebius strip' people (geometric impossibilities like a bottle with no interior; like the visual tricks beloved by the artist Escher) as they move in their own best interests by lateral thinking, by crab-like path-finding that *always* leaves them surviving.

How the rest of us wish at times for this faculty of deflecting stresses that are suddenly too heavy or too prolonged for our particular structure to bear! A Silk can collapse totally under his final straw of immense load; a Net never. The wider and whiter the Net reads in the iris, the more you can put your bets on this one being the last survivor in the lifeboat. Such people tend to live to the limits of their structural load capacity *all the time*. They sense that any additional load may not be taken and can be detached from their recognition of it through one of those holes in the net. A good night's sleep is usually enough to restore energy used the previous day: today's load will use today's available energy; no more, no less.

My second son's a combination Silk/Net. I have never seen him annoyed or even affected by stress—except for a pained look of surprise appearing on his face at some unusual failure of the filter system for a short time under extreme load. A few strands of the net tore! An abscessed tooth did it once; his dog's death did it again; and a severe flu was the third cause of the only three times I can remember the system breaking down.

Another Net-iris patient met any and every stress situation with an iced cream-cake! After he'd swallowed the last sticky mouthful his stress had gone. Diversionary tactics are common in instinctive patterns of animals. Human Net types show many animal characteristics, too. One could never call them simple and direct, though. They are complex, exceedingly so at times, and as stubborn as can be under their fairly calm exteriors. If it is not right for them, they won't have it, or even recognise its existence. It is not so much a sand-covered ostrich-head on their shoulders as a childlike one;

trusting, innocent, but protected by a remarkable self-defence pattern of instincts.

Net people take some knowing, even if you have had a quick look at their irises and labelled them accurately. Unpredictable in their structural strengths, they seem to be exhausted at one moment, then blazing with an energy to shame a Silk. Instincts govern these changes: a balance of output corresponding to resources from within at any given time.

I find Net people intriguing from a natural therapist's point of view. If positive examples of the type, they need almost no help or outside advice or treatment and appear to be self-regulating in their pattern. On the other hand, a negative Net type may filter *everything* through; may be so vague and out of this world that animal instincts revert to animal habits, too. Sleep, day-dreaming, and physical lethargy may give a negative Net person more the characteristics of the household cat than those of a contributing human being. Seeking only selfish comfort, warmth, and personal well-being, can create a certain tyranny of animal instincts over more humane qualities; but a Net person will usually behave like this only when sudden stress or shock tears the net threads apart. Pain, emotional or physical, is often the precipitating factor. The Silk type bears it with courage and acceptance of yet another burden; the middle Linen is used to small amounts of it here and there; the Net does not accept it, or if forced to by overwhelming circumstances, can spend long weeks and months, even years, 'adjusting'. Some Nets *never* recover from the shock of their apparently foolproof system letting them down once or twice in a lifetime.

In illness, Net types retreat, craving solitude until the pain is 'adjusted' out of their recognition. Even recalling such an illness afterwards can be quite disturbing for them. They should have filtered it out through a hole somewhere!

Many Net types seem almost as strong as the Silks and Linens, depending on the thickness of those fibre threads; but deprive a Net person of sleep and put pain in the same picture and the structural 'weakness' will appear. Endurance may also be present, but you could find that it's endurance by default: if one does not recognise all the stresses or allow them to touch the structure, it can be easy to 'endure' the remainder.

I often wish I had been born a Net person. Capacity to feel a little less, to work only when it is certain to produce results, to sleep and eat at the times most needed for the balance of the organism: this seems to me a more intelligent method of coping with life than most of us are equipped with. Maybe Nature is working at a new cycle of human development through the less strong structure patterns and back to instinctive self-defence of a different type altogether.

OTHER IRIS PATTERNS

O Zig-Zag Fibres

Many people of all structural types can show the sharp angles of zig-zagged fibre structure. Certainly, they are less likely to be found in a Silk iris than in any other type, because they indicate a reservoir of unused energy. If you are a Silk type, energy is used and used and used again. The less hardy Silk/Linens, though still remarkably strong, can show an odd fibre or two with this pattern if their energy is frustrated and unused. A Silk/Linen confined to a desk or a motor-car or a job where physical mobility is severely limited may begin to show zig-zag frustration of his normal energy-flow rate. The result can look like laziness if he then sits in front of the TV all the evening biting his fingernails when what he needs is physical activity. So zig-zag fibres equal *frustration* of available energy flow.

Even the more open weave irises of Linen and Hessian types can show this frustration pattern, fibres arranged like open zips all round the iris 'clock'. Ask such a person a few leading questions: 'Do you feel a bit frustrated; feel you should be doing something more, something different? Do you feel you'd like to run, and jump up and down and yell a bit?' When the answer is a clenched fist and a tight jaw, or a verbal release of pent-up energy, you're on the right track. However, the pattern of crimped fibres may stay in the iris long after any immediate release of energy. It can take some time to re-establish a balance, since such people tend to repeat or endure similar circumstances again and again.

I often find crimped fibres in irises of heavy marihuana smokers, particularly those folk who have smoked the drug too often, for twelve months or even several years. As well as showing certain disturbances in autonomic function (discussed later in this book), such an iris can indicate restriction of potential energy flow. A 'lotus-eater' can be the result: inhibition of drive and non-recognition of real energy capabilities, in a pleasant, illusory haze of well-being.

If you assess a person as quiet and slightly below average in energy, then find this zig-zag fibre structure in the iris, it can help to point out to him gently that he is not getting the best from himself, not using his structural strength and that he would feel and be much healthier if he overcame this inhibition of his real drive.

○ No Fibres At All Visible

If you're still waiting for this section heading to appear, you almost certainly have deep-brown eyes! They could be a natural brown if you're Greek or Italian or Egyptian, Aboriginal or Chinese, Indian or Polynesian; or they may really be basic blue eyes masked with varying overlays of brown discoloration. Look very hard with your iris torch. If even the faintest trace of whitish fibre-threads is showing, you may have much biochemical rearranging to do to uncover your genetic blue eye. The sins of your fathers and grandfathers may also have predisposed you to be born with what look like brown eyes: both father and grandfather could perhaps have kept their blue-eyed inheritance intact by better diet, better living habits, and an awareness of what good health needs for its continuance.

I have been discussing here only the apparent 'brown' eye which under magnification shows a few faint traces of blue and *fibres*, even if only one or two, amongst the colour patches. If your ancestry is *real* brown-eyed stock, a totally different picture is seen. The iris surface can have the character of brown velvet; a matt-finish surface texture with no fibres visible at all. Variations in tone and colour can be seen, but fibres—no! As you can imagine, irises like these limit the iridologist in assessing structure.

I believe this to be the reason why iridology, although it is known to ancient Chinese medicine, found less favour as a diagnostic tool than did pulse diagnosis, fingernail and foot diagnosis. It would be next to impossible to compile a grading of structural types from Chinese irises. Biochemical function may show as colour variation in areas of the body in which it has been less than efficient; but the genetic structure is not easily discernible.

Look hard at 'brown' eyes, no matter how deep the intensity of colour, and if a few fibres are visible anywhere you've got a basic blue ancestry some way back in the family tree. If the brown is really genetic, you'll need to pay more attention to the chapter on 'Colour' than to structure identification. Since all people of European descent have greater or lesser degrees of 'blue' ancestry (interbreeding with dark-skinned races will, of course, produce some real brown-eyed offspring), the odds are that white Caucasian readers will still spot a fibre or two in their irises. Much more fibre structure may become visible when corrective health measures are undertaken to remove waste metabolic residues and improve biochemical function. Many a deep brown-eyed, white-skinned patient has marvelled at the new light-hazel to brown-blue iris colour change as treatment progresses.

Different metabolic pattern

Much more on iris colours follows in the next chapter; but while we are still dealing with structure let me point out that no general comparisons can be made between the relative structure strengths of a blue eye and a genetic brown one not showing any visible fibres. The brown is certainly not 'weaker' in any way, but is basically reflecting a different metabolic pattern.

The fibre 'threads' so clearly white and visible in the blue iris are indicative of a metabolism that runs biochemically on varying combinations of calcium, magnesium, and phosphorus. Silica joins the other three minerals as a corrective agent for any great imbalance in *structural* health.

As less and less fibres become visible under *functional* disorders, the blue iris reflects a change in biochemical emphasis towards the other mineral grouping: iron, sodium, potassium; and chlorine, with sulphur, as a balancer and corrective. The true genetic brown eye metabolises naturally in this direction, with much more emphasis on sodium, potassium, chlorine, and sulphur, and with another two important elements, iodine and bromine, as stabilisers.

Many racial *structural* differences (skin colour, bone weight and size, height, even body odour) can be accounted for by the mineral combination that is the most genetically strong. The long bones and fair colouring of European origin are certainly the easiest to read in judging the structural strength registered in the iris.

4

IRIS COLOUR

A Record Of Bodily Functions

Is it blue eyes or brown you prefer? Or are you turned on by quiet hazel-grey or blazing green? Your gentle doe-eyed girlfriend with the widely dilated pupils may be suffering from chronic constipation (not to mention bad breath) and be pathologically tired. The green-eyed, Titian-haired beauty at the bus-stop may have a sluggish liver, nausea after her evening meal, and gallstones ahead at forty. That Greek-god young man in the office with the ice-blue penetrating eyes may have a digestive-tract ulcer forming, and catarrh, and offensive perspiration.

Let us look at iris colour a different way from just genetic blue or genetic brown: it is also a record of the *function* of the body day-to-day and year-to-year right through life. The easiest way to check on overall body function is to observe the many different colour patches, spots, clouds, streaks, and circles, visible in an iris, and to note which parts of the body (as set out in the iris chart) are deviating from the overall colour pattern of the iris.

A bright red patch of colour over the liver area in an otherwise clear blue eye can indicate functional inefficiency of the liver; a white foggy haze in the lung area in an otherwise generally hazel eye can show catarrh and mucus there; a grey-brown coloration all around the stomach and intestinal circle can point to hypo-function of the digestive tract, and if the rest of the iris is maybe a clear overall blue-green, then this digestive problem shows a *deviation* from general overall metabolic patterns and can benefit from therapeutic attention. Whether this consists of merely a cup of camomile tea each night and a couple of foods like ginger and yoghurt included often in the diet, or whether more extensive corrective therapies should be undertaken, depends on *how different* is the colour from the rest of the iris.

Let us look at colours on the scale from white to black and pale to dark. (Strictly speaking, irises show *tones* and *shades* of colour, rather than absolute colours as found in the spectrum.) Just as the good cowboy has the white horse and wears a white hat, whilst the baddies always ride the darker horses and wear darker colours, so too, does the white end of the tone scale theoretically show more positive 'virtues' than the dark browns and blacks. The scale of progression of colour indicates the degree of severity of any ill-health symptoms: white is 'better' theoretically than black; yellowish-white is 'better' than yellowish-brown.

The logic of iris colours is just as precise as is its structural counterpart. The ideal colour is clear mid-blue or rich satin brown; but the number of eyes showing this perfect biochemical function is miserably few. New-born kittens, six-week-old babies, and an occasional strong positive Silk or Silk/Linen type country man or woman can show to the world the most perfect metabolic function Nature is capable of in each organism. Whether this organism stays in good function biochemically depends mostly on what it is fed with: nutrition is the formative colour producer in irises extra to their basic genetic one.

An efficient metabolism, taking in food, absorbing nutrients from it in a balanced way, and removing completely any residues and wastes, will show the clearest and best iris colours. As parts of the function fall lower in efficiency (a chill to the kidneys slows down uric acid removal; a birthday dinner overloads the liver and gall-bladder and pancreas; tension increases the need for magnesium, calcium and phosphorus), the metabolism endeavours to adjust in some way to meet the conditions. If it can do this using its own defence resources of rest and resistance and instinctive re-balancing, the colour of the iris will not change at all, or may register only the tiniest colour variation which is not visible except under very high magnification.

You all know what a sudden over-indulgence in alcohol can do to the colour of your eyes the next morning. A yellowish-grey iris film as well as a bloodshot 'white' give you that bleary look for many hours until your excretory organs can get rid of the excess load. A similar colour change occurs in viral attacks, prolonged illnesses, and terminal situations. The body cannot cope with the metabolic overload and becomes inefficient at rubbish removal, new cell re-building, and everyday maintenance of function: the vitality, the 'life quality', is lowered and chronic *functional* ill-health can be the result.

Best nutritional pattern

Just as the structure of the body reflects mostly its mineral balance, so the function of the body is mostly dependent on its vitamin absorption that enables the appropriate minerals to be used. It is certainly possible to swallow a whole pile of multicoloured vitamin tablets each morning and still have very imperfect iris colour and general health. The efficiency of *absorption* of these vitamins, which then activate the mineral-based structure, determines your functional health. It's no use taking yeast or wheatgerm oil or straight vitamin B-complex tablets if your small intestine is clogged and under-active so that absorption of the vitamin is slow and difficult. Nor is it of much benefit to you if your small intestine is ulcerated, tense, or too speedy: the vitamin B is passed through as an irritant substance too quickly for proper absorption. So much of your functional balance lies in the understanding of your own best nutritional pattern—different for each individual—and what types of foods and simple food supplements will best maintain peak efficiency. Sometimes therapeutic correction must be done in a hurry to eliminate very real illness symptoms; but after that a simple, suitable nutritional pattern should be enough to maintain the better balance.

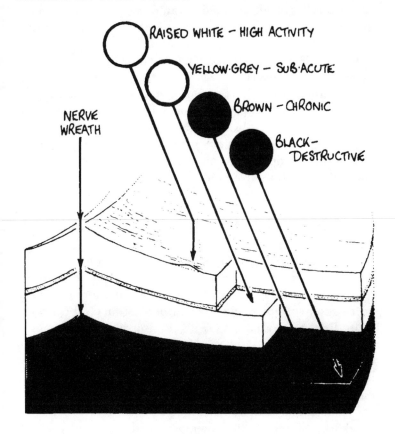

Iris Colour

The tone and colour range from white to black can be correlated to degrees of inefficiency of function.

1. *White.* The body is fighting hard to re-establish its own balance; to heal up, remove rubbish, and restore normal balance functionally.

57

2. *Whitish-Yellow.* The battle is becoming harder. Some body functions are showing signs of distress and constant overload.

3. *Yellowish-Brown, Yellowish-Grey.* Chronic and/or recurrent symptoms of functional disorders appear. There is gradual hypo-function of the affected organ or system, and need for constant or strong supportive therapy to regain initial function.

4. *Reddish-Brown, Grey-Brown.* The organ or function is under chronic, heavy overload, with possible tissue destruction and/or abnormal new tissue growth. The inefficiency of waste removal needs more prolonged treatment. The organ or system must be slowly re-educated.

5. *Black.* Tissue destruction; tissue removal (surgery, tooth extraction); complete atrophy of an organ (rare), parasitic infestation (worms, liver fluke, hydatids).

WHEN COLOURS DETERIORATE

We shall look harder at the evidence on eye colours reflecting functional patterns as we go 'around the clock' on the iris chart (Chaper 7). But let us examine here in more detail the processes involved as colours deteriorate from clear (showing white first) to darker shades if the disorder continues.

Normal function is a terribly abnormal occurrence in humans. Ideally, a perfect diet should produce a perfect biochemistry; but a perfect diet for one person is not only imperfect for another but may be actually harmful. While one person harmonises on paw-paw and lemon juice for breakfast, another needs raw muesli and yeast and yoghurt, whilst a third person could be severely functionally hampered for the day without a red, thick steak with an egg on top. This is where a practical iridologist/naturopath, with a good background of nutritional, anatomical, and physiological training, can determine for you your own personal 'perfect' balance nutritionally and explain how to achieve it and then stay generally within its broad limits. Iris colour should slowly change, maybe in a week, maybe over years and years, as you undo some pretty unfortunate nutritional mistakes committed mainly out of ignorance or from reading too many fanatical diet books.

Let's think again of a new-born kitten and its clear, brilliant eyes. Its initial chemistry may show a different type of nutritional deprivation many years later in the yellow-rimmed, grey-tinged, fearful eyes of the unloved alley-cat, badly fed and harshly treated. Emotional 'feeding' is necessary, too, and bad emotional conditions can also record functional colour changes as their end result. 'Man does not live by bread alone!'

○ A Balanced View

I shake my finger at some of my fanatically dedicated friends and co-workers in the field of natural health when they become too rigid and too puritanical to allow *emotional* feeding in a balanced way. Don't feel bad about that cream-cake sin at lunch or you may finish up with the emotionally 'bad' food of guilt as well—much harder to digest than the original indulgence. You may also finish up with a thick brown 'fog' over your liver area, as much from eating the guilt as from eating all that sticky, empty carbohydrate. If you must commit the occasional nutritional sin, *enjoy* it, and at least you are lightening a part of your liver's load. (Eat some dandelion greens the next day, in salad or steamed, and you have taken the load off altogether.)

Balance, as in every other natural process, can be achieved by knowledge of how to load and unload the scales. Colour deviations in the iris need not occur if such knowledge is applied practically with common sense. Of course, if you are going to eat two or three cream buns every day and apple charlotte on Wednesdays, and chocolate éclairs on Friday as a special treat, your liver's task is passing the 'white' stage and progressing down the colour scale. It may need not only dandelion greens the next day, but each day lecithin and vitamins B_1, B_2, B_6, plus vitamins A and D in balance, plus a change to dandelion coffee and lemon-grass tea—for quite a long period to tip the balance slowly back. Colour deterioration is more cumulative than sudden. While white and black signs can register almost immediately after physical trauma (surgery, accidents), yellowish, greyish, and brown shades appear imperceptibly and slowly as the nutritional and/or circumstantial balance is continually overloaded.

Many, many people who are walking around, apparently 'healthy', show abnormal dark colour patches and spots in various iris zones. 'I'm not sick!' they'll say if you look at their irises and comment on the murky colours. A little more probing may uncover a history of chronic constipation or frequent heavy chest colds. They may crawl out of bed every morning feeling nauseated, or urinate only twice a day, or have a constant craving for sweet foods which they are proud of resisting. All the signs of a chronic sub-health pattern are there. Most people believe themselves to be healthy when symptoms of ill-health are absent. This is not 'healthy'; this is *neutral* health. They may not be sick, but they are not well either.

One of the saddest comments on health I have heard came from an eminent member of the medical profession at a recent naturopathic/medical seminar. 'Let's teach them all how to live quite comfortably *with* their disabilities,' he said. 'That's life, after all.' It's not, you know; sub-health doesn't have to be accepted or adjusted to. Adjustment within ourselves to find, understand, and remove, small problems before they become big ones can result in *positive* health and a return, slowly or fast, to clearer iris colours when the body is able to regulate its own metabolism and homoeostasis balance day by day without outside support of any kind. Then you can commit occasional sins which keep you human and nice to be with—without suffering any more than a slight swing of your balance down and then up again easily.

WHITE

Purity, cleanliness, simplicity, innocence, light, brilliance: how do you think of white? In an iris it can mean phosphorus, calcium, and magnesium, structurally; vitamin C (and some A and D as well), functionally. It can also indicate no more and no less than an imbalance of these substances, sometimes too much, sometimes too little, sometimes enough normally, but after a sudden trauma needing a sharp increase. Let's take a theoretical example.

A fit young lad, nine or ten, gets wet through standing on the sidelines as a reserve player for his soccer team. He's reserve because he badly twisted his right ankle last week and it's not quite healed yet. Wet, cold and shivering, his ankle stiff and still painful, his body is about to show symptoms of actual illness. A look at his clear blue iris could show on the right side a white patch and whiter fibres at and around the thigh, knee and foot zone. Acute pain, inflammation, swelling and heat were present here last week, and the body, with rest and support, is fighting off the attack. To repair the damage, phosphorus, magnesium, calcium, vitamin C, and vitamins A and D, are needed in large quantities. If the boy's body is in very good health he can draw on his own internal resistance and heal up quickly. If the acute demand for these substances cannot be met internally it must be met by taking increased quantities of them therapeutically in the diet or in simple supplements. The ankle should then heal up quickly and completely.

However, he is still standing there in the rain, getting colder and becoming more susceptible to attack by viruses and bacteria as his body temperature drops in a 'chill'. Most of his resistance and adrenal 'fight-back' are being used solving his ankle problem, and a streptococcus invades throat and larynx without opposition. That night he shivers and gets a headache; the next morning he shows a temperature rise and a sore throat. By that evening he's in bed sweating and feverish, coughing, and without energy as his body tries to meet and overcome another acute attack from a different direction. If he is strong enough to do this, there may be only the smallest of white patches and/or a structural lesion at throat, larynx, and chest zones. There may be whiter patches around the sinus areas and bronchial tree, too, if the attack increases to bronchitis and upper respiratory infection. While his body can fight this off, the relevant colours will still be white. As his resistance is lowered and finally overcome, a yellowish tinge can colour the white patches.

He is approaching the second stage of disease: symptoms may hang on and on, with low energy and decreased resistance. And that ankle may take months and months to heal completely, because such acute demands for similar healing substances were being made elsewhere in his body at the same time. Even six months later, his ankle may still show white signs in the iris and may be tender and sore and unable to take its former structural load. It needs yet more of those healing substances it missed out on before. If it still doesn't get them, yellow colours may tinge the white here, too, drawing attention to the fact that the boy now has an inefficient right ankle. It will work, but it has limitations.

On the other hand, our soccer player may be a thoroughly well-nourished young man who recovers quickly from his ankle accident and whose chill produces no more than an overnight sniffle. Hardly any white signs will be showing, and the iris will register only the clear blue as before.

O Hyper-Function

White colours indicate always a state of *hyper-function*. Not only is the body working well: it may be working almost too well. Hyper-active children show many white areas in the iris. Stomach, head areas, spinal nerves, and limbs, may all show as over-stimulated, over-active. Their bodies are in a constant adrenal-stimulus state, irritating nerves which drop uric acid waste products from the nerve endings, flooding tissues and causing yet more over-acidity. The pale iris often found in hyperactive children is blue overlaid with the whitest of Persil-white. Every body process can be in a state of over-use. No wonder such hyper-activity can result in 'burning out', so that by mid-teens the opposite side of Nature's balance may be experienced: lethargy, slowness, dullness, and mental deterioration. Through years of the first process, the iris can stay very white, fighting a Quixotic battle still, unable to stop.

If you consider the conditions in which colours can be expected to be found, you will realise that many of them involve sudden shock and acute or severe continuing pain. You break a leg; strain your lumbar spine in the garden; get a toothache and have the dentist drill painfully deeply; you have a car accident and whiplash your neck; a sudden viral onslaught gives you a crashing headache; a sore throat makes it almost impossible to swallow. All these acute disturbances in function produce pain.

Secondarily they produce inflammation, the body's first line of defence *against* pain. The painful areas swell with fluid as a 'cushion': blood is rushed to the spot to burn up dead cell remains and live invading agents like viruses and bacteria with its iron and oxygen to start the fire, and *heat* is produced.

A white-coloured iris may be recording not only pain and trauma but also a high degree of body heat. Those people who poke their over-hot feet out of the bedclothes or wear only a shirt in the middle of winter often show very white nerve fibres and white patches and spots, too. Unfortunately, the negative end of the same pattern of a hot, dry metabolism and a whitish iris can produce the *negative heat* of arthritic and rheumatic joints, bursitis, fibrositis, and spondylitis. The fire can burn up too high altogether.

As an indicator of pain, whiteness is relative to the degree of the pain *recorded*, not experienced. Those fortunate Silks, with their high pain threshold, may not even recognise a pain that a Hessian person would find intolerable. Don't forget that the iris records the impression and expression at the level at which it is truly received or transmitted by the individual.

As pain recedes, white raised fibres relax and acute white patches disappear as the oxygenating 'fire' removes waste products. My own experience of a crushed lumbar disc after a severe lower spine accident showed in my iris the progression of acute white signs at the lumbar area of the back zone. As the pain released its claws, so did the white colour lose its brilliance and intensity. Under simple natural treatment and chiropractic adjustment, the white faded in a matter of weeks. But a tiny structural lesion remains as a warning that my body's resources were used to the limit to regrow that disc to its present functional level; it is not as strong as it was before the trauma occurred. This often happens after a 'white' type trauma. A structural lesion can remain as a record of a battle fought and won. A 'patch' has been made, but not quite well enough to blend in again as a strong/normal piece of body.

White can indicate another form of body defence, similar to the inflammatory processes of fighting off traumatic damage—mucus production. One of the lesser-known jobs of mucus—the thick excretion of colds and catarrh and colitis and vaginitis and bronchitis—is to repel harmful invading agents attacking the openings of the body: the eyes, nostrils, mouth and throat, ears, vagina, urethra, and rectum. A normal body reaction to attack on the mucus lining is to *flood* the area—if setting fire to it does not remove the threat! As the body senses a streptococcal, staphylococcal, viral, or spirochaete invasion through its soft, wet-lined openings (or even an invasion by pollutants in the air or cigarette smoke) it can produce an increased flow of mucus to literally wash off the attackers. This happens most obviously in the common cold. The sniffles and the sneezes, even the coughs, loaded with white mucus, are first attempts to physically dislodge the invaders before they can penetrate the vulnerable soft linings.

○ Weakening Process

Of course, if you *constantly* over-produce mucus, are always clearing your throat in the mornings and can't go out without a handkerchief, your body is over-reacting. That white flood is registering in the iris as unnecessary sabre-rattling. You shouldn't be under attack as often as that! If you *are* at risk it can be because your nutritional intake is heavily loaded with acid-producing foods like milk, processed cheese, white sugar, overcooked meat, white bread, and take-away foods—not forgetting alcohol and cigarette smoking. The end result of such poor nutrition can be a permanent state of panic induced in your body's mucus linings. They over-produce mucus, biochemically sensing their own vulnerable condition. After a while, this over-production can cause an actual pre-disease condition—clogging of the tissues with the sticky, acid mucus and a subsequent drop in structural and functional efficiency. The army that's always attacking shadows finds itself unprepared for real dangers. Crying wolf too often can bore the defences and a real wolf can get through unnoticed. Those who over-produce mucus may weaken the mucus linings so that a *real* attack can penetrate far too easily.

The same substances required for pain, for inflammation, and accidental structural damage, can also be required when white evidence in the iris suggests over-production of mucus. The foggy white clouds visible in various zones like bronchial tree, upper sinuses, throat, nasal and ear areas, can blow away on adjustment of the calcium, phosphorus, and magnesium balance, together with the vitamins A, D and C.

White iris 'fog' like this may take some time to dissipate while the body normalises its over-reactive pattern; but nutritional adjustment (cutting out foods that produce mucus such as fatty dairy products and sugary foods) can make the time shorter and the results more permanent. Such patients may also show the white, raised fibres of high adrenal flow. Natural 'fighters', they may need time, and patience as well, to calm them down and stop their shadow-boxing.

○ White Signals

Are you getting all the implications of white? Look at it, in any context, as *increased* levels of function, sometimes to deal with real threats, sometimes with imagined ones, but always fighting. As the whiteness returns to 'normal' colour the battle is won; as it deteriorates to yellows, greys and darker, help is needed.

A particular body area or function can be singled out for 'white' hyper-function. A white thyroid area can indicate an over-speedy metabolism where you burn up your food and flood out your rubbish so fast that you stay painfully skinny and under-weight. You not only throw out wastes a little too radically but also eliminate some of the good nutritional substances with them. Your white thyroid reflects chemical impatience.

A white adrenal reaction shows constantly in both irises of one of my favourite patients, a top barrister. He's not only constantly defending on other people's behalf but also prosecuting equally fiercely (I suspect on his own behalf). When the courts are in recess, his white adrenal glands boil and over-react with frustration and hyper-active inhibition of their normal outlet. His family sighs with relief when the legal year opens once again.

There is one more 'white' indication which may seem contradictory to previous statements that white colours are seen when the body is valiantly fighting acute symptoms of any type and winning. This is what could be termed 'chronic' whiteness. As the hyper-active child is not really winning either, just fighting too hard continually, so is the pale-all-over, ice-blue iris indicative of a continuous over-production, not of mucus maybe, but of over-*acid* end products of metabolic function. The white coloration of mucus shows in patches, fog-like and amorphous; an over-acid-producing metabolism shows more in either very, very white *fibres* and/ or almost solid white overlay between them.

The possessor of such irises almost certainly comes from Silk or Silk/Linen stock and has a family history of arthritic and 'stiffness' diseases. The acidic wastes lodged in body tissues may also result from the diet and too much acid-forming alcohol; but just as frequently these 'Antarctic' irises are recording another form of tissue-acid residue—*nerve* acid. Each time a physical nerve fibre is used to send or receive a message, it excretes a tiny droplet of acid from its ending. You can imagine the flood of acid saturating tissues at the end of the activity-filled days of Silks and Silk/Linens! This is another good reason why they should have a high fluid intake, to move such waste products quickly into and through the body's major elimination channels of lungs, skin, kidneys, and bowels.

Many Silks and Silk/Linens eat simple food of high quality, yet show the 'acid' eye so criticised by food fanatics as indicative of a poor diet containing too many refined foods and empty carbohydrates. The real reason for the high-acid residues lies between their genetic predisposition and their constant nervous activity. An awareness of the problem is often enough to stop its bad effects. A few simple dietary procedures (sometimes even alfalfa tea alone) can counteract all the negative effects of hyper-acid tissue wastes, and yet still leave the white 'chronic' pattern in the iris, because the next day that same level of nervous activity will be operative again. It can be *balanced* rather than stopped altogether.

More 'white' states of function in various body zones will be dealt with as we learn more from the iris map (pp. 131, 132).

YELLOW-WHITE

Our soccer player is still in bed, but listless, cranky, and off his food. He now has a heavy cough (with yellow-white mucus expectorated), and a few of his many sneezes produce yellow-white mucus blown out from clogged antrums and sinuses. An extra colour has been added to the fighting array of blue and white—yellow.

White inflammatory processes, or mucus, or pain flares,

may show in a *brown* iris as yellow-white too, the darker basic pigment masking the brilliance of white signs and making them appear more yellowish. Practice (and questions) will help you distinguish the paling of a brown iris that corresponds to the 'white' functional state more obvious in a blue one.

The yellow colour amongst, or apparently *on top of*, white signs tells us another mineral/vitamin combination is now joining the fight—sulphur, chlorine, and vitamins A and D again. The first-stage processes of resistance have not succeeded. Physical energy-raising by increasing adrenal output; physical fires and floods to remove the threat—extra protection by mucus at all vulnerable entry points: none of these simple forms of defence has been enough. The second line of defence is now called into action—chemical warfare. The liver and the gall-bladder and the bile duct, even the pancreas, work together to chemically 'surround' the invaders and inactivate them.

Have you ever wondered why sulphonamide drugs are prescribed medically for many chronic infections? The answer is partly found in the liver, the biochemical 'factory' of the body. Sulphur and chlorine work as a team here, helping to activate enzymes, producing digestive juices and hormones, reinforcing vitamins A and D, and potassium and sodium, in balancing cell fluids and *chemical* removal of waste by either metabolically 'eating' it or digesting and excreting it.

You can now understand why this second stage of an illness makes you feel below par, always a little tired, often cranky and touchy, too susceptible to stresses. Your body is forced to work too hard eliminating all this residue by metabolising it as well as the ordinary food you eat each day. You have a double load of function to carry. No wonder you're tired! This is also why a short sensible fast can often disperse, in a few days, illness symptoms that have hung on and on, unable to be entirely removed by other methods. Your body can concentrate metabolically *only* on rubbish re-digestion and removal, without taking on its usual load of new food as well. Fasting, with maybe one herb tea or one fruit juice chosen to support the digestion and excretion organs (celery-seed tea for the kidneys and 'acid' waste removal; carrot juice for the liver; fennel tea for the pancreas; senna pods infusion to help cleanse the bowel), can be a way to remove the 'yellow' symptoms and much yellow colour from the eye, too.

The chronic cough of our sick boy is going to make him thirsty. He will also instinctively want increased fluid intake rather than solid food. His skin colour may be greyish-yellow by now, too, contributing to the new recording of yellow colour in the iris. This iris yellowing may persist for weeks, months, years, or generations. Sulphur is a hard mineral to disguise and to remove from the body; and, since much of its work is done within cells and cell-fluids, its residues can tend to stay in the cell code-memory long after its work is done. Chlorine compounds can also have yellow-stain properties. As with the previous colour pattern, a yellowish recording in the iris can either indicate high activity of these minerals, or a great need for increased supply, or a need for balancing of their function.

○ Second Yellow Phase

The sub-acute stage of illness now operates. The body may not even know that it has not fully recovered, sighing, 'That's life!' It doesn't have to be. Many patients of mine tell me, 'I've never really been well since that flu two years ago'; or 'I can date all my tiredness back to after that operation.' Yellow iris colours could have shown at that time. They may be brown now, but this is simply a colour change from an earlier phase of the pattern when yellowish signs could have been seen.

There is certainly the possibility of complete recovery from this point, but it will take time and effort and an understanding of the processes involved. It may well take a very long time to achieve the state of real health in which the body *should* have been before that first chill started the downwards progression.

It is sad that many people will not give the time and patience, or make the disciplinary effort, required for complete recovery. In this 'yellow' stage they often reach for a tablet, or another cup of coffee, to perk up their failing energy, or ask their medical adviser for a tranquilliser to enable them to cope. These crutches may help in the short term; but they are artificial supports and should never become so permanent that the body relies on them to maintain what is only sub-standard health.

I believe this second 'yellow' stage of illness to be the hardest of all to correct. The person may not even feel ill, only generally below par and suffering from stress. A holiday, another beer, an aspirin, a sleep-in on Sunday morning; all or any of these things may *alleviate* the problem—but *correct* it? Never! Most of a civilised population seems content to remain in some state of sub-acute ill-health, never experiencing positive health at all.

Some of the conditions recording in the iris as yellow signs are indicative of this 'not sick/not well' state. Hay-fever may record in nasal and upper sinuses, in eye areas, and even in the bronchial tree, as a yellowish overlay on white. One hangover may not register, but a hangover every morning certainly will show as yellowish around the liver and its associated organs. An inefficient fat metabolism is one of the commonest causes of yellowed iris areas, and shows some signs in the 'white' of the eye (the sclera), too. Let's see how such signs can indicate sub-acute illnesses.

O Nutritional Measures

Of protein, fat, and carbohydrate elements in food, fat is the hardest to digest completely. Excess protein may load up your kidneys and constipate your bowel, but methods to stimulate both organs can remove the excess. Carbohydrates, like white sugar, white bread, and alcohol, can flood your body with acid waste products; but simple counter measures nutritionally can often neutralise the acidic tissue effect quite quickly. Fats, however, can remain as fats. Your liver, pancreas, and gall-bladder can process just so much at the time of ingestion and no more. The upper bowel feels the first load, and your 'tummy' gets a little flabby and larger. If the bowel can't remove these remains before another fat-flood hits it, it will off-load the fats into the bloodstream, to be carried away and deposited in other parts of the body which have no way of metabolising the greasy globules. Up goes your weight, and yellowish colours flood your iris, reflecting the body's saturation level. One good way to remove such fat is *exercise* to burn the excess fat as a body fuel. Eyes showing much yellow colouring should tell their owner to move harder, faster, and more often, as well as adjust his chemical balance.

Don't forget that blue and yellow make green! Green is not a natural body colour (unless one is a Martian!) and greening of irises shows a particular metabolic inheritance as well as a current functional imbalance. The green-eyed, red-haired Irish are examples. The Irish temper and the Irish ingestion of fats are both high. An eye that is really green is impossible to find. A good mid-blue eye is not going to indicate a fats or mucus problem over its entire iris. Neither will a healthy blue turn suddenly yellow all over under illness assault. So this build-up of yellow over blue, producing green, has a genetic base. The Irish consumption of fat bacon and pork and dairy products and their basic Celtic metabolic type have produced over many generations trigger-happy 'yellow' systems and acid waste irritation—an explosive mixture. That Titian-haired colleen with the pale green eyes is fiery for many real functional reasons. See how pale is any 'green' eye under your iris torch illumination. It's blue or white-blue overlaid with yellow, not real green at all.

There is another type of yellow coloration which can give warning of approaching 'brown' conditions: greyish-yellow. Any greying of a clear colour indicates a state of hypo-function (under function) approaching or already existing.

Grey-yellow patches over the bronchial tree can show that this part of the body has no longer enough energy available to remove waste products and regain normal function. A type of atrophy can result. The organ may lose its ability to shed dead cells and build new ones. It may transfer its functions to another organ or system, overloading it in its turn, or it may need a constant supportive crutch. A typical example is a greyish-yellow 'stomach circle' around the pupil. Such a stomach has lost its flexibility, its bounce, and probably its hydrochloric acid and enzyme functions as well. Under-activity is approaching a chronic state. Constant medication 'thumps' are needed to get a response at all.

The patient should be made fully aware that unless a function or organ is stimulated by *use* it will never get stronger. It may be only a matter of taking camomile tea at night to increase and balance calcium and phosphorus function, of nibbling ginger between meals and olives before a meal, of having high intake of B2 vitamin foods: but don't let such a metabolic slump continue. A low-energy area of the body is in danger of inviting other illness symptoms to gain hold. Don't just say, 'I've got a weak stomach ... I can't eat ...' and begin a long list of forbidden foods. As well as being difficult to invite for dinner, you become afraid of your own weakness—not a desirable precondition for eventual recovery. I see so many patients who are afraid of their body letting them down. Their stomachs or their bowels or their heads become tyrants, dictating a life-style to accommodate their 'weakness'. You don't have to put up with sub-health. It is an unnatural state, and understanding and simple correctives can remove it in the early stages, once the condition is recognised.

I get rather cross with patients who accept such sub-standard health as the best that can be expected 'under the circumstances' whatever those may be. Circumstances can be, and are, changed by healthy people.

Summarising 'yellow': The body is marshalling and then using its second defence system after the first has not proved adequate. Increased 'yellow' activity may mean difficulty with fat metabolism and clogging of the body with its residues. It may also mean that such problems have been genetically yours by inheritance; but there's no reason not to lessen such genetic patterns for children and grandchildren by corrective measures now. 'Yellow' also means you are falling too far behind in your future defence potential. Iron may become necessary if the 'yellow' process remains unbalanced or uncorrected. Iron compounds, the big guns of defence, may need calling out for the next process— browning.

REDDISH-BROWN, BROWN

If you thought the yellows sounded somewhat alarming, be prepared for the really bad news with the browns! Let us look at the iris structure anatomically and find out why a deteriorating pattern should register as brown, and a middling pattern as yellow, and an acute symptomatic attack as white.

Iris tissue, as well as recording structural and functional type, indicates the *levels* at which the structure and function are operating at the time of observation. An acute process of function will show in the surface layer of iris tissue. It may even show as raising of the surface layer into white 'embossing' (see diagram, p. 57). The body's hyper-function to remove acute symptoms shows as raising of the iris tissue, too. The yellow processes and functions last mentioned show as depressions, three-dimensionally, into the iris-surface tissue. Greyish signs show flat areas of non-activity or sluggish function. The browns begin to enter deeper areas of tissue, uncovering iris layers to reveal the degree of ill-health present. A 'brown' recording should be a reason for concern.

As we discover the logic of iris analysis, the 'fail-safe' recording of serious damage becomes a most valuable diagnostic sign. I have medical practitioners sending me patients when there is difficulty in diagnosing the *cause* of the problem, or even the basic problem itself. I look for brown areas in the iris to show me where the basic treatment patterns should begin.

'Brown' equals 'chronic'. Brown discolorations point to body areas where the body is not only below normal standards of function but may also be building up patterns of abnormal function (*different* function). There is a fine dividing line between low function and negative function. In the latter, the body is not only not going forward, it is actively moving backwards.

Let's look at an iris which is blue basically, but in which a greybrown overlay in some areas has deepened to dark brown over both kidneys. Such a patient, whether aware of it or not, is suffering from degenerative processes in these organs. Not only are the kidneys below par: they have deteriorated to the point where massive support may not be enough.

O Attacking The Problems

Undoing processes are necessary—elimination of waste products, removal of dead cells and tissue, burning out of rubbish, using *iron* as a major oxygenator; and such elimination may be quite uncomfortable. A patient experiencing white and yellow states of function should feel better as nutritional and therapeutic support is given. A patient showing brown signs in the iris may feel remarkably uncomfortable when corrective procedures are undertaken.

In this 'brown' classification are found many chronic illnesses in which repeated lowering of function has produced abnormal pathology and physical symptoms of severe disease. The patient who says 'I've had so many problems with my right ear. I had abscesses and repeated infections as a child, and I've never been able to dive or swim underwater without discomfort. The ear is always cold and sensitive, and now I'm getting a buzzing noise in it and it itches all the time ....' is showing symptoms of 'brown' chronicity. The ear has become a major trouble spot. By the time this has happened, the same patient may be showing many other symptoms like right-sided headaches, blocked Eustachian tubes, chronic sore throats, pains under the ear and at the back of the neck, neuralgia of the right side of the face, and even aching teeth as well. All these smaller symptoms could be treated continually with many other support 'crutches', but they would never clear completely. The old ear weakness is the thing to attack, not the resultant complications. *But*, direct action at the ear itself can produce real discomfort, even pain, and the necessarily severe 'undoing' may cause discharges, unexplainable sharp pains, even more headaches, dizziness and loss of balance, diarrhoea and general tiredness, making the patient feel, apparently, very much worse than before. But persistence can show real and lasting health rewards.

Of course the body will protest, and quite vigorously too, against such painful undoing; but those who stay with such a course can experience the very real rewards of reversing a destructive health pattern completely. I have ceased to use my own energy to reassure the patient during the uncomfortable patches. I explain, but I no longer try to support the patient completely. Those who are determined to persist will get the result; the others don't care enough or don't know enough about real health processes yet, and it is very demanding on the practitioner to keep continually reinforcing their lack of faith. Those who *do* persevere through the initial rough patches are a joy to treat. Watching the brown signs slowly fade in an iris as treatment progresses is exciting. Watching the *person* is even more exciting. Surprise from the patient is usual, but sometimes he is genuinely astonished at the efficiency of the body once it is given the required conditions for elimination, repair, and renewal. Total recovery from many severe ill-health conditions has rewarded those persevering patients.

Brown patches, streaks, and fogs, indicate a need for more iron, and usually vitamin C with it. The rusty red-brown coloration needs fast iron; the blackish-brown or grey-brown needs slower and more gradual treatment. Many of the 'brown' eyes, which are not really brown at all but brownish overlay on basic blue, belong to people whose bodies are quite inefficient at rubbish disposal. Their blood oxygen levels are always low, their energy is medium to minus, and their recovery after illness can be slow and incomplete.

It sounds a pessimistic picture, and many of you 'brown'-eyed Caucasians may hotly deny that you may be setting up destructive patterns in certain body areas which will get you in the end. Maybe 'in the end' is not so bad; but what if it's at twenty-seven or thirty-four that such ill-health becomes hopelessly apparent? Are you going to give up and accept major disease for another fifty years, maybe more? Spotting brown areas in the iris early, and undertaking strong restorative treatment before too much damage has been done, can remove many later fears and anxieties about health.

We left our soccer-playing lad in the yellow stage of his ill-health progression. We now find him out of bed, far too soon and contrary to all good sense, at evening soccer practice. He is dry-coughing, in some pain, his chest feels sore and tight, breathing is shallow, and he can no more do his three training laps around the oval than fly. His coach sends him home with instructions to see the doctor and get rid of his bronchial infection before he can return to play again with the team. After a course of antibiotics, he *appears* to be quite recovered a week later, and rejoins the game; but it is obvious to coach and supporters alike that he is no longer a fast-reflexed left-wing goal-scorer. Soon he is downgraded to the B team, his confidence falls, his cough returns, and he loses weight. Occasional days home from school in bed fail to restore his energy, and a new symptom appears— wheezing and difficulty in breathing on exertion. His illness has not been *removed* by the antibiotics, only *suppressed* for a time. Instead of his body vigorously expelling the remains of his ill-health, its fight has been 'called off' temporarily by the antibiotics.

In his iris begin the first brown patches in one lung and the bronchial tree. Before six months have elapsed, he is onto nasal sprays and more antibiotics. There is further suppression and no elimination. The basic principle of a body's need to fight off and remove remains of illness patterns has been violated. The problem is temporarily *buried*, not removed, and will return under stress conditions. We now have a formerly fit young lad condemned to quite severe ill-health symptoms. His body was not allowed (let alone ever *encouraged*) to eliminate and remove and excrete and *finalise* the process of illness. The brown discoloration of chronic poor health with all its limitations can be the result. If simple natural measures had been taken at the 'white' or even the 'yellow' stage to support the body's elimination systems, no chronic pattern need have developed. Major elimination at this stage can be impossible.

O Signs Of Toxicity

I have many patients who tell me horrendous stories of how their bowels move only once every five days, ten days or even three weeks! Some of these patients may have clear blue eyes if only the peristaltic signals to the bowel are missing. These are the children and adults with 'spastic colon' labels: their bowels just never get an accurate message to move when full. But others with similar constipation histories show in the iris around the stomach, the small intestine, and bowel areas, thick patches of brown 'mud'. These mud-puddles may spill over into iris body zones radiating out beyond that particular part of the digestive tract circle. Blobs of brown and reddish-brown overflowing from the transverse colon can affect many physiological and psychological functions of the head; brown bowel-fog may stretch from the sigmoid colon, out over kidneys, adrenal glands, and adjacent zones.

This browning indicates some degree of toxicity or auto-intoxication—rubbish—in the areas covered by it. You may still be hotly denying that such apparently severe destructive processes can be experienced by you without any obvious symptoms. Let's see how obvious these symptoms become under closer scrutiny.

Do you adjust circumstances to fit your sub-health or are you able to adapt your plus-health to whatever circumstances happen to you? Do you need your potatoes cooked a certain way before your stomach can handle them without indigestion resulting? Do you need a laxative every day? Do you have a severe reaction on sitting in a draught, lifting things, or sleeping on a different mattress from your own? Do you need early nights all the week and does even a happy, sociable weekend hold too much energy demand for you, so you stay home? Are your memory and concentration always poor? Have a good look at yourself, naked, in a mirror. Is your muscle tone all it could be, or does lower-back pain, stiff right shoulder, or sore left arm, compel you into a permanently awkward posture even to gain a small measure of comfort? Did you ever get that earache attended to or do you accept a sensitive 'ringing' ear as one of the inevitable consequences of being past fifty? Do you accept inefficiency and sub-standard performance from your employees, your grocer or your political party?

If you do accept such things, you probably also accept any limitations to your well-being in the way of chronic inefficiency from your body. Such acceptance may register in the iris as brownish areas of 'rubbish' which your body is carrying around with it, like garbage cans half-full or even overflowing. No wonder you feel tired and below par! As well as the stresses you meet in the course of each day, you are bearing extra stress before you even start. Your body has not completely removed dead cells, bacterial wastes, accumulations of pollutants, chemical residues from drugs, mucus, pus—from yesterday and last week and maybe from years past. Each of these areas of sub-standard performance can register as brown patches in the iris. What is worse, such areas can be deteriorating day by day.

As the body recognises such rubbish deposit areas, it can attempt to encapsulate them and isolate them from other adjacent zones which can still be functioning very well. A cyst or tumour may form (a sac enclosing all this rubbish) and such 'soil' can be fertile ground for the increase of random cells, those abnormal cells found in malignant growths.

⭕ Cleaning-Up Tactics

Let me stop you right now from panicking if you see deep brown fog all around your basic blue iris. Don't for a moment think that such signs necessitate an urgent medical check, with 'the worst' to follow. This would be an over-reaction to what can be recorded in the iris as a simple need for a general clean-up. Fast for a few days, drink some appropriate herb teas and juices, consult a professional naturopathic practitioner to find out whether you need therapeutic assistance or whether it's just a passing tummy 'wog', a lazy organ that needs a natural boost, or a real disorder that may need some simple herbal remedies, vitamins, minerals, and food supplements, to clean out the 'garbage-can'. But please don't panic! That will produce another stress which is probably quite out of proportion to the problem.

Differentiation must be made between the degrees of 'brown' in the iris. There are three main types: darkish brown fog, brown streaks, and red-brown 'angry' flares. There is a much more common type of brown known to orthodox medicine as 'pigmentation spots', but referred to as 'psoric spots' by iridologists. These are totally different in character, appearing not as brown coloration at the deep layers of the iris, but as sepia-coloured stippled flecks, dots, and patches, lying apparently just below the cornea itself, floating in front of the iris tissue. These psoric spots will be better described and explained in the section 'Special Signs'.

Brown patches don't always mean bad problems but they do indicate the need for *recognition* that the part of the body showing brown coloration is experiencing much less than its best potential function. The most common areas in the iris for brownish discoloration are the stomach and the bowel circle. Here is where your fuel should be taken aboard, processed, and its waste products removed. If foods are *not* completely metabolised and residues removed, rubbish stock-piles can slide into adjacent body zones.

A look at the iris will show you the problem exactly as it is. A brown cloud may be spilling from the sigmoid colon down and into pelvic organs, and over the rectum. Symptoms can be expected in these latter areas as well as in the prime cause site, the bowel itself. Many so-called 'mental illnesses' can be vastly improved by clearing the tranverse colon of its brown accumulation that affects the physiological and psychological functions of the head.

I remember a family GP in my childhood telling my mother: 'Teach kids to keep their mouths shut and their bowels open; it's all a matter of garbage removal. If stress doesn't come out one end it'll come out the other!' Maybe that's why so many of us nowadays are guilty of boring verbal diarrhoea: we have reversed this basic tenet of good health! Our heads are accumulating overflow rubbish which our bowels can't get rid of properly.

An iris showing you a brownish bowel and intestinal area is telling you something: increase the intake of substances able to burn out rubbish and stimulate the organ or system involved to regain structural and functional efficiency *without* continuing support afterwards. Naturopathic treatment like this is never aimed at providing a permanent crutch for a weak function, but at overcoming the weakness completely and permanently. In my practice, iris photographs taken before, during, and after treatment can show amazing changes in brown areas as the rubbish is gradually burnt out and removed, usually from the bowel zone first.

Grey-brown 'streaks' can run radially out through body zones. When this happens, the organ or area can be showing *atrophy* as well as waste accumulation. Areas of tissue are no longer working even sluggishly, choked by rubbish, but are showing necrosis (cell and tissue death) where new cells are not being built and installed as fast as the old ones are succumbing. You may have a kidney growing old before its time or a thyroid ageing you at thirty! There is no need to accept any degree of 'dying' when there is enough restoration of body energy and oxygen and iron to reverse the deterioration.

Iron, in many natural forms, can provide the energy; vitamin C is the 'glue' to bind the strong new cells firmly together. Vitamin C and iron aid each other's absorption, and the greatest efficiency is obtained by using high natural sources of both like rosehips; together with garlic and liquorice and red clover and sarsaparilla, and many other herbs extremely high in natural iron, which have a laxative effect on the bowel, speeding up waste removal.

So 'brown' is not as worrying as it might be, if the patient understands and co-operates in giving the body a massive clean-up through the processes of excretion. A skin rash, boils, diarrhoea, increased urination, and *tiredness*, may be the initial results as this happens; tiredness because the body is working hard again in an area used to slacking and must be re-trained; and any or all of the other symptoms as a result of the excretory organs dumping wastes through all available outlets. Some people have none of these symptoms at all, only a feeling of energy and well-being gradually returning as they clean up more sedately and gradually. A constructive pattern of waste removal can be recognised by the patient's feeling *better* after each day's runny bowels, better after coughing up green mucus, better after the dark-brown urine is excreted: a different pattern altogether from that of an illness, when each day of such symptoms makes you feel *worse*. One is a process of return to health; the other is a degeneration into illness, and anyone who has experienced both can immediately recognise the difference.

○ Revealing Root Causes

Sometimes removal of brown fog from an iris can show the basic cause or causes clearly as iron, oxygen, and vitamin C clean up wastes and leave the real culprit or culprits in the minus-health pattern visible.

One of my best examples of this was a patient with both irises obscured by yellow-brown fog clouds of waste accumulation. I gasped at his overload. His skin was under-active and greenish-grey, his expression was of tired resignation, and his energy was nil. He was nauseated and couldn't think or concentrate without enormous effort. After massive natural iron started to clear his iris, a huge angry appendix area was uncovered beneath. I ordered him off to Casualty straight away. Several hours later his almost-ruptured, swollen appendix was removed. It was filled with watermelon seeds; and to his certain knowledge he had not eaten watermelon for about two years. Surely rubbish retained too long!

After his release from hospital, his body became covered with boils and other eruptions, and his iris paled more and more towards its basic blue as enormous amounts of residual tissue rubbish were unloaded through all channels. When I last saw him, his iris was at the pale yellow stage of undoing, and big patches of strong blue were visible below as his real health potential was slowly regained. He typically had felt *better* each day as the boils came out, not worse, indicating constructive, not destructive, processes at work.

Red-brown flares looking angry and isolated in basic blue eyes are a different problem, though still a type of rubbish-level indicator. These can be signs of inflammation, irritation, and more acute tissue break-down—localised tissue erosion. Sometimes these signs can be directly produced by heavy doses of medical drugs, particularly those containing sulphur and/or iron of synthetic composition, which produce adverse side-effects for this patient. Such iris signs can indicate long treatment of a disease with sulphonamides and such-like, and even with sedatives in an attempt to allay symptomatic discomfort; but the basic *cause* is persisting untreated. Typical areas for such reddish-brown flares are again the intestines and bowel, especially the duodenum, the ileo-caecal valve, the flexures of the bowel (the *corners* where the large bowel takes a sharp bend: hepatic flexure, splenic flexure, sigmoid flexure). Sometimes the red-brown flares can persist long after such treatment has ended, the iris still recording the earlier deposition of unacceptable drugs in surrounding tissue. Brighter orange-brown signs are more likely to be of sulphur-compound origin than of iron.

An orange-brown or darker brown nerve wreath (pp. 9-11) can indicate quite severe disorders: of drug origin, of imbalance between the sympathetic and parasympathetic nervous system, and even of neurotic and psychotic conditions. Again, don't panic and rush through the gates of your nearest psychiatric hospital if your eyes show this type of colour sign: there are many reasons why the body records abnormalities of function of the nervous system in brownish colours. Seek expert diagnosis.

Since brown signs indicate deterioration in function, one of the best ways to treat them therapeutically is with *tonic* herbs and nutritional boosting, not only to improve function but also to remove waste accumulations more efficiently by providing better blood supply to and from the affected area. This is why iron is the main mineral needed. Its oxygen-carrying function 'burns up' those wastes.

O Conditions Not Diseases

Patients often ask me whether cancer can be seen recorded in an iris. It cannot, any more than can the common cold. Irises record body conditions, not medically named diseases. A body which is thick with 'brown' cell-rubbish, clogged and congested with wastes which remain too long, is providing a *condition* where random cells can proliferate. This certainly does *not* mean that such cells *will* activate and reproduce their kind; but it means that a body condition is present which one is certainly better off without. So many things can activate random abnormal cells into reproduction (a shock, previous weakening of a part of the body functionally and/ or structurally, poor nutrition, emotional hopelessness, lack of exercise, for instance); but once activated they need 'dirt' in which to grow. Remove the dirt as fast as it accumulates, and the odds against random-cell activity producing serious illness are much more favourable.

There are certainly times when the amount of brownish rubbish showing in an iris makes a practitioner wonder whether the patient has enough vitality, oxygen, iron, sulphur, adrenalin, and faith, to remove it completely *with safety for that patient*, using only naturopathic means. Each decision must be the responsibility of the practitioner concerned; but I often have to explain to a patient that it is not advisable in the circumstances to rely only on the relatively slower, though more generally effective, remedies available through naturopathic treatment. Faster methods must be employed to assess and remove the bulk of the problem when necessary. More gradual strengthening, regrowth, and repair, can be undertaken naturopathically afterwards. There are naturopaths who claim that *any* process or result of illness can be removed by fasting alone, or by drinking spinach juice or even one's own urine! For the patient's sake, it is often necessary to soften one's own beliefs and take faster and more radical measures first.

If you always thought you were as healthy as could be expected considering your work-load, your wife's nagging, your financial worries, and the state of the nation, and are now going to stare gloomily at your 'brown' eyes reflected in the mirror each morning and feel even more hopeless and sorry for yourself—*stop!* There is no way that brown colour needs to mean any more to you than 'Remember to put the garbage out!' If it's your left kidney that's showing as covered in a dirty-looking fog, read some nutrition books; ask your local health store folk which herb teas and which vitamin and mineral supplements help kidney function; consult a naturopath; be *aware* that the kidney is less than efficient and you will do something about it if you love yourself at all. It is not only atrophy that registers in an iris as brownish; sometimes *apathy* does as well. Hiding your head (or even not looking at your brownish eyes in that mirror) is not enough to make the problem go away. *Do* something about it!

I am always amazed at the fear than can keep human beings away from skilled help. Health check-ups are put off and put off for fear of 'hearing the worst', when a check can locate potential problems long *before* they get to the 'brown' stage.

Brownish residues often remain in the iris after surgery, after accidental damage, after serious infections, indicating a deposit of rubbish the body has not completely cleaned up. Such signs may remain for many years, the residues not moving but not (obviously) causing symptoms either. One of the commonest sites for these enclosed pockets of rubbish is the inner ear and the mastoid area; another is the appendix. Sometimes a tooth can slowly abscess for twenty years and all the person is aware of may be a sensitive 'jump' from ice-cold drinks, or a slight change in the bite alignment to avoid landing on the touchy area when chewing. An ovary can abscess or form a cyst for months, even years, and all that is experienced may be a slight pain on too energetic intercourse or a too-large meal or even hanging up the washing on the line. So many factors can be blamed for the symptoms: the wrong emotional partner, indigestion, fibro-sitis, 'old age', 'tension', constipation, may be diagnosed one after the other when the pain refuses to go. An iris analysis can narrow possibilities down to that one 'brown' patch over the right ovary as the basic cause. Treatment can then be more accurately undertaken right from the beginning.

The depth of the brown fog usually indicates how long treatment needs to continue. A dark, dense 'mud' patch needs longer and heavier correction than a light brown haze through which fibre structure is still visible. Watch for even a tiny area of brown in an otherwise clear blue Silk or Silk/ Linen iris. Remember that such irises may not record trouble as dramatically as the condition warrants because intense energy is being directed elsewhere and limiting the *range* of what is registered by the iris. What looks like (and usually is) a problem to be brushed aside or ignored as a minor event in the busy lives of the Silks may be proportionally worse than their minimal iris browning would indicate. Net people may also let a set of warning symptoms slide through their filter systems unrecorded.

Ask many questions when an iris looks so browned and overloaded that you feel the person should be in hospital instead of walking about saying 'I feel fine. What do you mean by saying my health's poor?' So many people accept sub-standard health as their lot that a run through how they really perform a few basic body functions can be enlightening for them as well as the amazed iridologist. I'm still reeling from a lady patient telling me: 'I have a bowel motion once every week or ten days. My doctor told me it was quite normal, seeing that all my family are the same, and not to worry about it.' She had come to me to reduce weight, and it took me a goodly part of the hour's consultation to explain to her where her weight originated. The amount of brown garbage showing in her iris was confirmed by the enormous spread of tissue and fat around the hips, thighs, and waistline. I explained how the high-iron herbs I would give her would also have quite a heavy laxative effect (aloes, liquorice, sassafras, senna, cascara), oxidising some of the wastes and stimulating removal of others. She had never correlated her weight problem with the exaggerated slow-motion of her bowels.

Bodies are quite remarkably efficient mechanisms when given high-performance fuel and good maintenance, plus a cleaning programme no harder to understand than everyday dusting of the furniture, vacuuming the carpet, and emptying the ashtrays, the waste-paper baskets and the garbage-bins regularly. Your car engine often gets more preventive care than your body does; your house may be beautifully clean and tidied regularly but a look at the inside of your stomach and bowels, and the results in other organs and functions of such incomplete cleaning, could horrify you. You shower every day and keep your outsides clean and attractive. Your insides should fare likewise. If they don't, 'browns' can show in the iris to warn you of possible problems ahead. Heavy browning may take months, or even years, to leave the iris, as treatment progresses. Symptoms of the original problem may recur during this period.

Vigorous house-cleaning can raise the dust. As the body empties rubbish-bin after rubbish-bin, some unpleasantness can be expected. A skin rash or itchiness; diarrhoea; increased urinary activity; coughing; sneezing and blowing; any or all can be experienced, and praise God if this is so. Your body is returning actively to normal function.

GREYISH-BROWN

Brown indicates stored rubbish, and grey with it can show that there is too little vitality in that body area to overcome the problem *on its own*. A grey-brown stomach zone is registering insufficient hydrochloric acid and enzymes to handle digestion of food for fuel, and therefore an over-whelming need to pass the problem somewhere else for attention. It's bad enough when rubbish can't be efficiently removed; but it's much worse when vitalising inwards fuel can't be absorbed. The result is predictable—low function to the point of 'starvation' of the organ. This stomach will let its owner know how delicate is its balance. There will be many *good* foods unable to be digested at all and therefore forbidden. There may be wind and pain and bloating. Pills and potions may be heavily relied upon for any kind of comfort at all. If you wish to be a slave to such a pernickety stomach, adjusting your life-style to pander to its whims, then you don't care enough about your health to take the steps required to normalise its function. On the other hand, if you are tired of being dictated to by your stomach, recovery may be simple and complete once awareness of the problem is translated into action.

'Grey' equals atrophy; functional loss resulting from underactivity. Most grey-brown signs in the iris react best to general tonic treatments *first*—before attempting to take more specific corrective measures. Lack of enough vitality in the affected part to absorb the correctives may otherwise make treatment ineffective. All the good vitamin B foods are not going to help your nervous energy and stamina one whit if your small intestine is too tired and/or overworked to absorb and process them. Get some iron energy in to clean out and tone up first, and then better function can gradually result.

Many patients tell me that their nutrition is good and they really are eating all the right foods at the right time in the right combinations. They may be; but greyish-brown areas in their digestive tract can show that the body is not capable of *absorbing* such good food for maximum benefit. Simple correction can help you get your money's worth from the wheatgerm and the bran and the sprouts, from the brown rice and vegetable protein, rather than have it all empty out again mostly undigested and therefore not available to the body as the good fuel it should be.

BLACK

True black signs in the iris are rare; understandably so, since they indicate absence of life in the part of the body concerned. Not many of us can still walk around when such conditions occur. Surgical signs (p. 24) are certainly black; and logic tells us that this should be so, since a part of the body is 'killed' when tissue is removed. Black signs can show when tissue is 'deadened' too (e.g. the spleen ruptured, a tooth extracted). They can also be recorded when parasites infest the liver, the lungs, the bowel, destroying cell-tissue in the host organ.

But most black signs refer to *structural* trauma, not function. For a function to register as black, it must virtually have stopped. Terminal illnesses may provide conditions where black signs can be expected to occur, and such is often the case close to death and immediately afterwards. By ancient custom, in many cultures, the eyes are covered immediately after death. No further recording of inside or outside conditions is possible. The soul is freed symbolically by placing a blanket over the head, coins over the eyes, even by just closing the dead eyelids firmly. One island culture places little pats of mud over the closed eyelids to seal the soul off from any more 'impressions' as it takes its three days leaving the body.

I *have* seen, however, near-black signs in the nervous system in severely psychotic patients, in drug addicts, and in the irises of two patients who committed suicide shortly after such signs became obvious. Nervous control is absent; dead, if you like. Survival is seldom possible for long once this has happened.

A layman will almost never see such black signs. These may be seen in casualty wards, in psychiatric admission wards, in narcotic addiction centres, and in the morgue, but seldom, if ever, in everyday circumstances. Dark-brown signs are much more likely, signifying low or inefficient function, but not *absence* of function or tissue destruction.

COLOUR CHANGE

There is no way an Australian full-blood Aboriginal will ever change his deep ethnic-brown eyes to pale blue or even muddy blue, unless generations of interbreeding with lighter pigmented races have slowly changed genetic patterns. There is also no likelihood of a red-headed colleen losing her 'green' irises to acquire deep-velvet-brown orbs of darker pigmentation. Basic inherited *pigment* colours can never be changed; but beware of accepting 'genetic brown' as your true iris colour unless you spring from a racial background of olive to darker skin, black hair, and deep brown to almost purple-brown irises. Many children with 'brown' eyes—born to pale-skinned, pale-haired parents of European origin— are only suffering from the sins of their forefathers function- ally and are not brown-eyed at all.

Patients who have persevered with the undoing processes of natural therapies have been amazed at the change of colour obvious in their irises. Photographs later in the book will show how dramatic such change can be as health

improves. Get into the habit of checking your irises occasionally in the bathroom mirror. Many colour changes are
apparent, even without a magnifying torch. Watch that
murky yellow-white overlay as a virus takes hold; see how the
red wine last night gave you a greenish-grey liver overload
this morning; check whether that pain in your foot/tooth/
ear/back is showing white signs or brown signs in the iris:
and you will learn more about how your body is handling the
problem and whether it is winning or losing. Don't forget
that proper diagnosis from skilled practitioners may he
necessary every so often. Your too-close subjective view
could result in unnecessary worry, even panic. Get explana-
tions if you are in doubt.

'Take a pair of sparkling eyes,' sings the tenor, and *clarity*
of colour takes on another dimension—light. Light reflects
best from a shiny surface, and the vitality of plus-health often
shows in this way. What you are feeling, inside and out, can
show as 'squeaky-clean' sparkle and brilliance at the iris
surface diffused by the corneal layer. Think of people you
know with this luminous quality in the eyes: they have a
dimension of intensity and vitality added to their good
health. Enthusiasm can produce it; so can love, and being
loved. So can passing an exam, winning the lottery, caring
for a child, a pet, or another human being in distress. It is
a quality of compassion and understanding which can forget
self for a while and feel and care in a larger dimension. Such
feeling radiates from the irises as light, producing sparkle
and shine. A good belly-laugh can produce 'sparkle', so can
intellectual fun. Unselfish happiness causes shine. Get
yourself into this fourth dimension of health!

5

REFLEX SIGNS

In Opposite And Adjacent Iris Zones

So far, we have explored several interlocking systems of segments and circles, and the two overriding conditions of basic structure (colours and fibres) and biochemical function. There is yet one more type of pattern to be considered, that of reflex indications in opposite and adjacent iris zones.

Human beings are more stubborn and more adaptable in their tolerance of external and internal stresses than most animals and all plants. If cattle are kept on poor pasture, starved of nutritional satisfaction; if water is in short supply; if climatic conditions don't suit them; if they are over-crowded and constantly harassed by being changed from one poor food area to another—what happens to them? They register their intolerance of the conditions by becoming diseased and dying off quite rapidly. Plants are even more vulnerable. The wrong amount of fertiliser; the water table too high or too low; the sun scorching, or missing under weeks of heavy rain; planting at the wrong time of year or in the wrong place: such adverse conditions can leave the plant shrivelled, brown, and dead within days or even hours.

Humans can and do tolerate many extreme conditions by using their head control to block off, forget, adjust to, or rechannel stress reactions so that the body can apparently override such trauma and continue on its daily round. The human will has developed at the expense of many of our protective animal instincts, so that a man may deliberately choose the self-destruction of drugs or alcohol while an animal's prime instinct is self-preservation and survival. An animal will not eat at all rather than eat food unsuitable for it at the time. Watch a dog eat grass when it's ill; try to get the same dog to eat grass when it's well again and see how far you don't get.

A civilised human has lost most of this self-preservation instinctive choice and can eat truffles and cream sauce just to be sociable when the body is really crying out—unheard— for maybe carrot juice and raw egg yolk. Any real 'cravings' like this can be overridden by a cussed and perverse head. A human can consume overmuch alcohol with good dinner companions purely because the head is so busy with the stimulating conversation that a still small voice from the instincts goes unheard amid the wit and good humour. If a dog is eating, it is doing solely that—eating. Almost all its other needs turn off for a while until instincts sniff out the food to see if it's suitable. If it is, Fido will eat sufficient and then stop, even if the bowl is not empty. Wouldn't it be glorious to have such clear signals in our own eating patterns? No obesity, no indigestion, no 'morning after' feelings!

So let us see whether iris analysis can help us re-sensitise ourselves.

○ Protective Reactions

Some long-buried instinctive reactions in humans can occasionally surface and play a protective role when external stress and strain have reached real danger levels for the survival of the organism. Many of these instinctive 'buck-passing' ploys are readable in an iris as they activate. Let's take a well-known example of instinct—the 'fight or flight' defence mechanism under the stimulus of fear. All animals, even humans, react to this one. In a healthy human, the adrenal glands can respond immediately to trigger off self-protective processes. Whether you run like crazy or whether you stand and fight, blood vessels will drain supply from non-vital areas, like the stomach, to vital control centres like the brain and the heart; muscles are flooded with glycogen from the liver to contract and harden, supplying extra physical strength; pulse rate and blood pressure rise to boost oxygen levels for thinking clearly. Your *instincts* produce all these processes irrespective of whether your *head* lets you take advantage of them. You can still decide to stay there and get clobbered!

In the right iris, the right adrenal gland is represented at 5.30-5.45; and in the left iris the left adrenal gland is at 6.20-6.40. Almost opposite the adrenal gland in the right iris is the 'anxiety and apprehension' zone, where various processes concerned with these emotional stimuli are monitored and dealt with. In iridology, such opposite zones are often inter-related, one throwing off its 'overload' (whether it be structural, biochemical or external stimuli causing it) to an opposite related organ to help carry it.

In the previous example, enough acute anxiety mushrooms into fear and/or panic; and when this happens the adrenal glands pick up the overflow and produce instinctive ways of removing the stimulus: run or fight. In the left iris, the opposite reflex areas to the adrenal gland are the locomotor/movement and the visual areas. The *sight* of something frightening, like a snake at your backdoor or a movie monster, can trigger all three reflex areas at once: fear/adrenal response/fight or flight. Have you ever wondered why a child snaps eyes fast shut at the scary bits in the movie? Even an adult watching the 'late show' on TV may avoid those really horrifying monsters by looking somewhere else. If the visual trigger is absent, the adrenalin won't pump out so fast. Here we have an instance of a *positive* reflex response. Shut your eyes and the fear can be less! The 'locomotor' reflex adjacent to the visual area can also avoid fear reactions by getting in first and moving you away fast from the object of the fear. That same late movie often produces a 'Let's have a cup of tea' and an acceptable movement-away reaction from the most timid member of the family!

Many of the patients I treat for chronic anxiety of various degrees have corresponding reflex signs not only in the adrenal gland zones but also continuing through them and into the kidneys. Prolonged disturbances in the anxiety zone have led to the whole possible instinct-reflex being activated. Here we find the people who are so constantly over-anxious that they urinate excessively as the stimulus rises. A child who has to go to the toilet five or six times before settling down to sleep at night is probably frightened of the dark, the solitude, or his exam tomorrow morning, and is still more subject to his animal instincts than a controlled adult is. Bed-wetting can often be traced to the same cause. Remove the anxiety pattern from the child and the reflex will gradually become inactive, being no longer needed to carry overload conditions.

O Suppression—And Expression

Another fascinating reflex pattern in the right iris, between 7.40 and 7.50, is found associated with the liver zone. I always check the liver area first when I look at a patient's iris, because it tells me the state of some thirty-odd body processes and shows whether emotions are coming out straight and uncensored or are being edited by the patient into a more 'acceptable' personality.

Directly opposite the liver segment is the tongue, mouth, and lower-jaw zone, the parts of the body that move to produce speech. It is a fascinating diversion to remark on the change in emotional pattern of speech of a patient suffering from hepatitis. Words and feelings come out that you would never have imagined to be in there, no matter how well you knew the patient previously. Often the opposite occurs during a hepatitis infection, especially in the early severe stages; a patient not only does not *want* to talk, but finds the effort of speech quite exhausting and prefers to be silent. The reflex jaw-and-mouth area is feeling the overload thrown across to it by the liver. *Neither* wishes to work hard.

It is also feeling a second overload associated with tongue, mouth, and lower jaw: the disinclination to move these parts in the business of eating. The low appetite with hepatitis is a common diagnostic indication of this illness. In fact, if the patient *does* persevere in moving the bottom jaw to eat, a reflex may go back to the liver again, now in no shape to handle any food, and vomiting and increased jaundice can result.

Now let's look at a problem which troubles many people—compulsive eating, the irresistible urge to raise the hand to the mouth with food in it. Here is where head control, possible in humans, has broken down and given way to a forceful instinctive reflex so loud that it should red-light a warning: 'Go back, you are going the wrong way!'

The whole pattern of a true compulsive eater can be seen spread across the iris from the liver to the reflex lower jaw and mouth, and bounced back again to the liver, in brownish discoloration or open structural parting of fibres, or both. The liver is the main organ feeling the *chemistry* of suppressed or censored emotional response. An alcoholic drinks because the rest of his emotional range of experience does not satisfy him, or because his real emotions are severely repressed by circumstances around him. His liver takes the brunt of his bottom jaw's inability to say what he really feels. At least the jaw flaps up and down a little more often as he swallows his tenth beer, and some pretty uncensored emotion may surface as the reflex is released.

With food, the need to move the jaw up and down is a constant mutually helpful reflex between mouth and liver. Enough *chewing* of roughage foods at a meal will tend to stimulate correct liver function in its metabolism. Reflexes operate both ways, remember. Just as strong, positive adrenal function can produce the *absence* of fear—courage (the inability to feel anxiety under pretty anxious-making circumstances)—so can chewing your way through honey-toasted whole-grain muesli in the morning stimulate healthy liver function for the day. Some raw carrot and celery sticks can do the same thing at lunch, rather than even the very best of liquid health drinks.

Now perhaps you no longer wonder why you set your bottom jaw hard to avoid telling the boss to go to hell! A vestige of that atavistic protective reflex, that survival instinct, remains when the situation really is demanding of caution to *inhibit* a damaging flow of real emotion.

ADJACENT ZONES

A spinal-arc transfer of nerve messages produces many reflex reactions in opposite parts of the iris; but overloads can be dumped in adjacent areas, too. Let's use the liver example first.

Adjacent to and above the liver zone, just below 8 o'clock, right iris, we find the right hand and arm represented. Many liver discolorations in the iris extend not only all over the liver segment but also to adjacent zones. One of the commonest in obese people is to find the brownish-yellow, sluggish liver 'fog' enveloping the right hand and arm, and maybe even the diaphragm and upper abdomen too (below the liver zone, at 7.30 on the Iris Map).

When enough sub-standard food nutritionally is eaten to make the liver's job enormously difficult (and many of us do this all day, every day); when emotional dissatisfaction builds up and we suppress it and do naught to change our emotional circumstances; then the liver may collapse, like a lumpy, obese lady itself, and *spread* the problem on either side. Protective reflexes, like 'biting back the words', are no longer enough. It becomes painfully obvious to others, as well as to the patient, that the overload is so great as to be out of control.

Stop and think a moment more about compulsive eating.

Do you live alone and get a desperate urge for carbohydrate binges from the fridge? It's your right hand that's putting the food to your *mouth*—to satisfy what? Think some more about it. Is it really to satisfy your loneliness—the need to talk to someone about your day; the need to feel wanted and loved; to satisfy the suppressed or unexpressed emotions felt chemically in the liver?

O Release And Relief

Are you clenching your *right hand* as you read this now? You may be experiencing an unexpected emotional release, even tears, as for the first time you feel the uncensored emotion of loneliness, not its pathological substitute (easier to bear perhaps), abnormal hunger for food, or drink. I find this often happens as I explain to a patient the *cause* of compulsive eating. The reason for it is the dumping of a huge, unrecognised emotional overload in other areas and functions of the body. Change your circumstances, find a buddy; take up tennis; yell and cry until you find the emotional block source—and watch your weight drop and your eating and drinking return to normal.

If you still feel obliged to *accept* the conditions producing the overload, there's no way in the world that dietary firmness or crash programmes or anything else will break the pattern permanently. There is certainly no need to yell and scream all day, or even to weep all through morning tea, as a means of breaking a compulsive eating or drinking pattern. Often it is enough just to realise why that hand goes to the mouth, and then to take steps to fill the 'empty hole' with its real need.

The diaphragm zone, adjacent to and below the liver, can also contribute its tension to a liver overload. If you are apprehensive your breath will move more shallowly and your diaphragm will endeavour to offload its 'spill-over' back to the liver again. This is how disagreements and aggression at the dinner table can interrupt the liver's proper job—the metabolising of what you have just eaten. If you're airing your stresses and problems of the day while eating, your liver is going to be much more concerned with emotional unloading and sorting out than with the biochemistry of digestion. Get rid of the day's stress *before* dinner, and your diaphragm will be relaxed enough to let your liver work without structural stress.

Another adjacent physical reflex is activated in the painful illness medically labelled 'gout', often called 'arthritis of the big toe'. Symptoms are redness and inflammation, heat, swelling, and quite remarkably acute pain on contact of the toe with the ground or even the bedclothes. After a day or two or more of this misery, the swelling gradually subsides and slow moving about can painfully recommence. Recurrent attacks are threatened by the physician unless the patient promises to stay away from port and sinning! Gout is actually a 'spilling' of uric acid from congested kidneys which can't pass it on and out through the bladder fast enough to cope with the intake of uric acid-producing fluids—*and foods*—at the other end. It's not always port that's the culprit! Red wine in excess can certainly give the kidneys a hard time; but so can too high an intake of animal protein, with its acid-forming residues.

It is usually such a meat-eating history that produces the gout sufferer. The eighth glass of red wine at the same meal may get the blame, but it just triggers the overload mechanism from the kidney segment of the iris into the adjacent knee/foot zone at 6 o'clock. It is usually only the big toe of one foot that is affected, as the gravity-fed uric acid crystallises and causes the swelling and pain. The treatment naturopathically is not only to cut down on alcohol but also on acid-producing foods (such as fatty dairy products and sugary foods) in the long term. People prone to gout should take the same care as arthritics to normalise kidney secretion and excretion of uric acid so that a 'spillover' to the foot just doesn't happen.

Many reflexes activate all around and across the iris in a

similar fashion. We will deal with them as each zone is more fully described in the next chapter.

WORDS OF CAUTION

Once again it must be emphasised that clinical diagnosis from an iris needs much more training and skill than a layman has at his disposal. Iris analysis is not a parlour-game. You can not only be wrong about some discoloration or 'abnormality'; you can also cause untold worry and mischief if the poor soul on the other end of your diagnosis believes you have had more training than is actually the case.

Ask the person first. My attitude on noticing a problem area in the iris is to be very cautious how I phrase my leading questions. 'Did you have a back injury some few years ago that still gives you twinges now and then?' 'Do you have a history of sore throats more often than just when you have a cold?' 'Is the base of your neck painful when you lie down at night?' 'Have you had your appendix out?' Asking such questions is much better than confidently announcing, 'Your appendix is in a mess', only to find that it was removed five years ago and what you are seeing is adhesions and scar-tissue causing bowel problems around where it used to be! *Ask* rather than *tell*.

You can still have the fun gambits—deciding whether your new girlfriend has a high libido, or if the life of the party is really as happy as he pretends to be. But be responsible and very, very cautious in physical diagnosis of *illness* from an iris. Better to leave it to those who've spent time and effort and experience in learning about such problems, and who have the technical knowledge of the body and its needs in illness.

6

SPECIAL SIGNS

*Diseases Of Body-Processes And
Systemic Diseases*

Midway between function and structure are a few special iris signs that refer to both. A chiropractor will tell you that structure governs function; a biochemist-nutritionist will state that function governs homoeostasis (the chemical balance of the body) and that structure is dependent upon efficient biochemical function. The iris, by some special signs, records a marriage between the two opinions, where structure and function are dependent upon each other and both have broken down. Two of these special signs are found in the outer rim of the iris, the circulation zone.

THE CALCIUM/SODIUM RING

You will certainly know someone showing a sodium ring in the iris. He or she would be over forty, a little too sedentary for peak health, a little stiff around the joints, a little slower than last year and the year before. Doesn't it sound familiar? 'Old age creeping on, I guess,' you'll get as a reply if you mention the symptoms. 'I'm slowing down, I suppose.' Such a person is not really slowing down but turning into a kind of human stalagmite. Stiffening, hardening processes are at work in the circulation as calcium compounds and maybe cholesterol deposit on the walls of major and minor blood vessels. Aches and pains can occur all over the body as this increasing rigidity makes it harder to move joints, harder to get out of bed with a bounce in the morning, harder to get out of the armchair at night.

Simple mechanics can explain the problem. It's much more difficult to pump fluid through narrow, rigid pipes than through wider, flexible ones; the pump must work harder and greater effort on the handle is needed to get it started and keep it going. The system is inefficient. Structurally, the bones and muscles may be as strong as ever; functionally everything may appear as before—the bowels move, the kidneys secrete and the bladder excretes urine, the digestion seems no different, no symptoms of actual illness can be identified, but the stiffness and tiredness increase imperceptibly day by day. Both irises of such a person can be showing the first signs of a sodium ring.

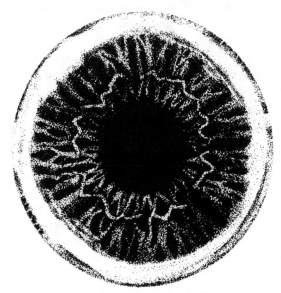

The Calcium/Sodium Ring

Different altogether from white fog clouds, white raised nerve fibres, and white flares of pain, the white of a sodium ring forms a dense, narrow band around the outside rim of the iris. When it covers only this outer circulation zone, no classifiable symptoms may be experienced at all. Even tiredness may be absent in the early stages, but if the pattern remains undiagnosed for what it is and spreads slowly into the muscle zone, the aches and pains of 'arterial rheumatism' can occur. Some people show a yellow tinge over the thick white ring. By this stage, cholesterol can also be depositing in clogged arteries and veins. The danger of sudden blockage of a 'pipe' can be high.

Sometimes this ring is called a 'calcium ring', or a 'salt ring'; but 'sodium ring' is more applicable, since sodium in natural forms can be the major corrective for such a problem. Calcium metabolism is very much out of balance, or the wrong sort of calcium (cow's milk, processed cheese) is being taken to excess and the body is unable to metabolise it as fast as it is being ingested.

One prime cause of a sodium ring can be too high an intake of *un*natural sodium—cooking salt. You remember how Lot's wife turned into a pillar of salt? I see many patients who are not far off such an immobilising fate! If you automatically sprinkle vast quantities of salt over your food, sometimes before you've even tasted it, or if you need a lot of salt before you can even taste the food at all, you could be unnecessarily hardening your arteries and hastening your demise. One of the greater joys of eating simple whole foods, without loads of salt, is that one can separate the fine nuances of flavour as the palate becomes more sensitive again. It is a sad comment that manufacturers of foodstuffs are obliged to add progressively more sugar and more salt to their recipes because customers complain that they can't taste the contents otherwise. Deadening of the taste buds can also result progressively as more and more salt is consumed. Try a good vegetable salt to cook with, and gradually re-train your taste buds to distinguish subtle variations of flavour and taste. Experience a new sensual delight at the dinner-table! Cooking salt is mostly 'pure' NaCl. Vegetable salt, even sea salt, contains many other mineral compounds to balance the sodium and chlorine naturally and to ensure that calcium is not deposited throughout the body in an unnatural attempt to keep sodium/calcium levels proportionate. Take in too much *unnatural* sodium and your body will throw out calcium into tissues to even the balance.

The 'sodium ring' itself is composed of particles of calcium compounds deposited even in the tissues of the eye. Many naturopaths claim that, for this reason, a sodium ring will never disappear entirely from an eye, even after treatment has removed symptoms and halted the problem. I have found, in practice, that such an indication *can* be reversed and removed as the body re-establishes its balance. Rigid arteries *can* be softened again and the calcium salts and cholesterol deposits thrown out in general garbage removal.

Vegetable sodium is the 'youth element'. Asian diets are high in natural sodium, especially in the use of seaweeds and typical Oriental vegetables like Chinese cabbage. Consult a good natural nutrition book to find your best simple sources of *vegetable* sodium. Even eating lots of celery (a particularly high-sodium vegetable) can start the ball rolling.

Sometimes a sodium ring can be 'inherited', almost; although the word does not completely describe what is happening. The person concerned may never be aware that more flexibility is possible. While I have never seen a sodium ring in a young person's iris, I have seen such signs appearing in hale and hearty forty- and fifty-year-olds' eyes without any apparent trauma at all; but *awareness* of their predisposition had made sure that it never caught up with them. Remember, you can fix *anything* with your head, even genetically coded signals deep in cell metabolism. Your iris will give up eventually and stop registering a condition you have decided not to accept.

Both blue and true brown eyes can show sodium rings. 'Civilised' foods have penetrated even to the depths of the jungles and the mountains of Tibet, taking their salt and sugar along in the can or package; but blue eyes are much more prone to show this sign, with their tendency to abnormal calcium patterns of 'stiffness'. The more supple, graceful bodies of Asians, even well into old-age, are less likely to stiffen and seize up if they continue with their ethnic diet patterns rather than join the take-away-food queues of Western civilisation.

Sometimes there may be only a small arc of sodium ring visible, rather than a whole circle, usually round the lower iris rim: just as heavy calcium sinks to the lower limbs and lower back first, affecting kidney function and leg, thigh and hip mobility. Excessive aspirin consumption can also produce this sign in the same areas.

Salt affects the body's fluid balance osmotically, retaining approximately 70 grams of fluid for every gram of salt taken. You often find sodium-ring arcs visible in the lower iris in patients suffering from fluid retention.

It is also possible to find a sodium-ring arc at the top of the iris, over the head areas. The heart pump is finding it difficult to circulate blood against gravity to the top of that rigid pipe system. The first symptoms may only be vagueness, loss of memory and concentration, and 'woolliness' of thinking. A quick iris check can tell you if the cause is calcification, or a 'dirty' transverse colon, or a low vitamin B or magnesium intake. Use iris signs to learn more about your body, your own private vehicle you drive around in in this world, and its maintenance requirements.

Senility can be a direct result of cerebral calcification. The general acceptance of degeneration of faculties as old age approaches is not compulsory. The Chinese revere the increasing wisdom of age. No hard cerebral arteries there! But then they drink sage tea and eat celery and cabbage and water chestnuts and raw fish and soy sauce: their sodium levels balance with calcium to avoid the problem.

A sodium-ring crescent over the head areas of the iris (often called *arcus senilis* by the medical profession) can also be treated by the same natural methods. You don't have to be written off at sixty by your grandchildren as a silly old fool. Show them the wisdom and experience supple, flexible cerebral arteries can transmit!

'Rheumatism' is the label usually put on sodium-ring symptoms by medical practitioners, and aspirin for the pain is often prescribed—one of the very worst substances to overload already labouring kidneys. Chew celery instead; eat bananas and yoghurt and coconuts and vegetable salt and feel that stiffness loosen gradually. Eat onions and garlic to loosen cholesterol and metabolise it, and feel your body grow more youthful again. You may not have rheumatism at all, only clogged plumbing.

THE LYMPHATIC ROSARY

There is quite a different sign which also appears in the circulation zone (and is found more commonly in the irises of young people), signifying lymphatic slowness and yet another pile-up of rubbish not being efficiently removed. Like the sodium ring, the lymphatic rosary can show as a complete circle, this time of glistening white 'beads' like pearls, around the iris rim (p. 106). A partial lymph blockage can show as just a few spots or beads at the outer rim of the particular zone affected. Acute lymph blockage at the right foot may show only a couple of white beads at the outer edge of the right iris at 6 o'clock. If the body is then unable to clear out this small rubbish pile-up, the colour of the beads can deteriorate through yellow (if swelling, pain and enlarged lymph nodes occur) to the brown stage—a much more serious situation.

Browns, as you recall, mean a chronic stage of illness has been reached where not only are the rubbish-bins not being emptied today, but there is not much likelihood of their *ever* being emptied completely without extensive muck-raking. Many serious degenerative processes of ill-health can start in lymphatic rubbish remains. But even if your iris is showing brown lymphatic beads, it is still possible to burn out the rubbish naturopathically, and iron is the element to help most, together with two herbs which work within the 'duties' of the lymph system—fenugreek and violet leaves. Expert help should be sought as to how such treatment should be undertaken. Mistletoe is another herb useful in some cases.

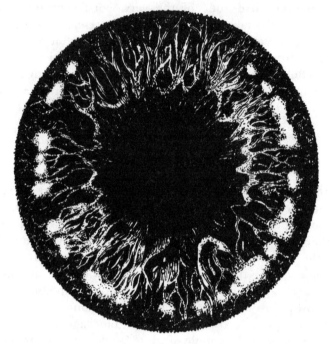

The Lymphatic Rosary

The white rosary beads may mean no more than a basically lazy metabolism which doesn't readily attempt menial tasks like rubbish removal. It may be found together with a slow pituitary and thyroid function and some degree of obesity, which can prove hard to shift no matter what dietary controls may be applied. This slow glandular function can mean that you're always a little behind with your body's 'housework', and much exercise, iron, and zeal, can be needed to speed you up.

The major job of lymph glands is to collect day-to-day cell rubbish, rather than digestive-system remains. They function quite independently of kidneys and bowels; but being visible, as they are, in the general circulation zone, you would expect them to have a working partnership with the skin, and this they do have. Some lymphatic load can be dumped out of the body via the skin, in sweat. Do you perspire heavily on exertion? Is that perspiration quite offensive? Do you need to shower two or three times daily and use deodorant powders and sprays, too? Are they still not completely doing the job of keeping you nice to be near? You may have lazy lymph glands!

Lymph collection points at various parts of the body should be delivering rubbish to the major elimination organs via the bloodstream. When this cannot be done, lymphatic fluids can be pumped out eventually through the pores of the skin, and your rubbish removal can be embarrassingly obvious. On the other hand, if you perspire freely and still smell like a rose this indicates good vital skin function without extra lymphatic tasks added.

○ Lymph Clogging

If you hardly perspire at all, take time and trouble to improve your skin function. This pattern can also cause lymphatic clogging just underneath a skin which can't breathe. The body envelope of skin can be made to act as a surface 'pump', helping physically to push lymph fluids around just by contraction and expansion. A skin-brush, vigorously applied before shower or bath, can also tone up small lymphatic circulation. Physical exercise can do it too, or a sauna, speeding up sluggish lymph movement all around the body. This circulation needs stimulation and continuous movement, just as do arteries and veins.

Many patients who have smoked heavily for years show chronic yellowish to brown lymph beads at the outer edge of bronchial, lung, and throat zones in the iris. Such signs can be indicative of deposits unremoved from tar- and resin-laden tissues. Lymph clogging does not of itself necessarily indicate cancerous or abnormal cell formation, but *any* long-accumulated pockets of such rubbish are better cleared. Again, there is no need for panic if your eyes show any part of, or a whole, lymphatic rosary. Get some professional advice on which is the best way to clear whatever part of the body is affected.

So-called 'rheumatism' may be nothing more than lymphatic congestion over a long period preceding the 'rheumatic' diagnosis. Aches and pains, and vague feelings of tiredness, dullness and heaviness, suggest that the patient may show a calcium ring or the white acid eye of some rheumatoid arthritics, but only a lymphatic rosary can be seen under the magnification of the iris torch. The symptoms may be almost identical, but the iris can show the difference in basic causes and therefore indicate the appropriate treatment.

One particular physical type is prone to show lymphatic clogging. This is the somewhat overweight person, either male or female, of placid temperament, slow-thinking, slow-moving, and with apparently little energy for physical tasks and outdoor exercise. When the irises of such people contain shiny lymphatic blobs or, worse still, yellowish or brown ones, my first treatment for them is tonic herbs, high in iron, to give them better energy to attempt the next step of their recovery process through *moving more!* Such people often astonish themselves as energy, never apparent before, begins to make their feet tap and their fingers snap and they *want* to do more physically and mentally as the iron quickly burns out residues. Many people of this type have the endurance and toughness of Silks once the lymphatic bogging down has gone. In fact, many of them can be Silks who've not had enough stimulus and challenge recently and have ground to a halt. I explain what has happened; I get fast iron herbs like nettle, gentian, garlic and rosehips into the diet (or in therapeutic form of extracts and tinctures), and watch the change.

Photographs 1a and 1b in Chapter 9 show a patient under such treatment. From a slowed, always tired, always oversleeping young lass, whose pupils were hugely dilated, she has now become a zappy dynamo mentally and physically as her lymph system, formerly extremely slow and clogged, has removed long-stored cell rubbish. Mistletoe, a herb beloved of the Druids, was the activator here in removing lymphatic wastes and raising the revs of the lymph-fluid 'pump'.

Many people who feel tired and lethargic, and are short on drive and enthusiasm and long on complaints and problems, may not merit that blanket diagnosis of 'stress and tension' so generally thrust on them by a medical practitioner. They may merely be experiencing the *boredom* of 'nothing interesting to do', so that all their systems slow down until some stimulus re-appears. Lymphatic slowness can make your body think it's tired and overworked when it may not even be trying. You don't need Valium: you need speeding up, not relaxing!

A recent case-history gave a classic example of lymph action and iris change. A child of ten months developed a large lymph node on the side of the neck when he was teething—and this *can* sometimes happen. But his mother had inherited a chronically slow lymphatic system and a brownish lymphatic 'rosary', and the child was born with what looked like a 'real' brown eye. The swelling increased day by day until there was a huge lymphatic 'balloon' some three inches in diameter. The mother persisted with carefully controlled homoeopathic and herbal treatment, and the sac finally broke and discharged an incredible load of greenish-brown muck. Just before this, the child's eye showed not 'real' brown any longer, but a dirty brownish lymphatic rosary and patches of fibre structure and basic blue underneath it.

This child's small body had collected all its inherited cell rubbish in one spot, and had powerfully expelled it by classic naturopathic treatment. The baby is now happy and thriving again, and the iris gets paler and bluer day by day. I wish I could have managed to get iris photographs before and after; but it was next to impossible to do this with a small child whose eyelids defensively clamped tight shut with apprehension at the camera's metallic strangeness.

Some people showing lymphatic rosary beads at the outer iris edge also show physical evidence of skin sub-health. Blotches, spots, pustules, even boils and carbuncles, may erupt and cause emotional distress at the appearance of the covering envelope visible to the outside world. Think of the processes involved here. One blotch or spot may be an infection after a scratch or break in the skin, but outbreaks lasting sometimes for years mean bloodstream inefficiency in use or supply of iron and oxygen, leading to an overload on lymphatics trying to pump an overload out through the nearest available exit—the skin.

Chronically bad skin often indicates long-standing lymphatic slowness. You may not be 'spotty'; you may be just greenish-grey or yellowish-grey or pasty white: evidence that more iron may be needed to clear the skin zone and the lymphatic channels below.

Some multiple sclerosis patients show lymphatic clogging in the *muscle* zones of the iris, some do not. I was interested to find recently that new medical research is basing a pilot study of multiple sclerosis on lymphatic efficiency. Some MS patients certainly do have lymph fluids different in content from the norm, and strange lymph signs in the iris; but I believe that much more evidence than this will be needed to tie a possible cause and effect together.

The minor circulation of lymph fluids can be a major health factor. Iris indications are invaluable here, since many symptoms can be attributed to malfunctions of other body structures and functions when they are actually problems of lymphatic inefficiency. Look for the tell-tale 'beads'— white, yellow, brownish—and, if they are present, you will know that the health potential for that person is not being achieved: his health can be improved.

NERVE RINGS

While the straight lines found in irises refer to one organ or structural zone, the circles indicate a more generalised effect on the body as a whole. The circles or arcs of circles of the calcium ring and the lymphatic rosary show generalised symptoms. Nerve rings follow the same pattern.

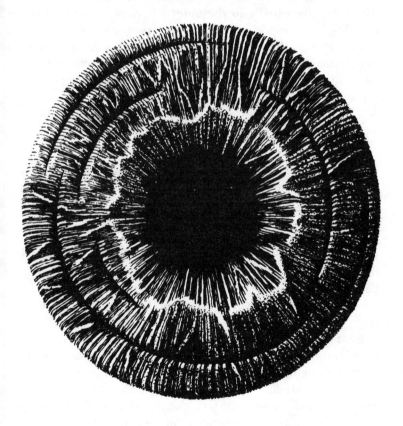

Nerve Rings

You remember how the nerve *wreath* showed the balance between automatic and voluntary nervous control? Nerve *rings* might be called secondary manifestations of the same control. Have you a spouse or boss or friend who sits forward on the edge of chairs, leaps about suddenly rather than flows, and is always 'ready to race'? You can find in the iris of such people fainter echoes of the nerve wreath, concentric with it, like the rings on the water when a stone is flung into a pool. The rings are usually in the outer iris zones of organs and muscles, and especially in the zones representing large muscle groups that are used in everyday movement. Shoulders, arms and hands are one group used thousands of times daily; hips, thighs, knees, and feet are a second. Back muscles tense and flex as stress loads are taken.

○ Tension Points

Muscles are easily recognisable as tension points by masseurs and chiropractors and hypnotherapists. Even an untrained observer can notice finger-tapping on the arm of a chair; a foot scraping the carpet back and forth, to and fro, while someone is watching television; hands clenched during sleep while the body is curled up in a foetal position with knees to chin; a child unable to sit still, with 'ants in the pants'. Continuous muscle contraction, when there should be *relaxation* of the muscle fibres, can produce nerve rings in the iris.

Some people-types are more prone to over-strong, overstimulated muscles than others. The Silks may tend to keep the engine revving long after the vehicle has stopped! Some muscular over-tension can also be the result of high adrenal stimulus, so Silks are doubly at risk. A *chronically* unbalanced muscle/effort ratio can produce iron bands of tissue permanently contracted. Physical relaxing for such people becomes a task for conscious will, for their muscles are not going to give way otherwise unless exhausted.

Nerve rings over organ zones like liver, kidneys, uterus,

can indicate a similar over-used nerve impulse towards muscular contraction of the organ. A liver which has two, three, even four, nerve rings showing across it can be tight and muscle-bound functionally and also show over-tight emotional control. A spleen crossed by nerve rings can indicate not only constriction in function and structure, but tight control over anger boiling underneath. A kidney with nerve rings furrowed across it can have limited function and occasional pain from the tightness of its contraction. This may sometimes indicate the presence of renal calculi (kidney stones). So nerve rings can register a *tightness* which should be able to be further explored and diagnosed by the practitioners who will try to discover how such a constriction and contraction can best be unlocked.

It is really necessary for all parts of the body to be in a flaccid, relaxed state when not in use. Relaxation makes the structure last longer; it allows the function to rest and/or remove rubbish; so there is increased efficiency next time an adrenal stimulus is applied and energy is needed. Muscles are particularly able to maintain contraction long past the stimulus/response period of use. Don't go to bed with all your muscles still ready to face situations which passed hours ago. If you do, sleep will be more like running round the block all night, or weight-lifting, than rest and recuperation. Do your 'fingers let go, arms let go, shoulders let go ...' or any other form of *conscious* de-control to relax muscles each night before sleep.

Children can show nerve rings for many reasons. Apart from the fact that their young muscles are flexing to find their strength, children can exhibit a degree of response not yet damped down by experience. They can be forever moving as new untried stimuli present themselves. Hyperactive children may show nerve rings in the iris. Over-active nerve-control centres condemn muscles to continuous contraction. Only when physical exhaustion has been reached will a hyper-active child sleep.

Asthmatics can show nerve rings over the chest and bronchial tree zones in the iris. Many types of mechanical asthma show these signs, as well as the more emotionally triggered kind in which degrees of anxiety, apprehension, concern, and even panic, produce muscular tension and contraction around breathing 'pipes'. Four and five close nerve rings crowded across chest areas can be relaxed out by herbs, therapeutic exercises, will-power, and understanding of the problem.

I see many patients who show a whitish nerve ring over head areas in the iris. My chiropractic colleagues use physical adjustments which can release such tightness, while herbs and dietary change can support the process. Although there are few muscles in the head itself, muscle contraction from the neck can literally 'pull your head in'. Whether this has happened before birth, during birth, or before the spine is structurally able to bear the relatively enormous weight of the head in infancy, a nerve ring later in life can show that pressure and tension have been applied and have remained. Sometimes headaches result, sometimes a feeling of heaviness is all; but *tension* in the head is certainly experienced. Skull adjustments of a sophisticated type can be the partial solution here.

Looking at the mechanics of nerve rings, one condition applying in the body is clearly in evidence in iris fibres—contraction. The points of contraction produce the concentric 'furrows' appearance. A simpler way to think of nerve rings may be as *spasm* indicators, whether muscular or organic. If you experience the joys of regular massage, you will know how knots of contracted muscle fibres can undo and release their tension under expert kneading. You may first feel a second spasm symptom—pain—before you get to do something about those tight muscles; and you may also experience pain as the deft movements of massage find contracted muscle bundles and prise them apart. My chiropractor doesn't have green fingers—he has black thumbs! As he undoes for me the painful after-effects of too many games of squash or a day's too-vigorous sailing, he may not find nerve rings at all in the iris if normal muscle tone is good. It is only when *persistent* muscle contraction occurs that nerve rings register the imbalance.

Sudden accidents producing pain can show nerve ring iris signs, too. Although the duration of the pain may be shorter than chronic, its *intensity* can cause muscular spasm.

Biochemically speaking, magnesium phosphate, calcium phosphate, and potassium phosphate are the spasm-release agents. Simple herbal teas, like camomile and valerian, contain balanced combinations of these salts, and can greatly reduce nerve ring iris signs. As with the calcium ring and the lymphatic rosary, structure and function are both involved in this circular type pattern. Both need attention to remove the signs effectively.

RADII SOLARIS

For many years I have quaked and trembled whenever asked to explain *radii solaris* as seen in irises. If a patient has the typical dark 'wheel spokes' of the sign radiating out from the pupil towards the iris rim, I try to assess such a patient psychologically before deciding on which level to explain the body processes involved. First, a purely physical happening can account for them; second, such a physical process is 'anatomically impossible' according to present-day medical thinking; and third, if I tried to explain the *other* levels of *radii solaris* interpretation I might scare the patient into a negative state of antagonistic disbelief, fear, even panic. No wonder I have myself christened this sign the 'Crown of Thorns'!

May I ask you to read the *whole* of this section before checking to see whether your irises show the pattern? (If you're heading for the bathroom mirror right now, at least I tried.)

An accurate description of this pattern must be understood. With all the other iris signs different iris-layer levels are visible, to a degree dependent on colour (white to black exposes deeper iris tissue as it goes); and *fibres* (raised white or less visible) can also be seen in the iris layers. *Radii solaris* seem to have been gouged with a chisel straight through colour and structure: V-shaped, blackish-brown, straight lines, geometrically stiff, and pointing directly along the radius lines of the iris circle (hence the name). They may be all around the iris in a pattern of long and shorter 'spikes', but they may also pierce through only one or more body zones, and they are most often found pointing to head areas. They can start even from the pupil and out through the stomach and intestinal zones; but this is rare. Mostly they originate just inside or just outside the nerve wreath. Naturopathically, they have their origin in the bowel. Psychologically, they originate in the head. In naturopathic practice, both origins are treated.

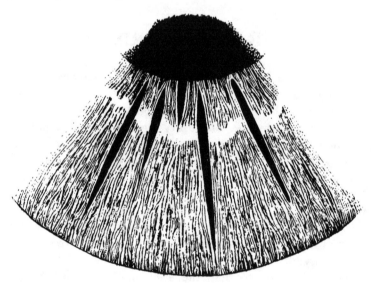

Radii Solaris

○ Reversing Destructive Patterns

How does one convince a resentful arthritic of sixty-plus to 'Go back to Square 1 and start again'? How does one even try to explain that the wrong road has been taken somewhere, and that both body and mind are *in the wrong pattern*, a pattern contrary to the potential one programmed at conception and birth? How can one reverse the self-destructive progression towards cancer or suicide? A practitioner can't look at the eyes of a child of ten or a young lass of twenty or even a mature patient asking for therapeutic help and yell, 'You've done it all wrong! You weren't supposed to do these things, to be this way, to suffer these symptoms!' How is it possible to re-direct health processes and overcome *radii solaris*?

Let's look first at the 'impossible' anatomical conditions producing *radii solaris* signs in an iris. Put simply, the problem is this: in a 'normal' bowel, the function of the large bowel is to extract water from sloppy food residues and pass it out through the bowel wall into tissues, there to be collected by lymph glands and/or eventually eliminated from the body via sweat and urine. The firm bulk of normal faeces is the result of this water-extraction process. When *radii solaris* appear, the wall of the bowel becomes permeable to toxic wastes that would normally be excreted. This is the 'impossibility', medically, which takes place, and the person begins to re-cycle his or her own wastes.

One recent theory as to *why* the bowel wall suddenly becomes more permeable to other substances is that it could have been weakened at some stage by some form of parasitic invasion. One of the high-level remedies I use is a powerfully potent form of *holly*, a herb which, in ordinary extract form, is rather too harsh on the bowel in its drastic purgative action. I believe that this herb has an anti-parasitic effect and certainly *radii solaris* fade and disappear quite remarkably with the high-potency tiny dose of it I use in treatment. I would like to spend time and effort to check this hypothesis, and to have some bowel tissue tested medically and pathologically to confirm the suspected parasitic weakening of structure and chemical function, and the resultant changed permeability.

You can imagine the results in 'target' organ iris areas pierced by a *radii solaris* 'spike'! There are symptoms of infection, pain, inflammation; though extensive physical and pathological investigation shows no trauma. Such symptoms are *always resistant to medical treatment of this target organ or function.* A slow sewage drain exists between the bowel and the body area pointed through by the *radii solaris,* so that most orthodox treatment can be ineffective against such a continuing waste flood. Naturopathic treatment to remove *radii solaris* from the iris and its cause from the body is always aimed at normalising the bowel wall with herbs acting specifically and strongly upon it. Violet leaves, mistletoe, and holly all have a place in treatment; but *very* skilful advice must be sought as to how such agents should be used.

Closing off the 'drainage gutters' of *radii solaris* removes in a different way the possibility of great loads of rubbish being dumped in some body organ or function. As our brown/black section in 'Iris Colours' has shown, you can reasonably expect trouble if such wastes accumulate and overload the target organ over a period of time. *Radii solaris* absolutely *do not* indicate cancer any more than any other iris sign combination. But the pre-conditions of waste deposits in tissues are present, and in continuing supply day by day, *irrespective* of the diet, general health, and energy, of the person concerned. Some patients who have had a history of cancer treated by medical methods have said to me 'I don't know why I got it; I've looked after myself; I'm happy, ...' *Radii solaris* recognition earlier could have closed off *one* possible contributing factor.

Again, please don't jam my telephone and mailbox with panic requests to be 'cured of cancer'! First, we are not legally allowed to treat cancer. Second, naturopaths and herbalists regard cancer not as an illness but as a potentially reversible body condition involving accumulated waste removal. Third, and most reassuring, *radii solaris* can be found in an iris for many years without likelihood of any such serious illness ever occurring. See how hard this sign can be to interpret and explain?

O Mental And Emotional Implications

Let's leave the physical aspect of the sign and look at the mental and emotional implications. Say you have a right iris showing only one *radii solaris* 'spike' through your 'anxiety and apprehension' zone. You are hurling a load of rubbish into that particular faculty! Your anxieties are unfounded; your worries are not really there; and your apprehensions about vague, intangible circumstances are all a load of rubbish, too! You are giving yourself a hard time unnecessarily; probably boring those around you, upsetting your own health and producing a negative track through the bowel wall membrane because of the 'Crown of Thorns' you have placed firmly on your own head.

The *radii solaris* may radiate outwards from the pupil, but it can be a channel from *outside* the body, too, directing rubbish of a different kind inwards. If you have ever had experience with mentally disturbed patients, you know it's no use at all saying, 'That's a load of rubbish', if they tell you they are the King of Siam or the Lord of the Night or Napoleon. It's also no use explaining rationally that there are no black spiders on their chest or Indian assassins waiting in the bedroom. I feel similarly helpless confronting a patient with *radii solaris*. How does one start?

'You are doing all this to yourself by biochemical choice.' No. 'You are really a selfish bitch but don't realise it, and your headaches won't go until you do.' No. 'You are not crazy, just re-cycling your own rubbish.' No, most times. Often I just give appropriate remedies at the first visit without even mentioning the problem, knowing that as treatment progresses the patient's awareness can change, and sudden (or slow) realisation of the former wrong pattern can emerge. Most of the battle is over when this happens.

You could also sub-title *radii solaris*: 'Negative destructive patterns superimposed by stronger outside or inside pressures than can be recognised and overcome without outside help.' By this time I've probably lost any reader showing such signs; but if you re still with me, it gets *better*. Often, awareness of the real problem can be enough, as treatment progresses, to reverse the negative processes completely. I have seen many patients who really have returned to 'square 1' and gone on positively from where they previously got sidetracked into negative, out-of-pattern body responses. I have also seen many patients who have intellectually recognised the problem but have made a deliberate choice to continue in the same wrong pattern. I have neither the enormous energy needed nor the professional time to continue with such people. Their 'rubbish' load is shouldered with individual acceptance of its possible results; and it is no longer my responsibility to try to take it from them or show them how to drop it as an unnecessary burden.

If a *radii solaris* spike points to the ego area in either or both irises, such patients may experience two aspects of the same problem: high or low blood-pressure symptoms, and high or low opinion of themselves: The one can cause the other, or they can be found together. All the *radii solaris* indicates is that both conditions will be resistant to medical treatment for blood-pressure imbalance, and to 'head talk' to improve the ego image—*until* the patient becomes aware of the situation, and changes it himself by any means at all. I prefer to think of *radii solaris* as an unaware iris sign rather than a destructive one.

The deliberate acceptance of a 'Crown of Thorns' passively, *knowing* the implications, has been the choice of many wonderful human beings. One lady often comes into my thoughts; a white-haired, gentle soul of sixty-odd, quietly spoken and looking at me with clear blue Silk irises where one fading *radii solaris* channel to the uterus marred the general perfection. She had had a malignant growth, and the organ itself, removed several months previously. 'Why did I get it?' she asked me gently. In the course of the consultation I found that her husband had been diagnosed as having a tumour in the throat some twelve months earlier. She loved him dearly and had prayed to 'take it away from him' if she could. And she did! The *radii solaris* recorded the danger in which her self-sacrificial love had placed her.

Being Scottish and practical by nature, I try to keep my feet on the ground in the general treatment of illness; but *radii solaris* often take me into areas of philosophy and metaphysics rather than health. Destinies can be changed by conscious exercise of the will; cancer victims can 'miraculously' recover; other apparently healthy people can *choose* to be ill and then set about finding ways to *be* ill. I'm sure much has still to be explored in diagnosis from *radii solaris* signs. Suffice to say they are totally different in appearance, effect, and disappearance, from any other iris indications. When the negative pattern is gone from the life of the person, the 'wheel spokes' just disappear! They don't heal over or gradually change like other signs; they are just no longer observable. The narrow blackish trench is filled in somehow, and disappears. Any spread of general brown through the zone (if it is present) can then be removed by the bowel, and no trace of the *radii solaris* will remain. Magic? No. Just another body system we need to discover more about.

If your eyes show *radii solaris*, think! Have you taken a wrong turning, made a wrong choice, suffered unnecessarily the burdens of others? It's not too late to make a better-informed decision now and reverse the negative patterns of health and well-being.

PSORIC SPOTS

Radii solaris is a difficult iris sign to explain outside metaphysics; and psoric spots, too, can lead us into all manner of discussion of their mysteries. There seems to be no rational anatomical reason why a tiny pigment fleck of brownish-black in iris tissue should have such massive influence as it does on the health of the body zone it covers.

Let's start simply with a description of a psoric spot. Most of the 'special sign' group differ in the layers of the iris where they appear, and psoric spots seem to lie above the surface of the iris. Under the 10x magnification of an iris torch, they appear almost to float between the iris and the clear corneal layer covering it. A group of tiny stippled dots, very close together, clump to form a dark fleck, or freckle, quite obviously different in texture, colour, and position from more generalised brownish fogs and clouds of biochemical rubbish. The flecks are hard-edged, certainly not amorphous,

Psoric Spots

and seem superimposed, even over other brownish, yellow or white coloration. Mostly, they stay for life in the position in which they were found at birth (or shortly afterwards); but they *can* move from one part of the iris to another; they can suddenly appear or disappear at any time of life; and they can sometimes be removed by the patient's working through the 'lesson' inherent in the spot location, which can be a traumatic experience.

The psoric spot is anatomically a pigment deposition and is usually thought to be inherited pigmentary coloration as genetics join brown-eyed and blue-eyed parents in various combinations of chemistry. I remember vividly a novel from my youth where the heroine's 'gold-flecked green eyes' had me wishing for such mysterious orbs too. Now I know the heroine could have had liver troubles, early arthritis, and all sorts of resistant illness patterns. Although under unmagnified observation the flecks may have seemed gold next to the green, the real colour of all psoric spots is sepia-brown to black. If they *fade*, the tone becomes lighter.

○ Significance Of Position

The position in the iris of such dense little blocks of colour is of the greatest significance. Just as normal vision can be severely impaired by abnormal pigmentation of the retina (even to eventual blindness), so flecks of pigment placed *in front* of various parts of the iris can interfere with the recording of accurate data from external and internal stimuli. Therefore the internal response to such stimuli can be inappropriate.

Take, as example, a psoric spot masking some of the liver area. Liver function may be inefficient and all sorts of liver illnesses (hepatitis, alcoholism, parasitic infestation, enlargement, heroin addiction) may be experienced by the patient during his or her lifetime. If a motor-car accident happens, the liver may be damaged; if it's a fall downstairs, the liver may be bruised or shocked into inefficiency. Emotional suppression affecting the liver may last a lifetime; or compulsive eating; or inability to process carotene from food into vitamin A. The liver is a trouble spot, prone to damage, and the damage may not register clearly in that section of the iris.

When a psoric spot is situated in the spleen iris zone, everything from inhibited anger to pernicious anaemia may be experienced. On the other hand, no evidence of any problem in spleen function may be obvious to the person— for there is a *block*, remember, to his awareness of the situation.

'I'm not an aggressive person at all,' one patient told me. 'I don't like to fight or make a fuss—seems useless.' His presenting symptoms were pathological tiredness and poor circulation for many years. He had no energy to defend himself against the constant petulant demands of his ex-wife who had divorced him years before as a chronically tired, low-motivated partner. An iris examination showed a deep brown psoric spot at the outer rim of the iris (circulation zone), in the spleen segment. No wonder he was tired and no wonder he was passive! His spleen recording of stimuli was blocked. He couldn't defend himself because he didn't know accurately that he was being attacked. His red blood cells and his white ones too were inefficiently processed and restored by the spleen; so his overall immunity was low and the quality of his blood was poor. Tiredness and lack of motivation resulted from his near-anaemic state; so did colds and viruses which hung about for months: all produced by a psoric spot.

Think of these spots as possible inefficiency producers, not as a sentence of gloom, doom and disaster. Some people have them and do not appear to have any problems associated with them at all. One lovely strong woman, who came to me for a check-up and iris-analysis only, was quite amazed to find that each now fading psoric spot in her iris covered a zone where she had had previous problems but had them no longer. Over her uterus was one spot (she had had several pregnancy terminations in earlier life and had had difficulty conceiving her first child). She had another spot over the appendix (at the age of 14 her inflamed appendix had ruptured, causing peritonitis). A third spot showed over her throat zone (as a singer in her teens, she had had many bouts of laryngitis and tonsillitis). At her present age of sixty-plus, she had had no further problems in any of these areas.

'I learnt my lessons,' she told me. 'I stopped singing; my voice had never been good enough. I resigned myself to having only two children (I had wanted four). I went to a naturopath years ago who fixed my abdominal adhesions after the appendicectomy.' I assured her that her problems were now in the past, for she had suffered all of them and learnt to 'see' from the situations experienced. Her present good general health was reflected in the rest of her clear blue Linen irises.

You see how difficult these psoric spots can be to interpret? Probing questions must be asked of the patient to establish the degree of inefficiency or blockage of function experienced. Mostly, the person feels that the conditions experienced in the body area covered by a psoric spot are the *real* ones; but in fact a better potential can exist. Some degree of impeded or abnormal reaction to external stimuli and internal response can always be found. The adrenal output can be too high under imagined fight-or-flight stimuli; the lungs can absorb coal-tar deposits too readily and inflate too slowly; the thyroid can produce alarming weight fluctuations even on the best possible diet; a kidney can atrophy or help retain abnormal amounts of fluid. Any zone under a psoric spot *can* produce out-of-balance reactions some or all of the time. But the unpredictable element in psoric spot reaction is always present. There may or may *not* be evidence of a health or emotional problem in the affected zone. Often, bringing the situation to a patient's notice can start off the 'clear-seeing' learning process needed for spot removal.

According to anatomical science, a pigmentation spot in the iris remains for life. In practice, this is not so. Such psoric spots can *move* from one part of the iris to another; they can also fade, and/or disappear altogether. I have had patients by the hundreds in whom such spots show quite remarkable travelling ability.

One woman who had a psoric spot over the pituitary zone in the left iris, when she first saw me, had the *same* spot over the bronchial-tree segment after months of homoeopathic treatment. She originally had had an incredible, unexplainable weight increase from twelve stone to nearly twenty-two stone in a few months. Even on nothing but water for ten days in hospital she put on sixteen pounds! Her pituitary gland was just not setting her body processes at the right speed at all. Under the rather sophisticated naturopathic treatment I prescribed for her, her weight began to drop as the psoric spot changed position. I could never tell where it would be next; but when it landed in the bronchial zone she had quite remarkable chest infections and trauma. The weight loss compensated her for such new inefficiency in another body process!

You could call psoric spots 'learning situations'. Will the person see *through* the inefficiently recorded zone? Will awareness of the *real* stimuli remove the spot? If someone can explain to the patient what is happening it's a question of will-power and a willingness to progress through limitations. Tune in again next week! See if the psoric spot has faded or moved!

O Spots As Atonement Areas

Many people show no psoric spots in the iris. Metaphysicians propound that they *see clearly*. Every stimulus is recorded accurately from outside and translated accordingly inside. Those who believe in reincarnation and karma often see psoric spots as *atonement* areas: functions that must be endured at inefficient levels in order to learn karmic lessons and progress to a higher state of grace. Certainly, once a lesson-learning approach is taken, the inhibiting effect of psoric spots can be minimised—even removed—and the spot itself can fade as the hard lesson is worked through.

I was born with a pronounced psoric spot over the liver zone, right iris. I learnt the hard lesson of accurate emotional response, but not until my early thirties. By that time the psoric spot had faded slowly, and then it disappeared. I am not sure which is stronger—the inhibitory effect of not 'seeing clearly' or the human will to overcome obstacles; but I would back the latter every time.

If you have a psoric spot over any iris zone, consider the implications. You will not 'see clearly' through this function. You can have problems and obstacles which you may or may not choose to overcome in order to remove the impediment to your accurate recording of stimuli. It seems to be a matter of 'choice'. How far do you wish to evolve this time? How much karma do you wish to earn before your next incarnation? If such beliefs seem nonsense to you, psoric spots can indicate nothing more than annoying vulnerable areas where health problems may occur, problems unexplainably resistant to normal treatment.

You are beginning to understand my hesitation in explaining psoric spots in terms of straight iris analysis? Of all the signs visible in irises, they are the hardest to classify in orthodox fashion. I try to deal with them at the level at which the patient is most interested. It's no use talking of 'lesson learning' and karma to a lady who just wants her chronic resistant cystitis fixed. It's equally useless to explain that *her* cystitis will be much more resistant and take longer and more involved treatment than usual because her iris has a dark brown spot at 4.50 in the right eye. An iridologist is often accused by those outside the profession of far-fetched diagnoses, but the proof remains with the patient: what happens is recorded in the iris.

If you have a multitude of brown flecks in your irises, don't despair of yourself as being untreatable and chronically behind the eight-ball in health. The iris areas so covered may still seem to be functioning normally, *but* be aware that it is possible for a different type of functional pattern to be experienced in such areas. It's up to you to decide. That irritation you experience—yelling at someone, 'Can't you *see* what you're doing wrong? Can't you see what's under your nose?'—can be unfair. *Over* the nose, recorded in the iris, can be the reason for the block—a psoric spot.

7

THE IRIS MAP

Charting Your Findings

So far, we have explored some principles of iris recording: structural fibre types; colours and biochemical change; special signs and circular zones marking body system boundaries. Now we must locate all this broad information in a map or chart, so that each small sector of the iris can be accurately assessed and analysed.

Accuracy of diagnosis is one of the major reasons for using iridology, so the art/science of iris-reading needs care and attention to smaller detailed indications as well as to the broader general personality and type so far covered.

You can read off much information in a ten-second look at the iris. You can say to the person, with reasonable accuracy, 'You have strong structure and very good health, but you keep too tight a control on yourself and swallow your stress. Your stomach is sensitive and highly acidic and your general health problems will lie in major circulation and arthritic tendencies. You are never likely to have migraines, but are prone to stomach-cramps after dinner at night. You had a rheumatic grandmother and you sit on a chair at work that is the wrong height for you. You don't exercise enough and your tiredness is only apathy. Any constipation problems are from your getting "uptight", so your bowel does too.'

While your subject is amazed by all this general knowledge, patients who come to see an iridologist therapeutically say, 'I have a pain *here*. I want it fixed'; or 'My left knee gives way all the time', or 'When I bend forward too long I get dizzy'; or 'Can you tell me why this little lump on my neck is so sore sometimes and not others?'

Finer accuracy is needed, and many years of experience by several practitioners have produced maps of the iris locating specific body areas and functions in great detail. A German iridologist, Kriege, has drafted a map which differs markedly from the American Dr Bernard Jensen's chart most commonly in use. I have found Jensen's chart more accurate, and use it with only a few minor alterations, but with the addition of *emotional* characteristics that register in organs and systems which share, produce, or feel, the result of the chemistry of the emotion.

Since each body varies in *proportion* (longer legs, shorter arms, an elongated trunk, rounder section, larger heart) the zones and boundaries of the map are slightly flexible, and they certainly are as mathematically inexact as each person is unique. People do not fit into mathematics and science; they vary. So do irises, and many scientific-minded medical practitioners condemn iridology as 'unscientific' for this reason. I claim its variability as a virtue; it fits *people*.

O   Iridology: A Tool Only

One important aspect of iridology must be understood. It is not a complete system of medical, emotional, personality, and type analysis *on its own*. There are practitioners who claim it to be so; but I have to disagree with them. It is a tool only, a screen from which to read off visually many things about the person. Questions must be asked and perception and observation of the patient used to fill in the complete diagnosis. Irises record body conditions; but interpretation of the pattern needs two people, the patient and the practitioner.

Some things cannot be determined from an iris alone. An eye photograph won't reveal gender (unless the eyelashes are thick with mascara—but you still never can tell!) or age. You certainly don't expect to find arteriosclerosis in babies or a clear china-blue iris in middle-aged 'civilised' folk; but around the years between, say, puberty and the fifties, it can be impossible to fit a disembodied iris into a particular age group. I have seen irises of sickly children which, viewed as irises alone, showed indications more reasonably to be expected in an eighty-year-old. The health of these children was poor, yes, but the irises alone could not have led to correct diagnosis. I have seen clear, china-blue Silk irises in eighty-year-olds whose abounding health and vitality was more like that of a ten-year-old. Relate the iris to the *patient*, every time, and you'll interpret the indications more accurately.

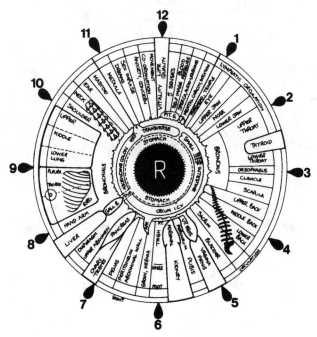

The Iris Map, right eye
(looking at another person's right eye)

131

Many natural changes, if all goes smoothly, do not register in irises. Puberty may show a little disturbance in endocrine function and some structural pressures as bones grow and body posture changes; but it's impossible to label the iris 'puberty'. Menopause (both male and female) doesn't show as such either, although some signs of functional change may be present to support a general symptomatic diagnosis. Pregnancy, if progressing well, does not show any different typical pattern. It still amazes me to see a healthy woman near the end of her pregnancy, bulging happily and obviously, with no signs in the iris of any change or trauma. Of course, if she has toxaemia, lower back pain, varicose veins, and anxiety, many signs will be apparent, but not 'pregnancy'.

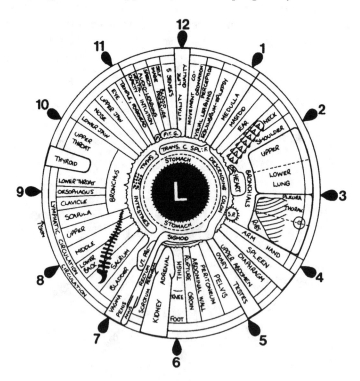

The Iris Map, left eye
(looking at another person's left eye)

Contents of organs or body spaces do not register either, unless the structure or function of that part of the body has been affected. So we can see a reason why pregnancy as such does not show: the contents of the uterus, if normal, are not visible in the iris. Kidney stones, gall-stones, gravel in the bladder, a cyst on the ovaries, or a tumour in the bowel, do not show in irises as such. Certainly, colour and structural indications may lead you to one of those diagnoses; but suspected contents of an organ or a space call for lots of questions and maybe further investigations in order to make an accurate assessment and recommend appropriate treatment for the patient.

The sixty-four dollar question is always 'Can you tell me if I've got cancer?' My usual answer is, 'No. But if you think you may have you're certainly more likely to get it eventually!' As I've stated elsewhere, irises do not record medically named diseases: they record body conditions.

RIGHT IRIS

O The Head

Between 11 o'clock and 1 o'clock lie iris zones referring to physical and mental structure and function of the head. From 11 o'clock to 12 noon refers mostly to processes of the physiological brain; 12 noon to 1 o'clock reflects *psychological, intellectual,* and *developed* functions of the physiological brain. The physiological zone is more obvious in its evidence than the psychological one.

We shall begin our exploring of the head signs in the iris with the Chairman of the Board, the control panel of the power station, the conductor of the physical orchestra—the medulla. This soft bulb of brain tissue helps to set your IQ, your structure type (indirectly), and the amount of physical control you have over this structure and its function. It is the physical message-transmitter from the brain directly to spinal nerves and their impulses to all co-ordinated body systems.

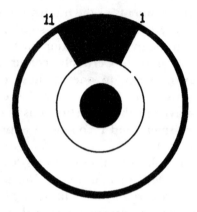

You can see why it's our most obvious starting point. Car accidents with whiplash, kicks at the base of the skull in sporting contests or outside pubs, and hits over the head with blunt instruments, can loosen the directness of this control and cause incoordination problems. Parkinson's disease often shows first in this area of the iris, and later in the locomotor zone. The gentle art of hanging (breaking the neck at the first cervical vertebra) kills the victim by severing the connection between the medulla and the spinal chord, cutting off all body function by throwing the master switch to 'off'.

If white signs show in the zone, you can expect a well controlled individual physically (maybe *too* tightly controlled), able to make the body do what the head tells it. If yellow or brown signs appear, there may be a fault in the control mechanism which is only sending low-power signals to the body.

This kind of person lets the body rule the head. Inefficiency in the body can also reduce the high-powered signals from the medulla, so that its messages do not get through as directly as they should. Chiropractic adjustment of the spine can often re-activate a sluggish medulla which has got tired of sending physical spinal impulses not correctly translated by the spinal nerve centres. Patients often feel an obvious surge of renewed energy to and from the head after adjustment of the cervical vertebrae stimulates the medulla.

Structural lesions in the iris at this point can show a record of past physical trauma, or can merely show that you have 'pulled your head in' under stress and that *compression* has resulted. A good stretch of the neck each evening before bed can take the weight of your tired skull away from your physical major control centre, and let it rest too.

Directly across the iris on a 'reflex' diameter lies the bladder zone. Children who wet the bed long past infancy may have medullary pressure or insufficiency to blame for their misery. Their non-control of the bladder is a symptom of this medullary imbalance—not a 'psychosomatic' problem but a real physical one in this case. Many natural therapies treat the control centre for such problems.

The medulla controls some intellectual and emotional processes, but its major job is to synchronise, co-ordinate, and transmit down the spine, signals to and from the brain dealing with physical happenings.

Sexual impulses zone

Adjacent to the medulla segment lies a fascinating zone labelled 'sexual impulses'. In the same zone we find a second classification, 'hallucinations'. Some iridologists of the older school also label this zone 'perversions'! Let's take these one by one.

Sexual impulse equals libido, equals *interest*, not necessarily *action*. It is possible to have a high sexual impulse which is seldom used or a lower one used quite often. This zone refers only to the level at which the *head* is occupied with sex. 'If you're not doing it, you're thinking about it!' says one of my randier friends; and the white flare out from his nerve wreath and through the sexual impulse zone tells me he's truthful. A dark lesion or brown or yellowish-brown fog would have told me he was *un*truthful and over-compensating for it. In other words, he was 'hallucinating', 'having himself on', the alternative response possible in this zone. Walter-Mitty-like dreams and fantasies can sometimes *replace* action, but are often a part and parcel of the action for many of us. Sexual fantasies play a large part in fixing the head level of sexual activity at 'white' response.

'Perversion', so-called, I would limit to the psychopathic definition of 'causing actual harm to another sexually, either physically or mentally'. One man's perversion is another's stimulation. Trouble only occurs when two differently oriented sexual partners accuse each other of 'perversion' or abnormal behaviour. If they both have the same 'kink', normality applies. If both you and your partner have a white hyper-active sexual impulse zone, fine. If you both have a brown fog or lesion showing, and feel that once every couple of months is normal, fine again. But beware of mixing the two extremes. In choosing partners, responsible checking of irises can help (not as a parlour-game or just a fun-thing) to estimate whether real problems are likely to emerge later.

Hallucinations and fantasies induced by drugs can show signs in this iris zone. I find that many drug addicts either lose their sexual impulse as they hallucinate, or find *apparent* increased sexual pleasure as they hallucinate. Both results show as brownish colours or structural lesions, or even interrupted nerve supply, proving that such sensations are destructive and negative. The message from the physiological brain has been incorrectly translated by a nervous system toxic with heroin or opium, even with marihuana. Such 'wrong' responses can register as dark colours, fibre disturbance, or imbalance in the nervous system. You may feel good, but it is an illusion. A white sign, by contrast, means you really *are* feeling good.

Take a diameter across the iris and you find the zones of uterus and vagina in the female, prostate and penis in the male. Obviously, this reflex is often called into use. When signals become too high for comfort in the head impulse, the body rapidly goes into action to counterbalance the overload.

If there are no visible differences in this zone from the rest of the general iris balance, you are probably a level-headed 'normal' person sexually, putting sexual activity in its place with other body functions but with no special emphasis positively or negatively.

Looking back for a moment to the calcium ring (p. 101), especially when it appears over head areas as *arcus senilis*, you will understand how many body functions can be affected by the inefficient circulation it causes. Your libido may be down because your cholesterol and calcium deposition is up. If only poor blood supply is available to the head, its physiological functions can be just as impaired as its psychological ones.

Anxiety sector

Next, in the adjacent zone, lies an area which affects some of us all the time and all of us some of the time—the 'anxiety' sector. I must tell you of a case history here which has remained memorable because of its obvious and extreme manifestation in the iris.

A child of nine years, labelled 'autistic' and permanently institutionalised because of it, was brought to see me by his mother. He sat for most of the day in a corner of a room, would eat only bananas and drink only lemonade, and could not even be approached by his parents or his brothers without extreme responses of withdrawal and fear cutting off all communication. (Don't forget we are still in the zone of the head where medullary control operates on certain physical functions.) He would back into the corner with apprehension, even terror, at the approach of anyone. After he had been given much loving care in the institution, and much understanding and patience by his family, I got to the point of sighting his iris. A huge fibre lesion extending from the medulla to the next zone after this one (the 'movement' zone) showed me the extent of the problem. Fear of pathological proportions, hallucinations, paralysis of movement, and lack of medullary control, added up to autism. He was born in a functional state of uncontrollable anxiety, and his defence was to deprive himself of movement to quieten down the panic. I have never since seen such a clearly delineated lesion of such huge size. Naturopathic treatment of a sophisticated kind has enabled his fear to be *controlled better* by the medulla. He now mixes with other children, puts out his hand to trusted adults, and eats more normally. The lesion in his 'anxiety' area has criss-cross healing lines over the greater part of it.

The rather polite classification 'anxiety' softens what is happening chemically and physically—a fear response. It is more acceptable to hear, 'Mrs Jones, you are suffering from anxiety', than 'Lady, you are scared stiff!' Whether there is much difference in degree will depend on the size, shape, and colour of any lesion appearing in this zone. Mostly, the indications are structural first, leading to the hypothesis that there are physical as well as circumstantial causes of anxiety states. There is sometimes a flattening of the iris perimeter across these head zones. Birth difficulties and even pre-natal trauma can cause the iris rim to flatten at any zone where enough pressure has been applied structurally to soft bones and tissue.

Another anxiety patient of mine showed a marked straightline iris edge, instead of an arc, at some head areas and across the cervical vertebrae. Her father had launched her at the wall, head first, when she was only three weeks old! I believe many of her later mental attitudes, especially pathological fear, could be attributed to such obvious structural causes.

The process of birth itself can be a drastically traumatic one. An organism which has been parasitic for nine months is suddenly required to become self-supporting. As the diaphragm flexes and the lungs inflate, a paroxysm constricts the chest and breathing is forcefully commenced. The pattern is very similar to an asthma-spasm onset. The first experience structurally of the world outside the womb can be 'fear' of not breathing, and an even greater degree of this fear—panic—as the new child struggles for oxygen. If, as well, the atmosphere in the delivery ward is noisy, hectic, anxious, can you wonder that a child over-responds in later life to anxiety stimuli?

The Leboyer method of childbirth should produce a much more balanced lot of adults. A darkened room; quiet; slow unhurried movements of others around; gentle touching and handling of the child rather than the 'hang 'em up by the heels and slap 'em' method of starting breathing: such a setting should minimise fear in the child as its first human emotion.

Some iridologists label this same zone 'inherent mental capacity'. If your IQ is high you should expect to find white signs—flares or fibres—in the area. The oft-repeated pattern of the brilliant student overworking before the exam and 'cracking up' with delusions, anxiety, and apprehension, can be traced in the iris. The adjacent zones may 'blow a fuse', too, and open a fibre lesion which then can become foggy and brown progressively if the anxiety continues and grows. A brownish streak down the centre of the area can indicate the biochemical or functional aspect of anxiety—an adrenal imbalance; a lesion or fibre disturbance plus white signs can indicate some physical cause for the level of anxiety. Often this latter can show the *hyper*-activity of a worrier, a person whose head never stops thinking, never turns off. Mental over-use like this can result in insomnia or that annoying habit—waking at three or four o'clock in the morning with the head alert and churning with thoughts although the still-tired body craves more sleep. There are herbal remedies available which help to 'switch off' these over-active heads.

If a brown cloud is generally dispersed over these last few zones, you can decrease your anxiety, increase your sex-life, and improve even your memory and concentration, by improving the function of your bowels! The transverse colon area, situated immediately below the general head section, can, by its function, affect many head processes. More of this later.

'Apprehension' can also be classed as a form of sub-acute anxiety. Do you know anyone who always appears to be looking over the shoulder at something lurking behind? In one type of herbal medicine the corrective treatment is aspen, that member of the poplar family whose leaves quiver and shake and turn at the slightest breeze. Apprehension sufferers feel vaguely uneasy, not able to put a name to their fears, but sure of their existence. The worst is always about to happen! Some of these people show dark colours and lesions, but often a pale 'fog' of yellow brown is all. Some carefully prescribed natural B vitamins can banish both the colour pattern and the apprehension.

Lesions of some magnitude in this iris zone can also indicate mental retardation of certain types. 'Slow learners' may be wrongly classified if there is only *colour* abnormality here. Improvement in biochemical function can vastly improve learning ability for many; but if a fibre lesion persists after the colour is improved by treatment the problem has only a limited reversal/success probability.

In the chapter 'Reflex Signs' (p. 91) you have read of the adrenal/anxiety reflex. The adrenal glands are one of the fastest reflex zones to operate. Instantaneous response under fear is common even before a situation has been rationally comprehended.

A *radii solaris* spike (p. 117) to this zone can indicate a more serious problem with anxiety that is quite out of awareness control, and therefore out of medullary control, too. It can also indicate another form of worry—over-concern for the welfare of others. As a consolation, a *radii solaris* sign occurs here in some really nice self-sacrificial people; but the sign can also persist as a signal that the over-concern is an *unnecessary* burden and detrimental to health.

I know one dutiful daughter who never left home and never had a relationship because 'Mum couldn't do without me'. I know another lady who felt every day of her father's terminal cancer pattern as symptoms in her own body. Another patient became quite mentally disturbed himself after a year's work in a psychiatric hospital. He said he could feel all the hopelessness and defeat of the inmates in his own body, and he tried continually to raise their 'vibes' with his own energies, tried to 'do it *for* them'. A *radii solaris* spike showed through the anxiety zone of all the above people.

Some people can carry the loads of others without damage; other people find the burden very heavy. Guilt can produce an over-compensation like this. Even *apprehension* about *possible* guilt or responsibility can produce damaging over-concern classifiable as 'anxiety'. A *radii solaris* line should be brought to the notice of the person as an over-concern reaction. Rest assured that such over-concern also has herbal remedies available for its treatment. Such correction does not suddenly turn a concerned patient into a Scrooge or a Simon Legree; it removes only the damaging *over*-concern which is depleting energy unnecessarily. That dutiful daughter may just say quietly, 'Mum, I'm going out tonight with some friends. I've arranged for Mrs Smith next door to sit with you for a few hours.' Concern has become more balanced, that's all.

Locomotor zone

The next zone in this head group records physical co-ordination and movement. I once undertook a survey of irises of spastic children and found that only a proportion of them showed negative signs in this zone. Some of the others were lacking the ability to absorb vitamin B_6, apparently even from before birth; others showed epileptic-type nerve responses; still others had head areas so flooded with brown bowel muck that it was no wonder their limbs moved jerkily and their muscles clamped tight. There were a few showing such lack of magnesium phosphate that never, from birth (or even *in utero*), did they have a chance of normal neuro-muscular response. Iris analysis is a simple way to find out what proportion of the medical labels stuck on a patient is accurate.

Any illness involving uncoordinated movement will show in this iris zone—if the cause of the problem is in *head*-control of movement. A bad fall hurting one leg may limit its movement physically for a while; but if no damage has been done to head control the only sign showing should be at 6 o'clock in the leg zone. As the leg heals under massage and osteopathic treatment, full co-ordination should return. But

141

if the damage to the leg is so severe that a permanent limp results, then a small inco-ordination sign may appear in the 'locomotor' zone. If the muscles of the leg weaken and atrophy over ensuing years of limited use, further fibre lesions, and maybe a brownish discoloration, too, can be recorded.

Fear can paralyse if strong enough. In many people it produces only an adrenal reflex and the urge to *move*; but in others the fear spills sideways into the adjacent zone of 'movement', and negative movement—immobility—can result. The fear can overflow back into the sexual zone, too, so that a compounding of the problem may result: fear of making the wrong move sexually inhibits many people so that their sexual impulse does not make any move at all. Involvement of these three adjacent zones can show in the iris.

Movement is restricted in some physical diseases. Locomotor ataxia is one, Parkinson's disease is another. Many hyperactive children show white flares and raised white fibres in the 'movement' area of the iris. Some physical 'senses' are also recorded here. Sensitivity to degrees of temperature, to atmospheric pressure, to heights, will show as whitish signs again: an over-reaction to 'movement' or change of external conditions surrounding the body. People who find flying uncomfortable often show white or yellowish signs in the movement zone. Their barometer is upset by a change in height and pressure. Maybe flight crews should have their movement zones checked in both irises periodically in case the adjacent zones—vitality and anxiety—become affected.

A *radii solaris* line to this zone may indicate that the degree of movement (or non-movement) is damaging. One of my patients dubbed 'psychotic' by the medical world showed many *radii solaris* lines to the head areas, but especially so to the movement sector. She was obsessed with moving objects around the house into different spots each day (sometimes each hour!), and her own frenetic movement while doing this registered not as hyper-activity but as negative damaging activity over which she had little medullary control.

In a psychiatric hospital I have seen patients whose catatonia (*absence* of movement ability) left them sitting in a chair staring at a fixed spot on the wall for many hours. Even eyelids did not move in blinking. You remember that blink-rate gives a measure for sensitivity of reaction to stimuli? A person who hardly blinks at all is *in*-sensitive (non-flowing, non-co-ordinating, non-flexible, non-empathetic) and does not move with circumstances. Dark signs can be expected in the iris.

A reflex from the movement zone across the iris points down the dividing line between 'leg' and 'adrenal' areas. Some folk move only on adrenal stimulus. Many Silks who have fallen into rusty disuse patterns, have done so only because of lack of challenge, lack of adrenal stimulus. Something exciting needs to be promised or they may not move at all! Signs of brownish colour may appear in both the reflex and the stimulus zones.

Vitality sector

The 'vitality' sector is represented at high noon on the clock. The degree of available energy and any limitations affecting it show here very clearly. Strong white fibres and white flares reflect the high energy charge along nerves and the equally high rate of input from brain-control centres. The vitality of such a person is obvious and bubbling. It makes you feel tired to watch all that inexhaustible energy spraying out from the top of the head. If the 'last straw' of load for those same Silks is added and they crumple under the burden, a fibre lesion can appear in the vitality sector. As a warning to them, it can appear even *before* they drop with clanging armour in an untypically helpless collapse. The iris can register 'Overload, overload' long before their stubborn heads give in.

Dark streaks, even *radii solaris*, can warn of danger of more permanent vitality loss. A brownish fog (often bowel-induced again) can show that the *true* vitality is fogged as well, and inefficient use of potentially good energy has resulted.

If you are too tired to get out of the armchair, think of the reflex zone opposite—the leg and foot. Too tired to get on your feet? Get your weight *off* your feet and re-vitalise! Happy feet can reflex back an equally content message to the top of the head. More of this when we discuss the foot zone.

Many of the brownish fogs seen in head areas are produced by chronically lazy bowels, and pathological tiredness thus caused can be treated with bowel/head combinations like yeast, molasses, bran, with enormous improvement to head energy and vitality.

If you show a calcium ring over head areas, your vitality will have dropped quite noticeably from its former level. A fading back or flattening-off of the iris perimeter can indicate lowered blood supply or low blood *pressure* to the head, and a different kind of vitality drop. Sometimes chiropractic adjustment of cervical vertebrae can raise your vitality if you 'pull your head in' or 'stick your neck out' under stress, straining the upper spinal vertebrae out of correct postural balance. Re-positioning of the load of your head correctly on your shoulders lets energy flow again unimpeded.

Top-of-the-head headaches often result symptomatically from hyper-white signs at 12 noon. That white-hot head energy of high vitality people can produce quite a 'hot-head' in more ways than one! Blood pressure in the head can also rise, and a thumping, skull-probing headache can arrive, indicating a need to 'put the feet up' in a reflex off-loading of the problem. Ten minutes of rest may be enough to cool down the condition, by *earthing* all that spiralling energy.

Five-sense area

Between 12 noon and 1 o'clock we find recorded many aspects of *psychological* brain function and structure. We will look at the radial sectors first, leaving the bowel and stomach zones beneath them until later. The sausage-shaped 'pituitary' and 'pineal' zones are also found beneath the next four segments.

Anatomically, the psychological brain is the cerebrum, the physiological the cerebellum. In practice, many humans exert both parts of the brain in overlapping functions. It's amazing how repeatedly the human organism flies in the face of science. Anatomically unscientific processes occur often. 'Miracle' cures take place; surgically sealed Fallopian tubes regrow together again; cripples suddenly walk; cancers 'disappear'—all at some unscientific bidding of the psyche. I have found in practice that enough will and determination exerted here can change *any* illness process into one of better health. The pituitary gland has a lot to do with it, and so has the pineal gland.

Looking at sectors one by one, we find the 'five-sense' area next to the 'vitality' zone. This follows logically as well as functionally. If one's vitality is high, one enjoys all the stimuli of the five senses: taste, touch, hearing, smell, sight. Enjoyment of the good things of living—a Bach cantata, a wild Pan flute; the smell of hot bread, or garlic sizzling in butter; the touch of silk against the skin or of a loving hand first thing in the morning; the sight of a returned loved one, a real Picasso, a red-gold sunset; the taste sensations—all can be stimulated by the pituitary and the vitality adjoining zones into sensory pleasure.

If you believe that one needs to *suffer* to be healthy, or to be 'saved' from the pleasures of the flesh, then maybe dark colours and even *radii solaris* in these zones will record your hair-shirt philosophy. Every animal, especially the human one, is designed to feel pleasure as the other side of pain; and gratification of the senses is a pleasurable experience. My friends often call me (after Ogden Nash) a 'sybaritic softie' because I rave on about the smell of lavender oil in the bath, the first sip of a lovely old wine, the gentle voice of a colleague, the aroma of onion soup with parmesan cheese, the way to touch a patient. They accuse me of trying to make life too *easy*. I counter by pointing out that there is enough pain to go round and afflict us all without looking for more by self-denial of its antidote—sensory *pleasure*. Nature's balance applies here too, with the added intellectual capacity of humans to *know* what they are experiencing.

I often ask patients who are busy looking after children, aged parents, responsible jobs, and household chores, 'Yes, but what do you do to make *you* feel good?' The question often surprises them. 'I don't indulge myself.' And they look rather disapprovingly at me as if I'm about to take off my clothes in public or Spanish-dance on my desk! Many established religions use the adjacent iris zone, the 'ego' area, to dampen human pleasure responses. '*Mea culpa*,' says Catholicism; 'Lord have mercy on me, miserable sinner,' says the Church of England; and *guilt* about human failings inhibits pleasurable responses. Such self-denial often registers in the iris as *radii solaris* to the five-sense area. To make a barbed comment (there are strong Scorpio influences in my natal Sagittarian horoscope!), I find that such people often find their 'pleasure' in giving other people pain—distortion of Nature's balance, which may show as brownish signs in this iris sector.

On the lighter side, white colours here can show super-response. That sunset is an orgasmic delight; the Picasso makes you cry; your lover has you speaking your fantasies in the sensations of touch; pleasure is enhanced by the *intensity* of its recording.

Fibre lesions in this zone can point to one or more of the senses suffering structurally from trauma or circumstances. If you have hyper-acute hearing and your flat-mate persists in playing the wrong kind of music at top volume, structural signs of stress can appear. The fibres part and a darker layer of damage is exposed. If this sound assault persists, permanent hearing damage, even though slight, may result. If your taste-buds are deadened from over-use of salt and sugar, a lesion may show; even a calcium ring may eventually fog over your taste sensations. A brownish cloud, emanating again from the bowel and diffusing into head areas, can lower your sensual responses, maybe permanently, if you let it persist. Many patients who have progressed with treatment to the point of having this bowel fog removed have said to me later, 'I *feel* so much better. I am getting more enjoyment out of life. I can taste my food again, I can hear better, I want to sing in the bath and laugh more; you've over-stimulated me.' 'No,' I tell them, 'you could have been there all the time, potentially. Now you've realised your potential, that's all.'

Some forms of deafness show dark signs in the five-sense zone as well as in the ear itself, and maybe at the second cervical vertebra of the neck, too. If the signs appear only in the five-sense sector it is most likely that the person has been obliged to listen to loud or oft-repeated stimuli un-pleasant to hear. This could be from a nagging spouse, a grumbling boss, traffic noise, or one ego-shattering remark! I don't separate illness into mental and physical causes, but so-called 'psychosomatic' deafness could be the only reason for the hearing loss unless other supportive signs of real deafness appear in the iris.

Enjoy sensual pleasures and improve your vitality and your 'self-image', its adjacent iris zone partners!

Confidence zone

'Self-image' is perhaps too broad a title for the next sector. 'Confidence zone' may be a better label. 'Ego pressure' is the one chosen by Dr Jensen for his chart. They all add up to a common total—one's opinion of oneself. Blood pressure, wheth-er high, low, or normal, or even fluctuating between all three levels, also shows a definite indication in this iris area.

I find this zone the one exception to the rule that dark colours indicate low function whilst light colours record over-high function. In this one sector, dark signs can mean either high or low blood pressure, high or low confidence, high or low opinion of oneself. Dark colours or dark fibre lesions need more explanation from the patient, more questions from the practitioner, to find which out-of-balance condition applies. That's all you can see from this zone: when dark colours are recorded, *imbalance* is present.

Let's take a typical case history. A sixty-year-old accountant, about to retire, tells me that his blood pressure has reached over the two hundred mark in systolic reading, and one hundred and thirty in diastole. This I translate as 'Danger-ously high levels for both—severe *pressure* of some type inside or outside the patient.' It is then my job to ascertain the cause of the pressure. He's still an ambitious man; still 'As good as I used to be' he tells me defensively. (If I'd taken his blood pressure then it could have been abnormally high—or abnormally low. He could have had an uneasy lack of confidence in the truth of that statement.) Many highs and lows in blood pressure reflect ego-assaults. One general body defence against stress is a rise in blood pressure to the head to enable thinking processes to be speedily assembled to meet the stress. So a raised blood pressure can produce an ego response, or an ego challenge can raise the blood pressure. If this pressure *stays* high after the situation has passed, the body is over-disturbed and over-reacting, and treatment is needed.

You all must have known, when at school, the class bully. This child (usually male!) terrorised the rest with his swagger and his strength and his cruelty to those weaker than himself. *But* ... if a *really* strong child stood up to him, all his braggart noise and fuss could be shown to be over-compensation for his doubts and fears as to his ability to succeed otherwise. *Low* confidence produced over-confidence as a defence bluff, and his iris could have shown dark signs of imbalance, even at an early age. The 'sergeant-major syndrome', I call it: lots of shouting and bluff and bullying for a purpose.

Control of one's aggressive, assertive emotions to the detriment of one's blood pressure is another common human failing. Brownish signs can show in this zone if the pattern persists.

There are, of course, many physical reasons, too, for blood pressure imbalance, and the iris can register these in various patterns in this sector. A calcium ring is the most obvious one to show blood pressure *rise* as blood is forced through narrower pipes. White flares may also record a passing blood-pressure increase on jogging seven miles or running up a mountainside or three flights of stairs; but the darker signs mean 'This condition is chronic.'

I have also seen dark signs, even *radii solaris*, indicating *low* blood pressure and even lower ego-image. A few minutes with the person should show the practitioner which is which.

The high-ego compensator will seem confident, crack jokes, and look at you squarely—with a veiled plea—'Please don't uncover my weakness' in his eyes. The truly confident person doesn't bother with all that, and their iris doesn't either. It doesn't register confidence imbalance either way. A *low*-ego person may start apologising for everything even as he enters your rooms: being late (when it's a minute or so past the hour); taking up too much time (he's paying you for it!); rambling vaguely (when you need him to explain fully). 'Excuse me for living' is the thread through it all.

Such people may sit quietly, hands folded, and jump when the phone rings. 'Doormats' they may be; but underneath the constant giving-in you will often find resentment and a perverse pride in being humble. They can make you feel a real monster after a while, as they crawl lower and lower under your feet asking to be kicked. It is not surprising, then, to find *radii solaris* or dark signs in the ego area. A *low* blood pressure can go with these signs. The person is tired, lacking energy, lacking fight, always a 'loser', shoulders hunched waiting for the next crack of the whip from life. It can be most rewarding to improve such a pattern naturopathically and help such a person find a space in the sun.

A complex zone, this one. Ask questions *gently* if at all. This is the ego area, after all, and the person is entitled to privacy within the bounds of it.

One interesting reflex is found across the iris towards the appendix. Have you noticed how many acute appendix symptoms occur at most inopportune times? It may be before an exam, half-way across an ocean, after moving into a new home, and with each situation there can come an ego-threatening doubt: 'Can I handle this?' Sometimes the poor innocent appendix distends with the reflex overload, and if the bowel is not in general good condition rubbish can quickly accumulate and cause an 'attack'. Pain may be the only symptom, as 'ego-threat' is thrown into an unwitting appendix. Conversely, if dark signs appear in both these reflex areas, a functional problem with an overloaded appendix may be the cause of periodic high blood pressure.

Speech area

Beside the last zone is another area related to it—'speech'. A person who speaks from a secure ego base says real things. There is no 'bull', no waffling on, and there is often an outstanding ability to use speech well and straightforwardly. White fibres and white flares here can mean that an Irish mother, or at least a visit to the blarney stone, has bestowed the gift of the gab. Such people become the Winston Churchills, the Laurence Oliviers, the Billy Grahams; speech is *positively* hyper-active. On the other hand, the same white signs may be found in hyper-active kids who never stop talking and asking questions.

Structural lesions and fibre disturbances in this zone can mean that speech is under stress load. People showing such signs can find themselves too tired to talk at night after talking hard through business deals or meetings—or even naturopathic consultations!—all day. Some actors and actresses can't say a word after the performance. I myself find it impossible to answer questions after a three-hour lecture, not because my brain is tired but because my speech is used up. Actually mouthing words becomes an enormous effort. A tiny lesion in this zone tells me I talk too much most of the time.

This zone could also be called the 'communication' sector, since it relates to your learning capacity. Many people learn best by listening to information—*audio* learners; others need to see pictures, diagrams, and practical examples, and become *visual* learners. If you have plus-active signs in this zone, both learning processes should be easy. If dark fog or *radii solaris* or dark streaks appear, then you may be a negative cousin of the Three Wise Monkeys, seeing nothing, hearing nothing, and saying nothing. A 'closed mind' is my diagnosis of such signs: 'This person does not want to learn anything more than he or she knows already.' Change is resisted, growth is limited, and anything new is suspect.

A calcium ring over this zone later in life will also inhibit its function and make it harder to learn, harder to remember and concentrate, than before those arteries started to clog up. And low blood pressure and/or low self-image (shown in the previous zone) can affect this adjacent learning zone. I find that patients whose learning processes have been restricted by lack of confidence, lack of ego incentive, or by circumstances, can take steps to change once their pattern and its causes have been explained and treated.

Speech defects in children can show as fibre lesions spread across this zone. If the defects are very pronounced, the lesion may also spread into both adjacent zones, and retardation or restriction of learning faculties may result in low ego and even lower 'mental ability' potential (in the next zone). Restriction of hearing, so that speech by others cannot be correctly interpreted, also restricts learning.

One unusual iris, in a child of eleven, shows a quite uncategorisable 'crease' of iris tissue stretched in a flat arc between the anxiety sector and the learning one. Her hearing suddenly switched off at three years of age, for no apparent reason. Her *actual* learning is good, as her school-work shows; but speech and hearing seem somehow to be *disconnected*. I am still wondering whether some sudden shock or fear at that early age threw an unusual arc across and closed hearing and speech to avoid facing the menace.

This zone can be a barometer of how much stress can be placed on speech and listening before one or both begin to drop in efficiency. A white level is obviously good; but when overload and high nerve charge build up the fuse can blow, and a non-listening non-speaking reaction occurs. You all know someone, the animated life and soul of the party, listening intently to your views, speaking well and fully on many subjects; when you look for him again towards the end of the party he's zapped out asleep on a couch in the back room. Try to get intelligent communication from him now and see what monosyllabic inattentive response you'll get! He needs to rest his communication channels to let them recover from their recent hyper-function.

The following iris zone, the 'mental ability' one, is closely connected with the previous one in many ways, and often hyper-function or low function signs overlap or lie along the border between the two.

Mental ability zone

A high IQ is not necessarily enough, nor is the best possible academic record sufficient, to lead logically to *use* of high mental capacity. 'Mental ability' may sound similar to 'mental capacity'; but in terms of iris analysis the mental ability zone will indicate whether the level of *use* of the intellect is commensurate with its potential. There's no point in owning a high-powered car if you never drive it!

One example of such non-use of potential was a patient who had the whitest of white Silk head areas, marred only by one big black fibre lesion half-way out in the mental ability sector. At about thirty he had quit his law practice, stopped studying for the Bar, and taken his brilliant head to the local pubs each day—commencing at the 'early opener' and finishing only when the bars closed. He had also turned his highly intelligent head to conning pub-met people out of money and into intricate 'deals'. His iris recorded the negative use of what was potentially a highly positive faculty.

I have seen university students with white-level signs superimposed over quite ordinary irises as they studied up to their limits. I have also seen others who would never take any form of intellectual study through to its conclusion because some negative sign, like a psoric spot or a *radii solaris* or brown clouds and fog, restricted intellectual use. I would rather label this zone 'applied mental ability'. Many people of lower potential get better results as they apply themselves in practical use of the intellect, the 'absent-minded professor' can dream his life away in non-application of his undoubtedly brilliant ideas.

Sometimes circumstances terminate a course of study or educational training. Children leave school early for many reasons and can become adults stuck in jobs below their mental ability levels. The resulting mental frustration and dissatisfaction can lead to chronic dark signs and fibre lesions in the mental ability sector.

Again, low blood pressure or a calcium ring can mean that less mental application is *available* than is inherently present.

It is good to be able to tell a mum of fortyish or fiftyish whose children are almost self-sufficient that she has just as good a mental ability as when she left school, and should study something—anything: Caluthumpian history or urban psychology or perhaps whatever it was she wanted to study when she left school and had no chance then to pursue. People with white signs in this zone are quick to comprehend and get the point. They find learning easy, stimulating, and not a chore.

Pituitary area

Under the sectors of five senses, ego, and communication, lies a lozenge-shaped area—'pituitary'. This two-lobed gland lies within the brain itself. The medulla controls the physical strings pulling the human puppet; the pituitary controls the speed and balance of endocrine gland function. Hormone balance is also *controlled* here, although the thyroid, the adrenals, and the gonads, do the distribution.

Obviously, white signs—fibres or flares—out and across this zone are going to indicate high hormone levels, high glandular function, and therefore one form of high *speed*, a super-vitality. Many Silk irises show such signs. So do most Linens, when in good health. The lively charge of magnesium and phosphorus along white nerve fibres keeps the pituitary at a plus rate of action, and from this one control centre body metabolism rate is set for absorption and elimination. These are the people who can sin nutritionally and get away with it; can stay the same weight all their lives; and do not vary much in general living habits, either. The pituitary control being set at 'high' means there is always energy in reserve to cope with day-to-day demands from external and internal sources.

Some severe cerebral diseases can register pituitary colour change or structural disturbance in fibre lesions. Interpreting these signs is definitely a job for professionals and not for the layman. But a brown fog over this vital zone can tell you that either your transverse colon is clogged and inefficient, and/or your pituitary gland has potentially better function at a more positive speed.

A fleck or psoric spot over this vital organ has a different interpretation. Two patients come to mind who showed pituitary psoric spots.

One was a woman of forty-seven, whose overweight condition was totally resistant to all forms of treatment. She tried everything: fasting, weight-watchers, vitamin B17 injections, crash dieting, a change of husband, a new house, and a holiday in the sunshine away from the kids. She ate very good food or she ate junk—it made no difference. She tried yoga, spiritual healing, and herbal medicine—no change. Some therapies made her lose a few pounds for a while; but her general progress was backwards and her weight *increased* more often than not, apparently for no reason. The rest of her clear blue Linen iris pattern was strong, and her general health was very good, but that one little psoric spot blocked pituitary *recognition* of, and reaction to, stimuli. The *control* of her weight was impossible.

The other patient also had a psoric spot over the pituitary area,—a much larger one. This was an eighteen-year-old lad whose voice had still not broken and who had not started to grow or mature at all. The social effect on him was disastrous and was producing neurotic personality problems. The psoric spot had been there since birth, and he had always had a pituitary slowness in metabolism. The hormones refused to change as in normal puberty onset. Three and a half years later, he finished an abnormally slow and emotionally painful growth pattern. The psoric spot is smaller and less intense now, fading as the inhibiting conditions were naturopathically treated; but *resistance* to the treatment was the outstanding symptom.

A slow pituitary means a slow whole person: other glands controlled by it cannot set the pace any faster. You will see how in the chart it touches and overlaps the 'vitality' zone, and lies alongside a portion of the nerve wreath and the bowel. Boosting function of these body zones naturopathically can support a pituitary trying to 'walk a little faster'. Sunshine on the head can also help. The pituitary is particularly sensitive to ultra-violet rays, and is the control centre triggering hibernation instincts in animals in the short days of winter, and breeding instincts as spring lengthens daylight hours. Get sun all the winter if possible, so that you don't lose your summertime pituitary speed.

The 'hunch' zone: the pineal

One of the most difficult zones to interpret lies adjacent to the pituitary gland and immediately below the mental ability sector already described. This circle is allotted to the pineal gland.

Anatomically, the pineal does not apparently function and, like the thymus gland in the chest, seems to have only long-lost genetic reasons for its existence in the body. Occultists call the gland 'the third eye' and quote all sorts of ancient texts to prove that this gland used to function well and can do so again if reactivated by various means. This is the 'eye' your brain can see with in dream states, the 'eye' that instinctively sees deeper than the physical, the real 'window of the soul' in its unedited form. Limitations of physical eyesight do not apply to pineal 'sight'. One can 'see' the death of a relative across the world, the sickness of a beloved friend thousands of miles away or in the next suburb. When you pick up the phone to ring someone at the second when that person is thinking of ringing you, it's a pineal response. I call it the 'hunch' zone, recording deeper instincts more like those of animals than those of 'civilised' human beings. Surely you have made instinctive judgments: 'I just *knew*, I don't understand how, that you were sick or in trouble; 'I just felt it deep down that you needed help'; 'I instinctively distrusted that man, and I was right as it happened'—using a system of 'seeing' that defies rational explanation and scientific analysis. No wonder—for this capacity is not in the area of rationality but of *instincts*.

Obviously white signs here mean a highly developed intuitive faculty, using an *extra* sense not assignable to any particular body system. A fascinating example was one of the only real clairvoyants I have seen professionally. His irises both had wide white flares of a peculiar type starting from the nerve wreath and radiating out to the rim of the mental ability zone. He had experienced what he called his 'little pictures' since childhood, and the accuracy of his future sight was quite uncanny.

White fibres and white flares here usually indicate accuracy of instinctive judgment—good hunches. When I see people with such signs I tell them to listen to these instincts and make decisions on them. You have all experienced a situation where your head told you it was OK, but a deeper feeling rang warning bells against it. Trust the latter if you have a white pineal zone. Its function is close to that of an animal's 'scent' apparatus. If you say, 'Something smells bad in that apparently good offer; it just doesn't smell right', you are 'seeing' possible future events.

Children often show white pineal areas. The fairies and the pixies and invisible companions may be *really* with them through high pineal activity! A vivid imagination is not always the cause. Instincts are trained out of children in civilised formal schooling. Let your children run free intellectually at times to keep their instincts alive.

Dark pineal signs can sometimes appear after rigid scientific training has produced a person who thinks well but does not *know*. Many 'mental' illnesses, so-called, show abnormal pineal areas, white or dark. I have seen a *radii solaris* straight through this zone and the mental ability one in a patient who heard voices telling him he was the Lord of the World and should take over his kingdom. Destructive 'visions' will certainly show as dark signs.

This is a fascinating iris zone, and I'm apt to lose friends amongst my scientific minded colleagues when I try to explain its implications!

O Caution, Please

So many patterns of people can be seen recorded between 11 o'clock and 1 o'clock! Interpretation of these zones should be of interest to the layman, but I would caution against analysing the area as a 'fun' thing. Serious physical conditions, even brain abscesses, pituitary tumours, mental retardation, and other physiological abnormalities, also record as lesions and flares and colour change in this part of the iris; and an untrained person might confuse an intellectual process with a physical one unless a patient's case history is responsibly taken. More than in any other part of the iris, the head areas are open to many interpretations of the signs and colours recorded there. Please use any little knowledge you have gained *responsibly*.

O The Face

From about 1 o'clock to 2 o'clock lie the iris zones of the face: the forehead and temple, the eye, the upper and lower law, the nose, mouth, and tongue. I will deal with these as a group first, because so many inter-connecting passages and cavities are common to them all that what affects one is probably affecting all to some degree.

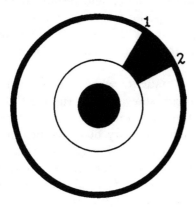

The anterior plane of the head anatomically, the face, is a mass of openings, tunnels, and specialised tissues like teeth and tongue and eye. A sensitive body area for invasion by bacteria, viruses, and irritant substances in the air, the face will also mirror the *personality* in its muscular holding together of all these quite different tissue types.

A clenching of the lower and upper jaws together can pull and push the eye shape, the nasal configuration, and the cheek contours, as well as narrow the mouth and keep it shut more often. Frowning from glare or vision inefficiency can tighten the forehead muscles and produce headaches, wrinkles, and sharp permanent forehead creases. Muscles so tightened then pull awkwardly, and the *back* of the neck and head becomes tense posturally, too. A clenched jaw can cause cervical migraines! Consciously study your face in the mirror. Try moving parts of it around: let some muscles flop, tighten others, see which expression feels most like you. Become *aware* of your face. It presents a translation of your personality for the world to read; and a 'happy' face means a balanced one, too, in terms of structure and function.

The forehead and temple zone can be a vulnerable site for people who 'lead with their head'. Children often show flares of white in this iris area, as they tumble head over heels, fall down steps, run into posts, and topple out of trees. Such acute trauma should disappear from the iris as fast as it is healed up and forgotten; but signs of any serious damage may persist all through life. The softer bones of childhood may not fracture, but just dent and retain the abnormal shape.

One migraine patient, who had resisted all forms of orthodox treatment, showed me a right iris with a flattened outside rim at this zone and a *radii solaris* streaking through it. Questions elicited a story of heavy beatings around the head as a child. An X-ray showed abnormal skull shape at the right temple, causing pressure extending to blood vessels and the optic nerve. Orbital migraines had resulted. They were able to be lessened in intensity but not removed, since the skull shape was permanently depressed. A *radii solaris* through this zone can produce headaches and vascular pressure.

In one patient, a fine lesion (hardly noticeable from the iris, but an obvious small scar on the right temple had made me look more closely at this iris sector) recorded a fracture history. Skull plates are thick and hard, but the hollow shape allows some flexibility. The head needs to be hit pretty hard to break! Hairline fractures are the most common. Standing behind a swinging golf club, a tennis or squash racket, has produced some interesting fibre lesions at the forehead and temple.

White foggy clouds over the general face area are more common than they should be, and mostly indicate mucus over-production on acute infection. They can also record more constant over-production levels in hay-fever patients or allergy-prone sniffers and sneezers, and indicate a precondition for blocking of some of the passages and cavities with thick mucus residues. The slightest tinge of yellow in these white fog clouds, and you have yellow mucus needing thinning and blowing out. You also have a higher risk of chronic clogging, pressure, and rubbish accumulating in deep pockets. Fenugreek tea may be all you need each day to thin the mucus chemically and remove it.

Symptoms and causes

Many patients say to me, 'I have sinus problems.' When I say, 'What sort?' they look puzzled and say, 'Well, just *sinus*.' I have to explain all the different things that can happen to cranial sinuses. As well as being over-wet with mucus, they can be bone-dry (and the word is accurately used). There is not much except bone and mucus linings in the upper forehead sinuses; so, if the linings are inactive (browner signs of fog and even fibre lesions may show here), a dry bone mass produces aches and stabs of pain if infection is present. Abscesses within the bone itself may even occur, and dull aches and pain become chronic. Naturopathic treatment to stimulate mucus linings and their function helps to remove such stubborn patterns.

Don't forget that the circular zones concentrically around the iris tell you which function of the part concerned is most affected, or is the prime cause of the disorder. At the outer rim, signs show circulatory or lymph involvement; signs in the inner part of the sector closer to the nerve wreath show nerve supply to be inefficient in one way or another; middle-zone signs mean muscular and organic malfunction.

A reflex across the iris ties 'forehead and temple' to 'pelvis'. Many frontal headaches, particularly pre-menstrual ones in women, can be tracked down to pelvic structure or function. If no abnormal signs appear at the forehead zone of a patient complaining of headaches there, check the pelvic zone opposite. A visit to a good osteopath will get structural problems corrected if necessary; functional disturbance (colours dark and murky) needs herbal and naturopathic treatment as well.

Ever noticed someone tapping or rubbing the forehead to help think better? The zone lies next to 'mental ability' remember? A little stimulation of the forehead and temple may help sluggish thought processes. On the other hand, thinking furiously all day can produce throb, throb, pounding of blood vessels at the temples as the adjacent zone feels the load. One good way to turn down thought energy in the head is to massage a soothing herb oil like rosemary or lavender into those pulsating temple 'hotspots'. Relaxation of the pressure can occur within minutes.

The 'eye' zone records physical and functional trauma to the eye itself as an organ, rather than vision abnormalities. These latter are more to be found in the left iris in the 'visual' zone. Of course, if both conditions are present (visual disturbance caused by physical trauma), signs in both zones are to be expected.

Let's look at a fascinating reflex: across from eyes to pancreas. Many diabetics have eye symptoms of functional disorder. Infections (viral, mostly) causing acute pancreatitis can also cause severe inflammation and soreness of the eyes. People with hypo-function of the pancreas can have watery weak eyes. As a diagnostic pointer towards either high or low blood sugar disorders, eye symptoms may be confirmatory. It certainly does *not* mean that everyone with eye problems is a potential diabetic—far from it; but there is often a connection. When we discuss the pancreas segment you'll see why such a reflex is logical in loadsharing or overflow.

As you would expect, white signs in the eye zone record inflammation, sensitivity, and irritation; yellow to yellowish-brown mean more destructive processes are at work. Physical injuries to the eye usually leave fibre lesions as a record, even if the tissue later heals and restores function. 'Darned' lesions are common.

As the iris is such a sensitive recording device, you would expect many disturbances in eye tissues to affect the ability of the iris to record accurately. The section 'Eye Diseases' will explain many reasons for physical disturbances elsewhere after damage to the iris.

A *radii solaris* to the eye segment means trouble. Not only are physical problems to be expected, but the eye is not *truthfully* recording what it sees. A 'load of rubbish' intervenes between true seeing and circumstances. Have you ever tried to argue or discuss with somebody and in frustration yelled, 'Can't you see what I'm talking about?' It may be that such a person can't 'see' well at all. Physical eye problems may be the cause; but check the left iris 'visual area' as well for *mental* blocking. A psoric spot at the eye zone may give similar symptoms: physical eye sensitivity, and an inability to 'see' things clearly.

'Upper jaw' is a different entity altogether from 'lower jaw'; its function is as an immovable object against which the lower jaw continually hits. The 'nose' zone separates both in the iris, and we'll deal with each jaw separately.

Upper jaw signs show after tooth extraction there; after a punch under the chin; on continual tolerance of a badly-fitted denture, and often after problems in the diaphragm or upper abdominal area (reflex zone) have not been quickly and completely resolved. One of the worst signs appearing here can be after wisdom tooth extraction, and even the adjacent zones both sides (eye and nose) can be affected. A surgical sign here may take many moons to disappear if the patient has been severely shocked by the experience. I remember a wisdom tooth extraction of my own, when my high magnesium/phosphorus/silica/calcium chemistry had produced a few too many teeth for my Anglo-Saxon narrow jaw to accommodate. The surgeon gave me a local injection only, and several hours later was still hacking away with a hammer and chisel at an iceberg of a tooth with three roots, one twisted several times around the jaw-bone! The surgical sign persisted for months afterwards, then disappeared altogether as the other teeth moved along and filled the slight residual space.

Infected teeth may cause slow-leakage symptoms in other parts of the face and even into the throat/tonsil area. A quick iris check can isolate the triggering area and therefore the cause can be removed more effectively.

Shallow breathers don't hit their bottom jaw against their top jaw often enough. Children who sleep with the mouth open are having difficulty using the diaphragm correctly. Upper abdominal distress, like indigestion, can cause snoring. Look at the reflex zone here to elaborate on these statements. Too much food, distending the stomach which then presses against the diaphragm, can cause mouth-breathing and thence snoring. If your sleeping partner snores, don't feed him/her so well. That upper jaw/nose combination can be sleep-destroying. The adjacent reflex zones across the iris of liver, gall-bladder, and duodenum, can also become part of the jaw/nose/mouth pattern.

Upper abdominal discomfort and mouth/nose symptoms are directly related through *chewing* processes. If the bottom jaw is not hit often enough against the top jaw in the process of chewing, upper abdominal indigestion can be a reflex effect. Train children to chew! Many secondary symptoms in later life can be avoided early if good chewing of food becomes a habit.

The 'nose' zone will of course register as white colours for physical broken noses, mucus-filled antrums, even a hyper-acute sense of smell (in which case a confirmatory whiteness may appear in the 'five-sense' zone already described). You all know someone who can smell leaking petrol, forest fires, or burned toast, long before anyone else can. No doubt the five-sense area is white, and the nose area should also be showing the white fibres of hyper-function.

The 'perfume' senser, the olfactory nerve, has its sensitive ending behind nasal passages from which signals are transmitted directly to the brain. I like Kipling's verse—

> 'Smells are surer than sights or sounds
> To make the heartstrings crack.'

A white fibre pattern at the nose zone should keep you smell-happy. Darker signs mean your sense of smell, and therefore taste, too, could be inhibited. See the adjacent zone next ahead: the tongue, mouth, and lower jaw. Taste and smell are intimately related. Hyper-function in one usually means similar function in the other.

The shiny white spots of a lymphatic rosary may appear around the outer iris rim in the general 'face' section. Those chronically watery individuals, sniffing, sneezing, and blowing, may develop white or yellowish-white lymph spots as rubbish piles up faster than it can be removed. Chronic lymphatic congestion can give you a swollen nose, puffy antrums, and heavy jowls, as well as a thick throat. All the adjoining areas below the nose can be gravity-affected by the lymph drainage problem.

Nose-bleeds may not register in irises at all if they are a rare occurrence; but a chronic nose-bleeder is blowing a safety-valve through the small capillaries to relieve cranial or facial pressure elsewhere. Sometimes a nose-bleed can prevent a migraine by relieving the vascular pressure in the head. Signs of such happenings may show so minutely in the iris nasal zone as to be almost invisible; but head congestion and general facial sinus clogging may show in various ways from 11 o'clock right through to as far as 2.30, indicating a basic reason for the nose-bleeding.

Sneezing and blowing the nose are the usual ways to clear

all this nose-and-above part of the face. From the lower part of the face, coughing and spitting out is the body's removal reflex.

The 'tongue, mouth and lower jaw' sector shows many readily identifiable signs but not the *causes* for these signs unless many questions are also asked. Is that dark brown lesion a sore tooth, a mouth ulcer, or a tongue which doesn't move enough in speaking out? Is it peridontal infection, or a badly-fitting lower denture? Is it a lower jaw that flaps up and down too often in compulsive talking—verbal diarrhoea—thus losing friends? Is it a reflex overload from a liver and/or gall problem? As I have often repeated to questioners from the 'scientific method' side of diagnosis, iris analysis cannot stand alone as a diagnostic tool without the presence of the patient—the only one who can verify and clarify recorded iris signs.

As expected, white signs and fibres should indicate enthusiastic use of the mouth and lower jaw; but they may also indicate an acute molar abscess. White fog here is going to mean mucus and its possible overload into the next segment, the throat, in a post-nasal drip. Yellowish signs and lymphatic choking show longer-term congestion and the brownish colours indicate tissue destruction and rubbish accumulation of one kind or another.

I have dealt with compulsive eating elsewhere (p. 95) and its reflex emotional component. If you think of the lower jaw as the hammer and the upper as the anvil, you can trace many movements of the jaws to emotional causes. Grinding the teeth with rage; clenching the jaws to suppress anger; 'running off at the mouth' as emotional release occurs; giving garbled descriptions of a shock situation; even stammering (convulsive movement of the lower jaw): all of these reactions can be direct pointers to emotional imbalance.

One chiropractor I know states unequivocally that *all* spinal problems start initially from the lower jaw! He explains the logic of this as an unnatural strain posturally being thrown at cervical vertebrae (from the tension in the lower jaw), which then reflexly affects lumbar spine posture, and perhaps he's right. Check how tight or loose is your lower jaw after the day's stresses. It can be illuminating!

○ The Throat And Bronchial Tree

From 2 o'clock to around 3.30 in the right iris lie the zones of the throat and its moving parts, and the bronchial tree and its nerve supply. The efficient function of these areas is especially important to public speakers, singers, actors, and teachers, or to anyone whose voice is used continually. An operatic soprano who has been trained correctly to produce her magnificent voice within the anatomical limits of her throat and head should show few signs of strain here; but a singer wrongly trained—forcing her voice—may show white flares or even brown or blackish destructive lesions, which are sure to give her difficulties with the voice and its use.

Nodules appearing on the vocal chords, or sore throats before opening night, may point to overstrain and unnatural use.

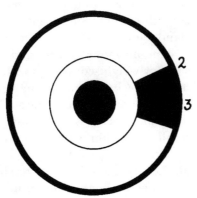

White flares over the general area can mean tonsillitis, laryngitis, or tracheitis, in any of us; but in the iris of a *coloratura* soprano they may indicate super-normal function.

Lymphatic spots (at the iris rim) are common in these segments,—especially in the irises of heavy smokers. Don't think you can keep on smoking without consequences if your iris shows yellowish lymph spots anywhere in this zone. And don't smoke at all—as from tomorrow morning—if your iris shows brown lymph spots here. The rubbish has accumulated, irritated and congested your throat and bronchial tree, and you can be heading into predictable danger if you persist.

Irregularity of the nerve wreath over this zone can mean the problems experienced in throat and bronchial tree are compounded by a poor spinal nerve supply to these areas. Some chronic asthmatics show many abnormal colour and structure signs here, but often only the spinal nerve supply is the triggering cause of an attack. Chiropractic or osteopathic adjustment can help such 'mechanical' asthmatics tremendously. Look to the iris to find which type of asthma it is—infective, mechanical, emotional, or a combination.

I do not separate the throat zones as to function. What affects the tonsils affects the vocal chords; all related parts become out of balance if one part is severely affected. But in the middle of this throat group lies a major gland—the thyroid. This 'second-in-command' gland takes orders from the pituitary gland, and translates them into day-to-day metabolism and some hormone control and distribution. A key area, this one, for weight-control and rubbish removal, as a setter of body *speed* in the metabolic process. Underfunction of the gland can produce lethargy, drooping eyelids, obesity, and an enormous need for sleep. Hyperfunction can result in a thin streaky individual buzzing constantly, never sitting still, eating like a horse but never gaining a pound. An important iris area to check! Structural lesions here may need a medical referral. The thyroid is prone to node and lump formation, and any swelling or abnormal shape should be checked out thoroughly.

See the position of this gland in the iris? Right in the middle of the general throat area, and obviously to be affected in function by the adjacent zones. If you have a chronically sore throat, or smoker's cough, thyroid function may eventually feel the overflow load. Your skin gets dry,

166

your hair lacks lustre, your energy drops. Conversely, thyroid troubles can *produce* sore throats and a hoarse voice. The body is a mass of interconnecting compensating systems.

Part of the bronchial tree area lies below these zones in the iris. Of course, bronchial function contributes to and is affected by throat function.

O Shoulder Girdle

Let us proceed to the next two segments, 'clavicle' and 'scapula', which are closely related to throat, thyroid, and bronchial tree anatomically. An osteopath or chiropractor will tell you that a broken collarbone (clavicle) can give you sore throats later if wrongly set or incompletely healed. He may also adjust your shoulder-blade (scapula) to let your collarbone slide back into place—to stop your sore throats and thyroid problems. Most iris signs appearing here are structural lesions and fibre disturbance; but if dark colours *do* show, you have rubbish to remove as well, either from the bronchial tree or the circulation to and from the area.

Reflex zones across the iris cover the lung, the bronchial tree again, and the rib-cage. A direct reflex from the thyroid to the breast zone links hormone and glandular response between the two, especially in the female. A slow or congested thyroid can give you large breasts. A hyper-tuned thyroid can mean your vital statistics lack one dimension. Slow down a little to gain an inch or two!

O The Spine

Since the clavicle and scapula are indirectly supportive of back function in the upper torso, they lie adjacent to the next group, 3.30-4.45—the spine itself. Here is the area for osteopaths, and particularly chiropractors, to check in patients' irises. The chiropractic tenet 'Structure governs function' means that if the spinal vertebrae are freely and accurately able to move without pressure on nerve supply and blood supply to body areas served by each one of them the person cannot help but be healthy. In many years of treating sick people, I have found this precept to be like so many others—correct in principle, but not always able to stand alone in practice. Certainly, adjustment of bones is necessary when they are out of position chronically or under acute trauma; but the bones move about all day every day (and night), as the muscles and ligaments pull them. That is why I believe massage and general strengthening of tissue *around* the bones—as in osteopathic adjustment—to be vastly superior to spinal vertebrae adjustment only. An honest chiropractor will tell you that five minutes after getting off his table—even as you bend down to put on your shoes, or straighten or cough or sneeze—your spine will move again. The muscles and ligaments must now pull all those vertebrae and the discs between into alignment once more.

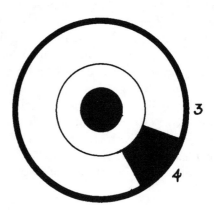

Signs to look for

The iris segments showing spinal structure must be viewed to discover which *circular* zone is showing problems. Is it the nerve supply (nerve wreath)? Is it in the muscle circle (outside the nerve wreath)? Is it in the lymphatic and circulatory zones (just inside the iris rim)? Is it the skin layer (the extreme edge of the iris)? Or is it the 'load' you carry on your back?

Is life compressing your spine as it beats you down into the ground? Are your shoulders sagging under the strain or is your dorsal spine hunching forward under the weight of circumstances? Check these iris zones, then look at yourself in a full-length mirror. It can be horribly obvious that your spine is continually being pushed or pulled into abnormal position.

If a white colour appears in the 'back' segments, think of arthritis and calcification and discs wearing or growing spurs. Think also of the person's job and the load carried or structural stress applied in it. Even an uncomfortable office chair or car seat or TV armchair can produce white discomfort signs in the iris.

Structural lesions here are common. Ask questions about falls and accidents. Get a *look* at the person. Assess posture and balance. Like most other illness patterns, much of the problem can be overcome once awareness of the *cause* is reached.

As the iris chart shows, the upper spine and back, down to the lower lumbar spine, sacrum, and coccyx, lie predictably top to bottom in the iris.

Brownish and yellowish colours here can often mean that biochemical clogging of tissues in the back requires massage and exercise to loosen rubbish deposits. Move that spine! Jog, play squash, sail or ride; but move tissue mechanically when darker colours show here. Regular massage, I feel, should be a health insurance policy. Physical movement of tissue, by those trained in the understanding of bodies and their function, should be a part of everyone's weekly programme. Apart from being sensuously and aesthetically pleasant, massage can remove little problems before they become big ones.

The coccyx (the 'tail-bone'), vestige of the tail humans have left behind, hangs uncontrolled at the base of the spine. It can be a trouble-maker if broken or bent in a severe fall. I remember some excruciating moments when I fell back on the cockpit seat of a heeled-over yacht, and crashed my coccyx down on the edge. It did not make matters easier when the skipper bawled me out for letting the mainsheet go as I nearly blacked out with the pain. We did not win that event, but I did not care. If you have ever experienced a hard fall on the tail-bone, you'll understand my inability to move. The next day my favourite osteopath did a painful rectal adjustment, and solved the problem. Without this, constant pain could have resulted for years, and bladder disturbance (in the next adjacent iris segment) as well. Get falls and car accidents checked by your osteopath/chiropractor *the day after they happen*. Don't endure unnecessary consequences.

Black holes between iris fibres can indicate disc deterioration. These cushions, or pads, between the vertebrae ensure freedom of movement by acting as buffers against structural loading. Consult your health practitioner if such lesions appear in your iris. Discs can be re-built by naturopathic means.

I would re-phrase the chiropractic gospel to 'Structure and function *support each other*'. I do not believe that any one modality of natural treatment can, or should, stand alone as the answer to all ills. I often refer patients to chiropractors when a preliminary examination suggests that more than biochemical treatment with herbs is needed.

O Abdominal And Pelvic Areas

Now let us observe the most difficult and complex of all the iris areas: the lower abdominal cavity and its contents and the pelvic cavity and its organs. Sorting out which segment is which, and which colour refers to what, can be, and usually is, a job for experts. So many organs fit in these cavities, overlapping and interacting in function and position, that a diagnosis made by a layman could be dangerously wrong. Let us look at the individual segments first, and then treat them broadly and generally. We will exclude a sector appearing in the middle of all this: the thigh, groin, and leg area.

Think of a bone-supported cavity, filled with a mass of pipes and initially hollow organs—some inter-connecting and some not; all capable of movement as muscles, voluntary and involuntary, contract and relax again. In this area are parts of the bowel and intestines, the bladder and kidneys, and the reproductive organs. If you have a large, strong frame, it is more likely that your muscle-tone will be positive enough to keep these organs in their usual positions. If you overstrain the lumbar spine, or have poor muscle-tone, your abdominal and pelvic organs may drop, twist, retrovert, or adhere to one another. Am I making you more consciously aware of all that hollow space? Good! Most people live in unawareness as far as their lower-body processes are concerned.

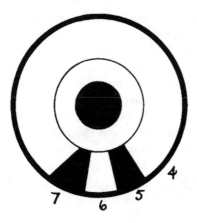

Do you know where your stomach is? It's not below your navel, where most people with 'stomach' troubles point to. That's your intestines down there, absorbing nutrients and eliminating waste products. Your kidneys may give you pain just below the bottom ribs of your back, but *referred* pain can occur at the front of your body, too. All these organs-in-a-hole are great ones for producing pain somewhere else, as well as at the site of the disorder. Reflexes go leaping about; overloads spill from one to the other: all because the organs are so close together, and what affects one may affect two or three others. Nowhere is the body's inter-connection between stimuli more obvious than in these iris segments between 4.45 and 5.45, and 6.20 and 7.30.

Some possible problems

If we start with the bladder, and its adjacent predecessor, the coccyx, you will see why I hurried to my osteopath after that boating accident. I could have had recurring cystitis, or frequency, or urgency, *forever*, if I had not had that necessary adjustment. The bladder is a loose sac in the pelvic cavity, very susceptible to pressure and reflex irritation. A reflex across the iris takes us to medulla or mastoid-bone zones. The next adjacent sector is the uterus and vagina. If any of you ladies have experienced 'honeymoon cystitis', or pregnancy urgency, or urinary difficulties, your body may be off-loading from one sector to the next. If my reader is male and has had bladder problems interfering with erections he will now understand why. On the other hand, a full bladder may give him an erection! See how the body shares its loads if one system is too heavily stressed?

White signs here in bladder and vagina/penis, uterus/prostate zones can indicate a chronic non-specific infection or irritation, annoyingly obvious, in both sexes. Get some advice on how to treat this. It may not be a result of your sexual activity (or lack of it). Many people of both sexes put up with unnecessary discomfort in these vital zones when the symptoms and their initial trigger can be treated and removed.

These sectors of bladder and reproductive organs, and the next structural zone—peritoneum and pubis—, often seem to need toning and repair treatment. Many people ignore these parts of the body and hope the discomfort will go away. Others try every medical treatment available for symptoms and prefer not to look for causes. Still others assume that discomfort must be accepted as a fact of existence. *No* body condition should be accepted as 'normal' when it is *not* normal. Many women say to me, 'Well, I know it's a Pill cystitis' or 'an IUD discharge', or 'pre-menstrual tension', and accept their lot as 'life'. Much of my day is spent explaining that such acceptance is not only not necessary, but can worsen the illness as fight-back fades.

White signs around these last three sectors should be treated as acute and dealt with at once. Brown signs here need thorough diagnosis and appraisal.

Many women show a rust-brown spot at the vagina/uterus junction (the cervix), after having taken the Pill for many years. The body is a sensitive recorder of abnormal stimuli in these zones. It confirms my theory that the contraceptive pill, in all its forms, is more cumulative and disadvantageous to the cervix than to any hormone function of endocrine glands.

Those unfortunate sufferers from *herpes genitalia* (that blistery nerve-rash affecting both males and females in genital areas, and becoming more persistent and more resistant to treatment every day) can register brownish spots and fogs, as well as fibre disturbance, in the iris. A low-energy condition usually applies before such a disease can take hold.

Many disease conditions are reflexes from initial pelvic causes. We have dealt with the 'anxiety' cause already, and how the head/body reflex operates sexually. Emotional disturbance can also cause reproductive area iris signs. I treated one woman who showed a black surgical diamond in the iris after giving up her illegitimate child for adoption. She told me much later she felt full of guilt, and as if a part of her had been removed. Her iris registered the emotional effect as surgical removal.

Many homosexuals, and women with pronounced lesbian tendencies, have a psoric spot over these sectors. The normal animal characteristics of male and female attraction have a 'block' through them. Sometimes this can be lifted, sometimes not; each person has the right of choice.

Let us bypass the thigh and leg zones, and the kidney and adrenal gland, and proceed to the next few segments, the cavities themselves, and some of the other organs in them.

Sensitive, complex zones

From 6.30 to 7.30 lie other organs and structures also related in function. Here we find the abdominal wall and the peritoneum (the lining around the abdominal cavity). We also find adjacent to it the pelvis (its bony structure and some functional indications) and the appendix. What a site for troubles is the latter! Headaches, nausea, abdominal cramps and spasms, pain and pimples—all can have as one possible cause an inflamed, enlarged appendix. Check the iris to make sure.

A reflex from the appendix crosses to the blood-pressure zone, right iris. We have already discussed how a rise or fall in blood pressure may be caused by appendix trauma. Headaches to the left side of the head may he similarly caused. The iris will show if this is the case, and treatment can be more accurately given. Unprocessed bran, and a diet rich in roughage (raw foods), can help ensure the health of the appendix. It was invented before stoves! Even if hard seeds do lodge there for a time, the scouring action of raw food should remove them safely.

The iris can identify for you that occasional pain in the right side of the abdomen. Is it appendix, or is it from adhesions formed after your appendix was removed? White thickened fibres may show if the latter condition has resulted. It's a 'picture' of the body, remember? The body functions and the iris records.

Motor-car accidents in which the pelvic girdle is crushed by the steering column are common producers of white pain and inflammation signs in this zone, followed later by yellowish-brown sensitivity. A psoric spot may have covered this area from birth: You may not have 'seen clearly' the accident pre-condition.

Part of the next zone (the right ovary in the female and the right testicle in the male) can obviously be affected by accidental damage to the pelvic structure, and *function* of ovaries and testes can be shocked or impaired after such trauma; but most ovarian and testes symptoms are produced by hormonal imbalance. The 'oestrogen headache' (a common pre-menstrual symptom) can result from a reflex pain curving across the iris at the forehead and temple area—showing that ovarian function, or structure, is less than good, and that the body is off-loading again.

I am often asked if cysts and tumours in ovaries are recorded in the iris. The answer is, 'No—not as such.' Some new German research into signs visible in the sclera (the white of the eye) may be able to shed light on this diagnostic question; but I would say such indications are as yet 'unproven'. However, there is often a pattern of brownish rubbish showing in the iris—which could indicate possible cyst formation. When there is doubt, Red Clover tea in the diet may help prevent, treat, and remove, *some* cysts. Seek skilled aid, though, for more therapeutic correction.

If you've been on the Pill for a long time (and many women have had ten to fifteen years of it), your ovaries can have become 'lazy'. Used to being thumped into action once per period cycle, they forget how to function on their own. A lazy organ allows rubbish to accumulate, remember? Have medical checks often if you've taken the Pill over long periods of time.

Many male children show testes disorders, some from birth or shortly afterwards. Ligament tightness or abnormal muscular function can result in undescended testicles. The iris records exactly what is experienced. The nerve wreath shows a retraction inwards towards the pupil, registering the tight condition pelvically.

Inflammation of testicles (hydrocele, orchitis) can be seen as white flares and fogs over testicle zones; and if function is chronically impaired as a result of ineffective treatment brownish signs can be expected.

So many interpretations can be put on signs in this zone that laymen should beware of worrying people unnecessarily by making diagnoses based on half-knowledge. Such sensitive and complex areas of the body should be treated with care and responsibility.

○ Thigh, Leg And Foot, Groin, Kidney, Adrenal Gland

Let us return to two zones adjoining the pelvic and lower abdominal areas in the iris. The first of these two zones records limb function below the pubis. We have already seen the reflex result here, as fatigue can cause inability to put one foot after the other, or even prevent one getting to one's feet at all.

6

Many structural weaknesses, and results of accidents and falls, appear in this iris zone. As with all of the iris boundaries, anatomical logic decrees that the thigh is record-ed at the top of the zone, the foot at the bottom. Arthritic knees, torn cartilages, and sudden structural overloads, will usually register as white signs and/or fibre lesions midway down the zone, or extending right through it. Brownish colours can mean that you feel the need to sit down often; and they can also mean that pressures from parts of the digestive tract, or from pelvic organ prolapse, are affecting your leg energy through a biochemical overload as well as the physical one.

The hip and thigh do a tremendous structural job mov-ing your body from place to place. One of the major load-bearing joints—the hip—can be very sensitive to bad posture. Get to that mirror again, strip off, and take a critical eye to

176

the *level* of each hip. Tape across the mirror, if necessary, then check that level again. Is one hip lower than the other? Most people will answer 'Yes' to this one. A chiropractor may be needed to get your body weight better balanced between both sides. *Two*-sided sports (running, swimming, jogging, riding, bicycling) balance the body better than one-sided ones do (tennis, golf, squash, pole-vaulting, fishing). If you are very active in one-sided sports, those hips may need attention before imbalance leads to unequal pressure and loading.

Lymphatic congestion around the foot zone, showing in yellow-white beads, can reflexly indicate a possible 'thick' head, too! People who refuse to go where their feet want to take them may actually suffer congestion and chemical slowness in the feet. Move your feet to get motivation back to your head!

As the foot is the lowest part of the body gravitationally, it bears the *actual* body weight even more than does the hip. Care for your feet if you value peace at the top of your head! Don't persist in wearing uncomfortable shoes or your energy will slump with every step. Go barefoot as often as possible.

Lying beside the leg area in the iris is the second zone referred to opposite: the groin on one side, the adrenal gland and right kidney on the other: the well-being of each can depend on the energy in your legs.

An inguinal hernia can result in both male and female if the thighs are not used correctly in lifting weights. Herniation most often shows in the iris as a tiny black 'hole' (long and narrow) in the groin zone, just as the actual hernia protrudes through a ligament or muscles in a 'slot' of torn tissue. Strains in this area will show as fibre disturbance; rashes, fungal and bacterial infections, will show more as colour change.

Some people show a calcium ring over this lower part of the iris as circulation becomes more difficult owing to arterial hardening. Movement is the answer again, painful though it may be at first.

The adrenal gland, as well as setting your defence response pattern, controls many hormone functions and determines your vitamin C needs. Strong adrenal flow means less need for vitamin C; inefficient adrenal function, and you will need more vitamin C to keep you healthy. In this gland, cortisone production and distribution around the body are controlled and monitored. White signs here and you are probably a zappy individual with good resistance to infection and high will-power energy too. A brown streak through the gland and your 'fight back' may need constant stimulus. Cortisone treatment medically for many illnesses is aimed at increasing adrenal function artificially. Naturopathic treatment is based on restoring again the loss of function, so that an artificial 'crutch' need not be permanently necessary.

The kidney, covering a large iris area, is directly linked in function with the adrenal gland. Under-action in one can produce under-action in the other. Sluggish kidneys, reluctant to move uric acid, can be the direct result of low adrenal fight-back stimuli. Coldness of emotional response can show in the kidneys, too. You may not only be non-anxious and non-apprehensive about life: you may be insensitive altogether to situations in which you *should* care and be concerned. Selfishness is based in the kidneys! A dark 'selfish streak' may register obviously in the iris through these two zones.

Physical ills and chills in the kidney are most likely to record as white signs in the early stages. Adrenal response in the adjoining zone should be cortizol production to fight off the illness. If the adrenal gland is also below par, a second way into arthritis is opened—kidneys overloaded with uric acid and unable to remove the residues because of a secondary infection. Such a kidney 'habit' can be established after experiencing emotional 'coldness', either from a chill, a lover, or a friend, or a family. 'Keep your kidneys warm, dear,' was a favourite exhortation of my wise grandmother, her blue eyes twinkling under white hair as her instincts protected her brood of children and grandchildren. The one daughter who rebelled, and didn't, became arthritic!

Some cystitis symptoms can be traced through iris signs as attributable to a low-grade infection in the kidneys, not producing real illness, just a general feeling of chronic tiredness accompanied by below-par drive. The kidneys should be treated in these cases, as well as the urethral tubes and inflamed bladder below.

○ The Liver, Gall-Badder, And Pancreas
The Upper Abdominal Area And Diaphragm

I call the first group above the 'chemical factory' of the body, pouring out digestive enzymes and bile and metabolising the food partially broken down by chewing and salivation. We

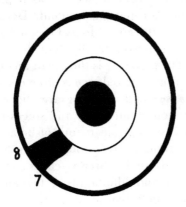

have already discussed 'emotional indigestion'—suppressing or censoring of emotional response—and the tendency towards compulsive eating to fill the emotional hole. The liver's anatomical placement also makes it adjacent to the pancreas and gall-bladder—and the diaphragm. Take a deep breath between courses at your next dinner party, and lighten your liver's load of rich food and wine! Good breathing patterns increase efficiency of digestion as the diaphragm relaxes and lets the liver get on with the job without physical tension. Nerve rings over the liver zone can show that diaphragmatic tightness is present, too. Never shout at the dinner-table: the diaphragm tightness may extend right out through liver and gall-bladder to the duodenum, and ulceration may be the eventual result. Don't talk excitedly at dinner about the day's doings, either. The emotional unloading can cause too great a flow of bile and digestive fluids, and the stomach can become over-acidic and windy. The drink before dinner, in the garden or on the terrace, a pause while the day's events are gradually dropped from the shoulders, can banish stress and strain before digestion commences. The liver's load is then considerably better balanced.

The pancreas can show many structure and colour disturbances in the irises of diabetics. The initial *cause* of the diabetes can often be clearly seen. Was it pancreas shock, inherited tendency, or genetic accident? Does a psoric spot or *radii solaris* cover the zone? Is bad diet a major contributing factor? Is the person totally 'out of balance' in life circumstances? The pancreas is the organ recording 'balance' of chemical function. The balance is often disturbed in travel sickness, and nausea and vomiting are triggered off by the pancreas. Many household herbs and spices can help make the pancreas less susceptible to out-of-balance conditions. Cinnamon and nutmeg are good; and so is fennel (as a vegetable or as seeds used in breads, cakes and soups). Celery and aniseed; kelp and alfalfa (as a tea and/or sprouts); liquorice and camomile tea: all can support pancreas function without disturbing blood sugar levels.

The pancreas can also process sugars a little too fast and produce hypoglycaemia (low blood sugar). Imbalance in this direction needs dietary awareness and eating of the 'a little and often' pattern. Emotional imbalances, even neuroses and psychoses, are often directly attributable to low blood-sugar levels. Get professional help for accuracy of diagnosis and treatment here.

White iris signs in these areas can indicate a good speed of response and eventual recovery. Darker colours may need much more prolonged treatment and control. Fibre lesions may mean that structural pressure or stress, or inefficient nerve supply to the organ, has caused the problem. Such differing causes need very different correction naturopathically. The pancreas is not given a permanent crutch, but is encouraged, gradually and safely, to regain normal function.

The gall-bladder stores bile made in the liver, and delivers it through the duodenum as digestion requires it. If the gall-bladder is removed surgically, the liver (the adjacent zone) predictably takes over and produces bile on intestinal demand.

The gall-bladder feels the chemistry of *resentment*. Gallstone formation can be the proof of a 'hardening' of anger past the point where it could still have an opportunity of being released. Something 'galled' as the anger lodged deeper. 'I became quite *bitter* about it,' say some patients. Their gallbladders show in the iris the degree of resentment experienced. Sometimes a long dark colour streak splits all three zones—liver, gall-bladder and duodenum.

A person who is chronically burying real frustration and anger will shovel it into all these organs, so that very little escapes in an outward emotional display.

We will deal more with the duodenum in the 'digestive tract' section of the iris chart.

O Hand, Arm

An 'open-handed' person is usually emotionally open, too. Look at hands as you talk to people. They can tell you much about emotional function through the liver. A clenched fist during a consultation can give the lie to the patient who says, 'To be quite frank with you ...' He is holding back the truth of the emotional pattern in that clenched right hand! Fingernail biting may be 'eating away' at yourself emotionally in self-blame or self-inflicted stress—as well as being symptomatic of low silica levels.

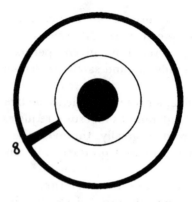

Sometimes the right hand does *not* do something the liver needs to have done. It can put wrong foods in the mouth, it can fail to hold the hand of a friend or lover: for hands can be *not*-used symptomatically, too. Have you ever wondered why creative pastimes using the hands can relax your emotional stress and strain? The iris may reflect the answer when the hand zone takes some of the load from the liver.

Hold hands with someone you care about, touch people you love. Hands can express the emotions that the liver may be too full or tight to let go otherwise. Massage is a wonderful way to relax tension and strain. Let someone else's hand take the overload from your liver! Touching, holding, and caressing with the hand, can release many emotional inhibitions which the liver may have carried as a burden for too long. How simple is the body's compensating interlocking system when broken down into iris-recorded patterns!

White flares and white fogs in this hand and arm zone can indicate an old badly healed fracture, a sprained wrist, an 'arthritic' finger, or too enthusiastic physical use that has strained ligaments and muscles for some time. Painting the house, bricklaying and gardening, may help *take* a load from the liver in physical exercise, but may also *give* a load to the liver, or the following segment (the chest) if overdone. Have you ever felt sick and nauseated with tiredness after such excess? That's your liver, begging you to stop.

Rheumatic elbows and hands may show whitish signs if

painful, more yellow and brown colours if chronically stiff and limited in movement, but the iris may show only parts of a calcium ring across liver and hand and arm, even back as far as kidneys. The 'rheumatism' is arterial hardening and calcification. Lymphatic spots, yellowish or brown, are 'rheumatism' indicators sometimes. Movement of the joints affected is the answer here—to remove the aches and pains that are of rust and rubbish type, not real rheumatism at all.

The forearm and just above the elbow register in this zone, the shoulder and its muscles higher up the iris can be seen at 10 o'clock.

◯ The Ribs And Thoracic Cavity, The Breast, Pleural Cavity, Lungs And Bronchial Tree

Comparatively simple, after the complexity of colour and structure to be found in the lower part of the iris, is the chest area. The diagram shows the anatomical layout as the iris records it from the body. The commonest abnormalities found here are from obvious illnesses like bronchitis, pleurisy, 'smoker's cough', emphysema, pneumonia, tuberculosis, and many structural accidents like broken ribs, collapsed lung, and the mechanical results of asthma. As you would by now expect, white colours indicate acute trauma, infection, pain and inflammation. Darker brownish stains mean more chronically seated troubles are present.

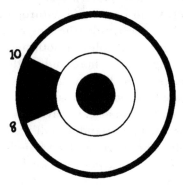

Many heavy smokers show yellowish or brown lymphatic 'beads' around the edge of these segments, as well as at the opposite side of the iris in the bronchus zone there. It would be enough to put many people off smoking to look at the muddy, clogged iris representation of the state of the lungs and the bronchial tree! I recently saw the lungs of a man of thirty-eight, whose alcoholism had led to such nutritional deficiency that a combination of pneumonia, meningitis, cirrhosis of the liver, and dehydration, had killed him one night in a city park. He had been a very heavy smoker, and both lungs, awash with fluid, were banded with dark stripes of tar deposit along the lines of clogged lymph channels. Inefficient breathing apparatus would have made the pneumonia harder to shake off. If your eyes are showing brownish discoloration and lymphatic spots around this zone, stop smoking right now!

The sharp pain of pleurisy registers here with white flares out to the pleural cavity. Generalised white fibres and fogs may also mean asthma-proneness, as mucus builds up and clogs breathing passages; but the clearest asthma indications show in the nerve wreath arc adjacent to the chest area. A sharp retraction of the nerve wreath in towards the pupil records the *tightness* of this body zone and perhaps a continuing misplacement of dorsal vertebrae, too, which massage and adjustment can treat. After many long years of asthma, the nerve wreath may show a collapse outward toward the iris rim as a 'weak chest' pattern takes hold. Both of these distinctive patterns can be treated naturopathically.

A small circular zone amidst the ribs represents the soft tissue of the breast and nipples in both males and females. Many lymphatic signs show here and at the iris rim when lumps and nodules form. Brownish lymph spots should be further investigated as soon as possible.

The posture of the torso can have great effect on the firmness of breast tissue. 'Standing tall' can develop better breast tissue tone. There are no deep muscles in the breast, only around it. Good back posture can firm these muscles and give you better breast shape and size. I feel sad to see young girls enter puberty with a 'lazy' back curved forward and shoulders hunched around the rib-cage under the many emotional stress loads of teenage years. Get shoulders back and lift all that weight off them! Your vital statistics will show the benefit.

Across the iris in a reflex from the breast zone is the thyroid gland. If you are thin and speedy with a hyperactive thyroid, breast tissue will tend to be small and tight; if you are *hypo*-thyroid in function, you may be large and floppy. Treatment to normalise thyroid function often results in better tone in breast tissue.

O Neck, Shoulder, Ear, And Mastoid Bone

The last four zones in our trip 'around the clock'—between 10 and 11—show many structural defects in the first two, and many more functional discolorations in the latter two areas. As drawn, the cervical vertebrae, from shoulder to base of the occiput, register here, and man's insistence anthropologically on standing upright has caused him to carry the weight of his head atop these vertebrae rather than letting it hang forward supported by the stronger muscles of the upper back, as do four-footed animals.

Heads weigh heavy, especially when full of stress and strain, and those deltoid and trapezius muscles around shoulders and neck must take *compression* loads. This tends to wear hard on spinal discs—the buffers between the bones, and aches and pains and tension may need massage and adjustment to allow the head to 'lift' again from shoulders. If you 'pull your head in' under stress and tension, you are doubly sure to pinch nerves and blood vessels around the area.

Rodin's *The Thinker* is propping up his head with his hand and his arm with his knee, and his body is rounded and hunched with the 'weight' of his thought. See how often you support your chin with your fist while studying, tip your head to one side against your palm whilst adding up figures or filling in tax returns. If *you* are feeling tired, think how tired are your neck and shoulder muscles to need the extra support of your hand! Regular massage can help lighten your head's 'weight'.

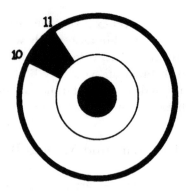

Problems and treatments

Arthritic spurs can form on these neck vertebrae because of the structural loading. Discs can wear thin and collapse. Road accidents with whiplash can temporarily or permanently damage structure and function. The neck is one of the body's most sensitive stress recorders. 'Speak not with a stiff neck'; 'stiff-necked with pride'; refusing to 'bow the neck' under adversity—such circumstances can cause the natural curve of the vertebrae to straighten and, by sheer mechanics, increase the apparent weight of the head. A flexible neck means a carefree head is on top of it. Sometimes a *hyper*-flexible neck means an *empty* head crowns it! The cervical curve should balance the lumbar curve at the other end of the spine, making the back a gently flexible compensating S-shape to absorb stress load applied to any part of it. A reflex across the iris shows this load-spreading provision. As any chiropractor, osteopath, or masseur will tell you, problems at one end of the spine, if untreated, invariably produce reflex problems at the other end. *Awareness* of stress load build-up can be the first step towards undoing it.

I advise people to buy chairs with head and neck support

if they insist on watching television. Lean back and take the 'weight' off feet and neck/head, and relax. Watch any exciting bits (are there any?) from a low-backed armchair, with narrow, uncomfortable wooden arms, and you have a completely unsupported spine as you slump forward, hunch shoulders, and take head weight down into the neck. Lean *back* with head support to watch television.

Small black signs in the shoulder and cervical zones usually mean disc wearing or misplacement has caused tissue damage. The pain alone should warn you to seek therapeutic help.

'Old age!'; 'It's to be expected as you get older, I suppose'; 'Not as young as I used to be'. When patients say such things I fire back at them, 'Never accept anything you don't want!' That old age equals obvious degeneration is not a precept of natural medicine. Wisdom should be acquired, not rheumatism; understanding, not limitation. If you haven't learnt much about your body and its life processes you can plead ignorance, I suppose. A lot of my time is spent explaining to people what is the cause of their deterioration in old age. Those with guts enough do something to reverse it, glad of the opportunity to feel better. Others accept their illnesses and say, 'It's too late now'—at the age of forty or fifty. It's entirely a matter of choice.

Brownish signs at neck and shoulder can mean that slow rubbish build-up has produced symptoms of rheumatism stiffness, aches and pains, inhibition of use. Clean out the rubbish and the 'rheumatism' goes too.

Stressed or badly-positioned cervical vertebrae can impair function of the mouth and jaw, the nasal area, the eyes, and especially the ears. Often 'ringing in the ears' ceases as the neck is corrected structurally. Deteriorating vision may be produced from C1/C2 misplacement (the two top cervical vertebrae). Even nightmares can be the result of structural misalignment of this area (the 'atlas' and 'axis') with the base of the skull. That giant—Atlas—carrying the weight of the classical Greek world on his shoulders, could have been blind, deaf and dumb at the end of his labours!

The ear is intimately connected with neck function as well as head function. Its zone lies adjacent to the top cervical vertebrae, and infections, irritations, abscesses, tinnitus, discharges, and hearing loss, can be direct results of cervical trauma. Very young children often develop ear infections as they learn to stand upright. It's that head weight again—a suddenly different load for a child used to crawling on all fours. The ear is feeling the adjustment stress of C2/C3 cervical vertebrae, and the infection can be the result of this overload.

A *radii solaris* spike here can show a mental or emotional reason for many ear problems. 'None so deaf as he who will not hear' could apply. A nagging wife for twenty years can cause protective deafness; an ego shock, as you hear some unwanted truth about yourself, can do it too. Fear of hearing blame or criticism; someone talking on a sensitive subject in an insensitive way; a discotheque at top volume next door; all can cause hearing loss. So can industrial noise, or living on a highway, cause *selective* hearing loss as the ear sends fewer of the painful signals to the brain.

Adjacent to the ear is the mastoid bone behind it. This sounding-board is a closed-in solid bone mass, subject to overload infection and inflammation from the ear itself. The next zone after it brings us back to the medulla again; so even low-grade ear infection should be watched and treated to avoid spread to mastoid and then medulla. Children have died from the spread of such acute disease before symptoms have been recognised. Check the iris during every ear infection, even during teething. Meningitis and encephalitis can result partly from an original mastoid disorder if this goes untreated.

We have mentioned the reflex mastoid to bladder, as well as medulla to bladder. Bed-wetting *may* be the result of disturbances here. Check the iris for an accurate assessment, and seek professional help.

This brings us to the last of the radial segment zones recording in the right iris. Let us now look at three circular zones around the pupil, concentric with the iris rim.

O The Nerve Wreath

In discussing the circular zones earlier, we found the most obviously visible circle to be that of the nerve wreath, a band about one-third of the iris radius away from the pupil. Ideally, this circle is regular and centrally placed, but how many of us have 'ideal' physical balance between contraction and relaxation of the body via the *physical* nerve messages down the spine to every part of the structure and its functional organs? Are you able to relax as well as you are able to work? Are you answering this one truthfully? Your iris will confirm or deny it.

Most people have tension spots or structural stress points which give recurrent troubles under load/effort. Often these will register in the iris as peaks outwards or retractions inwards around the nerve wreath. Take the example of a singer who is undergoing voice training. At the beginning, as tension and strain contract throat muscles and load vocal chords, the nerve wreath could show a tight pulling in towards the pupil at the zones of throat, vocal chords, even bronchial tree, as the effort of control was applied. If the same singer then overstrains the voice by continued muscular tension, stress, and forcing, a different pattern may occur, showing a distended, blown-outwards nerve wreath at these iris areas. The voice has been over-used and the nerve supply *over-relaxed* in tiredness.

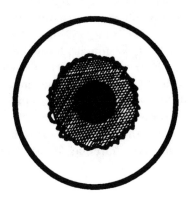

Many asthmatics show an early pattern of nerve-wreath retraction towards the pupil, followed by distension outwards after years of the illness. The *tired* bronchial tree has given up the fight, and medication has to be heavily relied upon.

Small peaks and valleys around this circle are visible in most people. Some of the body is relaxed, some other parts are in more constant use. If you work physically at jobs or pleasures that use the whole body in co-ordination (riding a bicycle, sailing, building boats, being a plumber or a garbage-man or a farmer) it is more likely that the nerve wreath will be closer in towards the pupil and much smaller and tighter around it. The nerve supply to the physical muscles will be good and strong and their ability to contract under load/effort equally positive. The Silks and Silk/Linens qualify here for the small-pupil/tight-nerve-wreath iris. However, the ability to *relax* the muscles after effort is also required. Most of the strong structural types relax emotionally by changing the effort *focus*. If the boat is being built during the week, sailing a boat at the weekend re-focuses effort in different parts of the body, balancing one load by taking another.

As we drop down in structure type to Hessian and Net irises, we find a disinclination by the body concerned to make much physical effort at all. The nerve wreath is found farther out towards the iris rim, and much more obvious peaks and valleys are recorded there. In a real Net iris, the nerve wreath appears to fill the whole space, its web almost touching the iris perimeter in some places. Some Net folk seem too muscularly weak to make much physical effort; but look at the *thickness* of each strand of the net (the whole bounded by the nerve wreath) to assess just how much effort can be applied if the stimulus is voluntarily 'caught' in their selective load/effort apparatus.

This leads us to another nerve-wreath attribute to be assessed, its *width* as a circular band, irrespective of its position in the iris.

190

Obvious indications

If you take common sense with you in your travels in the iris, you will again marvel at the obvious recording of body conditions. A nerve wreath tight up against the pupil may be very faintly recorded as thin and white, or it may show as a much wider ribbon, densely white, even yellowish-white. Think of what it is practically telling you. In the first case, the muscles are able to contract well under effort, but not so well if the stimulus continues overlong. These are the sprinters and the front-runners, able to take an enormous load for a limited time. If the nerve wreath is an obviously broad and thick band, you have a person able to apply endurance-type load/effort energy. Amongst such people you find the more phlegmatic of the Silks, and the more surprisingly energetic Nets—if their instincts decide the load is a good 'catch'. These are the people who can plod quietly all day under extended physical or mental challenge, and keep going steadily under prolonged stress conditions. These are the marathon runners and the mountain climbers and the old family GP on call twenty-four hours a day. They can make constant demands on the physical body for protracted loadcarrying.

My own medium-thick nerve wreath became surprisingly thin, almost to disappearing point, under a recent enormous physical work-load, renovating and decorating the lovely old building where our group clinic now functions. I stacked bricks, then built indoor gardens with them; I ran up and down sixteen-foot ladders; I painted and scraped and sanded and hammered and sawed—and for twelve to fourteen hours a day kept up the pace. In six weeks the building was ready. In six weeks my nerve wreath gradually became fainter and almost disappeared with exhaustion. Luckily, it remained thickest at the mental ability area: so my head got me there and told me to stop for a while when the work was finished!

Check your nerve wreath to see what type of exertion load you are best fitted to carry. You can't turn a draught-horse into a racehorse, and healthy people are those who become aware of their patterns of strengths and weaknesses, and live accordingly.

So far, the nerve-wreath examples mentioned have been white. What does it mean if a yellowish or brownish ribbon of nerve circle is recorded? By now, you should be assessing such signs as 'rubbish' and clogging of the physical nerves, with lowered function to many parts of the body because of it. We are discussing here only any browning of the thin band of the nerve wreath itself, although our next two adjacent circles, the stomach and bowel, certainly may be pouring brown streamers and fogs and spots out and over the nerve wreath, obscuring it from 'view' and therefore from efficient function.

Usually, a darkening here means that you are *not* within your true pattern of physical load function, and are trying to convince your nervous control system that it is what it is not. It may also indicate a history of narcotic addiction, or a clinical story of tranquillisers, sedatives, and suppressants, when all you really are is *unaware* of your real physical abilities. A bored Silk may be reluctantly dragged by the ear to a doctor by his worried Linen or Hessian wife, and be given tranquillisers or advised to ease up when the doctor hears what his day-to-day loads are. An unaware Silk or Silk/Linen may reluctantly take such medication, only to finish up even more bored, beginning to 'rust', and now recording a brown discoloration over his original broad white nerve-wreath circle.

I have seen almost black nerve wreaths on folk in a state of functional depression, and experiencing neurotic, even psychotic, behaviour patterns. Such people don't really give a damn what they can or can't do physically. Self-destructive impulses and the taking of irrational physical loads are recorded in the degree of blackness of the nerve wreath. Skilled help is needed in treatment.

People-assessment may require psychological tests and evaluations; but I would bet on the iris every time to verify such tests, or to disprove them. As a tool for judging the potential of staff and the qualities available for specialised use by employers, iris analysis can yield much useful information. A glance at structure type, discoloration, and the nerve wreath, could quickly slot personnel into the areas where they should be most efficient.

○ The Stomach And Bowel

Here lie recorded most of the nutritional sins and culinary excesses you don't talk about when asked, 'What's your diet like?' Here is the visible evidence of your addiction to chocolates and cream-buns, your carbohydrate-residue saturation, or your lazy acceptance of take-away foods and 'quickie'-type packaged dinners. It's a rare civilised iris that shows clear colour right throughout these two circular zones. I do not separate them much in the early stages of treatment, since what goes through the former proceeds inevitably to the latter, and on the efficiency of one depends the complete cycle of the other. Discoloration in these circles is much more common than structurally visible signs; but certainly if the *structure* is abnormal some lesions and gaps and variations in colour may often occur.

Are you a 'butterflies in the stomach' person under stress? Do you go off your food when emotionally tight? If so you are most likely to show structure-type iris signs in the digestive tract. Don't forget that the nerve wreath lies all around these two zones. The degree of balance of your stomach and intestines can *help* to balance your neuro-muscular physical responses. It can be astonishingly obvious in the iris that when correct individually based nutrition is followed the nerve wreath can do gymnastic feats of change: turning an apparent Net or Hessian type person back into the real Silk/Linen or Linen type he always was underneath that brownish, overloaded, inefficient digestive tract smog!

One man's meat ...

Remember, *nothing* can change the basic structure pattern you were born with; but how many people maintain, or even achieve, their potential? Clear away some of the brownish-yellow rubbish in the iris by seeking advice on the best nutritional pattern for *you*—not just a generally 'good' diet. There is no such thing! What a Silk can get away with, burning up the rubbish in an adrenal blaze, would flatten a Hessian with indigestion, wind, a hangover, and obesity to follow! A broad 'good diet' can still eliminate much iris rubbish, but the accurate best is what we are aiming for. One man's meat (needed for a metabolism using animal iron, vitamin B_{12}, and protein, as its working base) may be another man's rheumatoid arthritis, constipation, and acidity producer. People have as different fuel requirements as they have fingerprints, and the iris can tell a skilled iridologist which nutritional patterns is suitable.

Let's look for a little at the group of the last three zones together. The bowel and the stomach are certainly connected, and so is the nerve supply, to every part of the physical body related to nutritional patterns. But see, from the iris chart, how every part of the body structure and function has a section of nerve supply *and* stomach and bowel supporting it as it radiates out across the iris to the rim? The obvious inference is that the health of all the long convoluted twists and turns of the digestive tract has a bearing on the parts of the body sitting atop it in the iris. In practice this is confirmed.

Take the transverse colon, the portion of the bowel immediately below all the head area in the iris (from 11 o'clock to 1 o'clock). If a brownish-yellow fog is flooding out from this zone, covering irregularly many parts of the head area, you are not going to feel as 'together' as you potentially could. Physically, memory and concentration may be 'foggy' and unreliable and motivational energy low; mentally, you may be over-anxious, with a low sex drive, and have difficulty in making conversation or learning a trade or studying academically: all because your transverse colon needs unprocessed bran, vitamin B foods, and exercise! Many naturopaths start by cleaning out the bowel every time. There is much reason in this if the iris registers 'rubbish' signs there, but no reason at all if it doesn't. Blockages (particularly at 'corners' in the bowel: the hepatic flexure, the splenic flexure, the sigmoid flexure, the rectum) need the scouring action of raw foods or the burning out of a short fast to clear the bowel and free the iris segment above it from the results of its inefficiency.

Sometimes one isolated flare of brown may indicate that pressure of a particular kind has physically slowed the bowel at that point. A 'grumbling' appendix may be the only brownish area visible. A duodenum may show brown-over-white signs as ulceration takes hold. An ileo-caecal valve (at 5.10 o'clock) may be opening and closing erratically and producing brown fogs which flood into the uterus/prostate, vagina/penis iris zones below it. Off goes sexual anxiety again—maybe triggered only by the over-enthusiastic emptying of bowel contents from the ileum into the caecum.

The small intestines are recorded medially in each iris (towards the nose); the large bowel is recorded more laterally (out away from the nose). One fascinating link is established between the thyroid 'speed' of the person and the rate of assimilation of food nutrients, such a link being especially obvious in the iris. A small area, Peyer's patches, found in the small intestine, is placed in the iris directly below the thyroid sector. This bowel function can be affected either way by a too fast or too slow thyroid action. The thin speedy individual, high in thyroid function, hurls the contents of this part of the bowel into the next, the caecum, at a great rate. He may eat like an ox but remain as skinny as a rabbit. Food absorption is minimal, and his iris shows the white signs here of hyper-function. An overweight lethargic person may register brown signs right through Peyer's patches and out to the thyroid.

A slow bowel at the hepatic flexure (11 o'clock) can upset medullary function, or allow a mastoid-bone infection to remain longer than it should. An emotional stress load reflexing from the sexual/anxiety zones (to 5 o'clock) can have you wearing a track to the bathroom with diarrhoea as the ileo-caecal valve (at 5 o'clock, intestine zone) opens too readily and passes incompletely digested food into the larger bowel. A stomach distended with wind after a huge meal eaten too fast may not register in the iris if you do penance for your sins next day with lemon juice and yoghurt only; but if you continually overload the stomach with fast lumps of incompletely chewed foodstuffs there may be recorded in the iris a distinct difference in colour between the stomach zone and bowel zone. The stomach may be whitish as it secretes more digestive fluids, attempting to cope with the burden. It may later be brownish-grey as it gives up the fight and becomes under-active—while you become fat.

Clear colour right through all the stomach and bowel zone (blue or natural brown) means the digestive tract has processed the nutriment you are giving it very well, and is excreting the residues equally efficiently. Clear colours in the digestive tract are quite rare in a 'civilised' community.

It can be horrifying to view the state of the stomach and bowel of a person who believes he or she is 'healthy' on whatever the diet may be. The iris shows the truth of the matter. Even a short fast of a few days can clear away brown and yellowish residues from the iris, showing the immediate effect of the cleansing process. Such obvious iris change proves to me the whole of the theory behind iridology: irises *do* register body happenings, and comparative viewing before and after treatment can show how valid is the registration and its predictable change.

The digestive tract reacts particularly obviously in the short term. Longer treatment may be needed to remove the cause of the problem—emotional suppression and compulsive eating, low calcium/iron levels, loneliness, selfishness, or a Greek grandmother's kitchen! The iris will be slower to remove signs of the *cause* than of the effect.

Stubborn constipation problems

Radii solaris through any iris zone may break the nerve wreath and emanate from the bowel itself. A psoric spot may leave part of the bowel with inefficiency and a 'clouded' response to the peristaltic impulse to move, causing all sorts of stubborn constipation problems. Reddish-brown signs in the digestive tract can often be records of medication, over long periods, for such things as ulcers, cramps, indigestion, wind, and constipation. The iris, however, may still be registering a *cause* factor as untreated, so that the reddish-brown 'drug' signs may be mixed with yellow, grey, or brown, too.

Because the physical nervous system (the nerve wreath) surrounds the bowel zone, there is an obvious iris recording to explain why some constipation sufferers can't get the bowel to move no matter what kinds of diet improvement are followed. Gaps may show in the nerve wreath circle. It may not be completely *connected* all around the iris, and parts of the bowel may not be getting a peristaltic impulse at all. In such cases, unprocessed bran, vitamin B, or laxatives are ineffective: nothing gets the bowel moving again unless lubrication-type 'oils' are taken to enable the contents to slide out rather than be firmly pushed out.

Such a 'spastic colon' bowel can doom its possessor to difficulties with rubbish removal, no matter how good the diet may be. One patient, a fit, healthy, diet-conscious yoga teacher, came to see me in tears and desperation. 'I've tried *everything*,' she told me. 'My bowel just won't move.' Acupuncture treatment and herbs to support the *nerve* supply may help this type of constipation.

On the other hand, the iris can show the constipation to be due to the opposite cause—a *too*-good bowel control. If you are in an 'up-tight' condition, your bowel may be too tightly controlled by a tight nerve wreath. Many children hang onto faeces, if fear of the consequences of 'non-performance' become part of toilet training. Some children *use* non-performance as a way of upsetting mother or father if there is a will-power/ego tussle going on in the family. The stubborn habit of refusing to *move*, or let go, or give way, can persist through life as a chronically tight bowel. The bowels are as intimately connected with the type of person as is the fibre structure, and a look at the iris can give a very clear picture if there is 'a load of rubbish' present.

197

Other problems

Those of you who have visited or lived in Eastern countries may have had experience of 'Bali belly', 'Delhi diarrhoea', or 'Indonesian itch'. Intestinal parasites can take hold in the digestive tract from the food and water in such places. The iris records the exact picture of the disturbance: a collection, or small group, of little black dots here and there intestinally. Even threadworms (which cause irritation of the colon *and* the nervous system beside it) record the same signs, often found in the otherwise clear eyes of young children.

The duodenum (at 7.45) is one iris zone where a gap in the nerve wreath *should* be seen. Usually there is a brownish or even surgical sign if ulcers are present. Pre-ulcerous conditions may show only as white or yellow-white inflammatory signs; but tissue breakdown certainly records as darker colours.

A whole book could be written on the different signs and colours appearing in these two zones and the nerve wreath surrounding them. It is sufficient here to show the *supportive* role of the digestive tract to every other part of the body and its functions. Clear away any gastro-intestinal iris-sign causes, and you will improve the function of the organ or iris zone immediately above it. As the brown fog lifts, it may blow away towards the outside rim of the iris before it dissipates altogether.

The muscles, the circulation, the lymphatics, and the skin, may now all receive the bowel's 'load' in a spread of brown, and physical symptoms may result in these areas. Boils or rashes, muscular aches and pains, lumps and bumps and pustules under and on the skin—all or any of these may occur as part of the rubbish removal; and a much cleaner digestive tract will appear as this process completes itself. The iris registers clearing of digestive colour abnormalities from the inside outwards.

'Keep the mouth shut and the bowels open' should be writ on the forehead of every mother trying to do her best raising a child. The bowel is the way *all* stress should be removed from the body. If this is done efficiently, the mouth and the head above it will not have to be resorted to. Healthy minds and bodies are found in the same iris package of *clear* colour.

THE LEFT IRIS

As the right iris shows right-sided body happenings, so does the left iris record function and structure on the left side of the body. Most people are one-sided in body use. Unless you are truly and equally ambidextrous from birth, one side of you is going to wear out sooner than the other, tire more readily, take more stress, and be less clumsy. In a right-handed person, the right iris may be cluttered with all manner of signs and colours, while the left shows less of everything.

The left iris is a mirror-image of the right, with organ zones, function, and structure, reversed laterally to medially; but there are a few obvious differences if you compare the two iris charts. The liver is found only on the right side of the body and is therefore recorded only in the right iris; the divisions of the bowel fall similarly from right side to left side. The appendix, the gall-bladder, and some head functions, are all found on the right side of the body, and therefore again recorded in the right iris. I shall deal only with the different areas in the left iris, since all other structural, functional, and reflex indications apply as in the right iris.

○ The Visual Zone

Let us look 'around the clock' again to the first difference, at about 12.20—the visual zone. Here will show disturbances in *seeing*, but not necessarily physical eye disease. 'None so blind as he who will not *see*' can register often as a *radii solaris* spike through this zone.

A searing pain experienced behind the left eye may be a symptom of all manner of illness patterns, and the iris can tell you which one applies. Is it circulatory, functional, nerve supply, or just a blocked transverse colon, registered there? Many visual problems improve out of sight(!) on naturopathic treatment once the cause is accurately established.

As well as signs in this visual zone, there may be other indications of the *type* of visual disturbance in the five-sense zone and even in the eye area, too. Clear-seeing, perceptive people may show just a normal pattern of fibres and clear colours at the visual segment; true clairvoyants (and the *real* ones are rare indeed) can exhibit here a white flare, a nerve wreath peak, or a variety of uncategorisable hyper-function signs and colours.

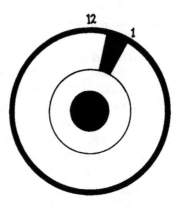

A psoric spot over this zone, and you may have to give in and wear glasses, or contact lenses, to help you 'see' more clearly through the pigment screen. You may be more an audio-learner than a visual learner, too, finding difficulty in remembering and recording visual impressions. A 'far-away look' in the eyes may mean your *inner* visualisation has replaced your eyesight for a while, and you are 'seeing' something other than what is there in front of you. Day-dreaming as a habit can prevent you from 'seeing' reality.

Visual response is particularly closely connected with the brain itself, via the optic nerve. Look at beauty and you give your actual brain tissue a tonic. 'See' the best side of everything and you'll live long with your faculties intact. See nothing but death and destruction and decay and hopelessness and you'll miss the golden dandelion flower on the rubbish-heap and the iridescence of pigeons' wings in the concrete jungle. 'Look' for beauty and you'll give your eyes a positive glow.

It is very important for children to be given the opportunity to 'see' in as many spheres as possible as they gain experience and knowledge. Exposure to television only will surely produce a child with limited 'seeing' day after day, and these impressions will persist as a framework right through life. Get children into *real* situations, gaining three-dimensional visual experience, with themselves *in* the picture. A 'clearer' iris will result and last all through life.

From the chart, you can also understand why a severe blow to the head can result in visual disturbance. The iris may appear flattened across the rim, and all the zones below this flattening can suffer restriction in use.

A reflex from the visual area across to the adrenal zone has been discussed before (p. 93). This reflex is a further reason for ensuring that children receive many visual impressions. A white, active visual zone means a better adrenal function in response to the stimulus. A macabre example of such a reflex is visual pornography. Adrenal hormones are stimulated by the sight of a sexual stimulus.

Sight and iridology are mutually dependent. What the iridologist 'sees' in the iris is a measure of his or her own clarity of vision.

○ The Equilibrium Zone

Adjacent to the visual area in the left iris is the equilibrium segment, where true epilepsy can be recorded. I have found few 'real' epileptics amongst those so classified medically. Many have suffered structural damage in falls, or circulatory blockages or strictures, all of which can give symptoms of epilepsy afterwards.

One of my patients became suddenly epileptic and blind two days after his first rebellious dose of LSD, and is still in the resultant pattern of illness six years later. Another patient had a fit every morning at 4 o'clock for many years, but no other symptoms were indicative of real epilepsy. His left iris showed nothing abnormal at all in the epilepsy zone, but there was an incredible squashed-flat iris rim above it and covering both adjacent zones as well. 'When did you fall on your head?' I asked him. 'Oh, yes, I'd forgotten,' he answered. 'When I was about four I fell from a two-storey building and was unconscious for two days, so I'm told!' His 4 a.m. fits, at the time when blood pressure is lowest, were now easily explainable. He was no more epileptic than I was.

By law, naturopaths are not allowed to treat epilepsy Explaining this to a parent must be done if *real* epilepsy exists; but if there is no long black line in the equilibrium/epilepsy zone it is doubtful whether the disease has been correctly diagnosed. Epilepsy used to be called the 'falling sickness', so its evidence in the balance zone is logical.

Off-balance illness

In this segment can also be registered signs of Ménière's syndrome, the off-balance pattern originating from the fluid canals in the inner ear. These three canals function like a gyroscopic top: three interlocking circles in three planes, which keep you from falling over every time you change position. Damage, like calcification or unequal fluid pressure, can throw these delicate canals off-centre, and you feel dizzy, and disorientated, and may veer across a footpath onto the road if the illness assumes acute proportions. One of my favourite patients, a jolly, contented, intelligent real-estate developer, developed Ménière's disease when he stopped all his former sporting activities and wedged himself behind a desk. Off-balance illness resulted. He has improved well after explanation and treatment; but his providing for his dearly-loved family has made him choose to continue the pattern. The disease will probably not be completely removed.

A reflex from this zone arcs across to the vagina/penis, uterus/prostate, rectum/anus areas. Many women develop Ménière's syndrome after a hysterectomy. The former balance for their femaleness has been removed, and physical imbalance results if the problem remains unsolved. Similarly, a prostate operation on a male, no matter for what reason, can often produce off-balance symptoms. His maleness has been disturbed. Conversely, an enlarged prostate gland may be spotted from an iris examination and treated ahead of time before it sets up an overload reflex.

As you can see from the chart, the splenic flexure of the bowel starts below this zone. An awkward bowel 'corner', this one, for blockages and slow function. If you are constipated and feeling a 'full' head and a little dizziness, it may be the splenic flexure at the base of it all. Keep that bowel moving briskly and often! You may also have experienced a dizzy feeling after or during a bowel movement. Splenic flexure again, and your equilibrium zone above it is disturbed until the bowel takes up its new position after moving out some contents.

The part of the reflex affecting the rectal and anal zones opposite often has to do with a fissure in these parts, or severe haemorrhoids (especially if infection is present), or severe inflammation. Some haemorrhoidectomies can throw a patient right off-balance permanently. I listen always to a patient's instinctive reactions for or against an advised treatment. One who says, 'Oh, no, I won't have those haemorrhoids out as the doctor suggested', and then veers over to one side as he's speaking, is going to react very badly to the disturbance of his balance if the operation is done. Even thinking about it produced a little dizziness.

Travel sickness may register as an abnormal peak or retraction of the nerve wreath at this zone. Proneness to balance upsets in cars, planes, and boats means that your gyroscopic compass in the inner ear area is very sensitively tuned. It is common for a seaman to have sea-sickness the first day out of port, then he's in balance again for the rest of the voyage. When he comes ashore again, he may feel as if he's still walking a ship's deck and be awkward in his gait on a city pavement, until the fluid balance in the vestibular canals adjusts to non-moving ground under his feet.

A strange but explainable reflex can occur if balance is so severely impaired that nausea gives over to vomiting and the total miseries of travel sickness set in. A reflex throws across to the *other eye*, and the pancreas, the organ which feels the chemistry of imbalance, produces the vomiting. Explainable it all is when you see the magnificent logic of the body: it is trying to *rebalance* itself by off-loading from left-side equilibrium to right-side pancreas. The load is physically endeavouring to balance itself both sides at once.

In my early childhood I used to watch a Chinese market-gardener balancing heavy loads in two baskets hanging from a rod across his shoulders. He was a living gyroscope as he bent and moved and reached and stretched picking his vegetables; and the baskets balanced his movements and he theirs, dipping and bobbing and swinging. He was a vegeta-mobile, adjusting perfectly and thus feeling little weight-load, even when this was clearly considerable.

◯ The Aorta And Heart

Here comes the sixty-four-dollar zone! Every patient past forty wants to know, 'How is my heart?' 'It's as good as you've trained it to be,' I reply. The heart, more than any other organ of the body, can adjust to its loading. Challenge your heart by exercise and know it is getting stronger! Even the medical profession has reversed its last-generation instruction to heart patients: 'Take it easy, rest, look after yourself.' Now the instruction is: 'Walk, exercise gently then more strongly, take up the load again as soon as possible.'

An athlete's heart can be trained to enlarge and pump a huge volume of blood at a safe pace, on demand. A heart can also enlarge after rheumatic fever, toughening its valves and its muscle structure to overcome the threat. But if a constant overload of the *destructive* kind is applied (alcohol, heavy, greasy food, coffee, cigarettes) the heart may pathologically enlarge and surround itself with excess fat and cholesterol deposition to avoid having to carry such an unwelcome burden.

In post-mortem work I recently saw a heart the size of that of an ox, enormously compensating after childhood rheumatic fever, and compared it with a pale, flabby, fat-saturated heart, enlarged for quite a different reason—*lack* of effort and nutritional overload. In the iris, the two would have shown marked differences. The first could show parting of the fibres and maybe some pressure either way by the nerve wreath: the sheer size of the heart would cause physical disturbance. But the second heart could show the yellowish-white or brown signs of destructive load, or even a greyish streak out and over it, through the nerve wreath.

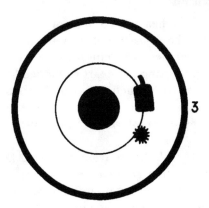

Here, more than anywhere else in the iris, it is imperative for the layman not to make pronouncements like, 'My word, your heart's not in good condition!' Differentiation between a heart problem and a muscular pain in the chest, indigestion, or a numb left arm, must be made by experts thoroughly trained in diagnosis. You could frighten someone into a heart seizure by such an irresponsible statement made with little knowledge. All you may be seeing could be a strained pectoral muscle, bronchitis, or a dorsal spine misalignment. However, if the heart area is clear, all the fibres straight, and colour difference is absent, you *can* tell the person, 'Your heart's in pretty good shape.'

For an iridologist to say 'heart' rather than bronchial disturbance, many questions must be answered by the patient. Some severe viral attacks record massive disturbance over both zones, and the fuzzy iris, apparently out of focus no matter how you move the torch around, can often be recording a viral invasion which has flattened the patient altogether. Anaesthetic shock can be felt severely by some people, and long after the operation a streak of grey or a fibre parting can still be seen. This can be so especially if an adrenalin injection has been given to pull the patient out of post-operative collapse. An electric shock can still remain obviously in the heart zone long afterwards, too.

Storing trauma

I'm convinced the heart has a 'memory' system as well as the head. It stores the *impression* of trauma, and repeated shocks can stop it altogether as it refuses to meet the same negative stimuli. It is subjecting the heart to sudden loads rather than weakening it by too much stress and strain that does the damage. It is a rhythmical system in there, and disturbance of the harmony of counterpoint upsets it more than allegro speeds.

It is quite possible to die from a 'broken heart'! Grief can be recorded here in a grey streak of misery and loss. So can the troubles of a dearly-loved one record in the heart zone. I have seen many patients showing classic heart disturbance signs in the iris, though all medical tests reveal no abnormality. On close questioning, I find that a beloved husband, or wife, or child, or parent, has recently been a 'load' which that patient has attempted to carry. A serious operation on the husband can produce a heart stress in his wife, and her iris records it as such.

One woman, full of *self*-love, showed a *radii solaris* through the heart area after her husband of thirty years had finally had enough and left. 'I *hate* everything and everyone now that he's left me,' she spat at me. 'I would rather he were dead than with that other woman.' Her iris recorded *negative* love, and her 'hardened' heart showed brown and angry-looking under the *radii solaris*. Already she had had unexplainable pains in the chest, loss of breath on exertion, and had contacted her removed husband every few days to tell him how ill she now was and how it was all his fault. I gave her no heart herbs at all, for there was nothing wrong with the organ. I did give her some sophisticated homoeopathic remedies for her self-centredness, self-love, and possessive negativity.

'Big-hearted Arthur', who picks up and 'shoulders' every burden dropped at his feet, may show a reflex sign across the iris to the scapula (the shoulder-blade), or a more angled reflex to the dorsal spine. If your posture is stooped and round-shouldered from too much sharing of others' loads, your heart may eventually feel the strain too. 'If you want a job well-done, ask a busy man' is descriptive of this type. Their broad backs not only can tire eventually, but can 'break' under the last straw of load and a sudden heart-attack can be the result. These are the people who can just drop dead, having had no previous sign of an ill health pattern. The Silks and Silk/Linens are typically at risk here. I believe that any exercise that flexes the upper back and shoulders should be regularly enjoyed by such people. Drop that weight of responsibility, and let your heart have a fair go!

A heart 'attack' can also be caused by an over-full bowel. The descending colon adjoins the heart area, and a sluggish elimination pattern can cause heart stress, even fatty degeneration of the heart as a muscle. See how important it can be to keep the bowels clean, and cleared often? Congestive heart failure can have one cause in chronic constipation. Folk who only have a bowel movement every four or five days may be told by a medical man: 'Well, it's not causing you any obvious problems. Just don't worry about it.' It's the non-obvious chronic enlargement of the colon that can one day *pressure* your heart into feeling *it* is sick!

'Heart-sick' people are more common than cardiac patients. Many of those in hospital wards are there after emotionally triggered burdens become too heavy for the individual to bear any longer. The iris can tell a professionally trained person the story.

O The Solar Plexus

Your 'sun-centre' is the point where if someone levitated you horizontally up in the air, back uppermost, you could rotate in perfect balance on a fulcrum applied just above the navel! Spinning around in mid-air, you could decide whether yourself and the circumstances around you were stable by your continuing gyration around this point. Have you ever watched a top, set spinning by an expert, hum at high speed on one tiny spot? A less expert hand will have that top noisily and erratically gyrating until it falls over and stops.

An iris recording of your solar plexus pattern can be illuminating. Are you continuing in the present cycle of stable experience, or are you about to cross the world, change profession, job, or spouse—or become a totally different person in life-style and thinking?

A white solar plexus zone can mean that change of a positive sort is just round the next corner. A brown solar plexus can show resistance to change and refusal to accept new experience opportunities; or it may mean that a change which could have been beneficial was offered and refused. A psoric spot over this zone, and you may not recognise an opportunity even when it's under your nose, let alone take it.

From the purely physical side, it may just mean indigestion! Interpretive skill and those questions and answers will determine which is which. The descending colon also adjoins this iris circle. Constipation can do it again! Hanging onto bowel contents too long can make you less open to change and growth by experience.

I often remark on the solar plexus indication to the patient, explaining the feeling of restlessness and frustration with present circumstances as a 'pre-change' pattern. 'There is a good new direction coming,' I can tell them when white active signs appear. Or 'I don't think you really will make that overseas trip,' I can tell them, if the solar plexus shows dark and negative.

No abnormal signs here at all and the probabilities are stable continuation of present circumstances—unless, of course, you become very constipated.

○ The Spleen

In Chinese medicine, especially acupuncture, the spleen is the organ of the emotions and determines whether they come to the surface or are buried. Interestingly enough, the spleen in the left iris exactly mirrors the position of the liver in the right. It may be that the racial differences between East and West have a *geometrically* opposite basis as well as a biochemical shift! In Western metabolism, the spleen feels the chemistry of anger.

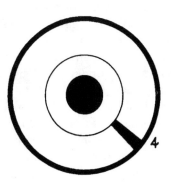

The anger may be of the 'righteous' kind: The crusader fighting for human rights, the active feminist, the protest-marchers, even the researcher, the detective, the surgeon,— may all be trying to right wrongs that have made them *angry*. Anger can be a powerful fuel, burning with intensity in the zealot, exploding disastrously in the homicidal maniac.

209

Anger at a situation can be the goad to get you out of it and doing something about it. When the incident is past, a white-hot spleen may then cool off and look normal again in the iris.

In some people the signs of anger may be totally absent, or unrecognised, because there is a psoric spot or a brown fog of dullness over the natural spleen colour. Then again, the bowel may inhibit the expression of real anger-producing stimulus if the sigmoid colon is full and sluggish. Mild, non-aggressive people may be sitting on a lot of pressure—from the bowel and its contents!

'Venting the spleen' can be a traumatic experience for the receiver of the anger-unloading. Have you ever dropped a violent unleashing of irrational fury on the head of a total stranger? Your anger may not have been able to be let loose on those near to you because you love them dearly and won't hurt them; but the postman might get it; or your secretary; or the income-tax department.

Anger and its release is a healthy balance of human experience. Aggression may not be a good thing if it happens twenty-four hours a day, but aggressive response and self-defence under attack are requirements for survival. If you don't even feel anger when an anger stimulus is applied, heaven help your immunity under attack by bacteria, viruses, bacilli—even cancer.

Low or suppressed spleen function can give you everything from leukaemia downwards. It can produce glandular fever, warts, and pathological tiredness. It can also lower your immunity so severely that such attacks remain unchallenged for long periods of time, and your self-defence is chronically lowered. The pale skin, acceptance of weakness, and loss of aggressive drive, of anaemic patients can all be traced back to the spleen and its low function.

Self-defence under attack should be the response of every living organism. I believe such diseases as multiple sclerosis can be the effect of spleen shock. The MS 'euphoria', so obvious in its later stages, the macabre joyous acceptance of a slowly crippling death, has its basis in negative aggressive response via the spleen. 'Fight,' I yell at my MS patients. 'Don't accept this illness!' A smile of negative docile obedience answers me. Spleen function in self-defence is obviously interfered with as a prime causative factor of this pattern of symptoms. Deterioration of the nerve sheathing can be a secondary symptom only of the person's basic *self*-destructive lack of anger.

What a joy it is for me to get vitality back to a patient with low spleen function! The 'doormats' start to look for their own sunspace, the born losers start to win a few times; the self-preservation instinct rises. They say, '*No*, dear', occasionally, and more respect accrues from those around them as they do. The mouse becomes the lion, potentially always there. 'Excuse me for living' is an attitude of the past. Haemoglobin rises; red and white blood cells balance; immunity increases; a healthy pink appears in the cheeks—and I go home happy. Acceptance of anything less than good health by my patients makes my *own* spleen 'angry'!

A fibre lesion over the spleen can be in evidence after physical damage. A car accident, a fall from a tree, a backwards skid on a banana-skin, can crush and bruise the spleen so that removal may be necessary. Following our previous line of thought, it is fascinating to find that the *liver* now takes over many spleen functions.

A fibre lesion may also register if a violent 'anger' is physically controlled well. I know many evolved human beings whose fury at the wrongs endured by mankind has made them do something about it. Love may cast out fear, but service given to others transforms anger in positive use.

O The Rectum And Anus

From the sublime, let us get back to earth via the bottom end of the digestive tract.

'A good shit is better than an orgasm,' postulated one of my more pragmatic patients! I did not agree with him; but the reflex across his iris to his 'balance' equilibrium area showed me why for him it was such a delightful experience. A *radii solaris* through his equilibrium zone pointed straight across to a huge brown cloud covering the rectum and parts of the sigmoid colon above it.

Haemorrhoids may register here (if internal) as a cluster of tiny blackish dots, or a grey-brown streak, or even fiery red drug spots after years of suppressive treatment. This zone is as hard to isolate from its neighbours as is the similar area in the right iris. Prostate inflammation can cause rectal pressure; vaginal infections can be caused by abnormal bowel flora; perineal or scrotum irritation can also cause or be caused by rectal and anal irritation. White signs here again mean pain and pressure; darker browns and blacks mean that cleansing of one sort or another is needed; white lymphatic signs can mean lumps and congestion; browner lymph beads need professional investigation.

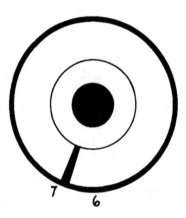

The 'itchy-bum' symptoms so many adults experience are probably not the threadworms or slight infections their children have. Excess protein in the diet can alter the pH levels in the bowel, and acid irritation can result. You all know the effects of too much curry and spice, too! The next day, a red-hot bowel will let you feel the irritant properties of such ingredients.

A diet high in white sugar, white flour, and other

excessively acid-forming foods, can produce an itch and a white irritable flare in this iris zone. Continuation of such patterns, and the rectal and anal areas may ulcerate. Over-acid body fluids in tissues can corrode the mucus linings of hollow organs, and mucus colitis can result in the large bowel. Especially is this evident in the rectum iris zone: white or yellowish-white over brown illustrates the actual conditions and body colours—brown faeces surrounded by whitish mucus.

Some severe epileptics, and sufferers from resistant migraines, find that anal suppositories containing sedatives and dilating ingredients are the only effective form of treatment. Here is a typical reflex example. Get that anal sphincter to 'let go' and relax, and the electric tension in the head (even the high 'aura' charge of epileptics and the flashing lights and haloes of true migraine) can be directed to the other end of the system, and earthed through the lower bowel.

○ In Conclusion

Taking both irises together, we have a side-to-side and front-to-back picture of the person. Top-to-toe completes another gyroscope of balance. If the circles are evenly circular, the straight lines nice and straight, and the colours are clear and bright, a well-balanced person lies behind the iris, receiving accurate impressions from external and internal stimuli.

8
EYE DISEASES

For The Medical Specialists' Attention

Many patients think my iris torch will let me see the internal structure and function of the eye itself, but only an ophthalmoscope can see the retina and the sub-structure of the eye through the pupil. 'My sight's poor on this side,' one will say as I hover with my torch, or, 'That eye is always red and sensitive'. Diseases of the eye need very skilled attention, and I often refer patients to specialists in this field. However, some eye symptoms do have a bearing on the iris itself and therefore come within the scope of our investigations.

PTERYGIUMS

About one-third of a civilised population shows the typical yellowish thickened tissue of pterygiums in the white of the eye. Usually, these are placed laterally (towards the ears) rather than medially (towards the nose). The yellow cells of opaque tissue appear gelatinous under the iris torch; and if the affected area of sclera covers some of the iris, symptoms of physical illness will surely appear in the zone so obscured. What more proof does anyone need in assessing the validity of iris analysis?

A pterygium edging over the liver area can point to emotional and metabolic problems, if over the lung, then asthma may appear out of the blue; if over any zone at all, the function of that zone will be inefficient and obscured. Like a psoric spot, a pterygium can 'pull the blind down' over the part of the iris affected.

One patient had a massive active pterygium medially, and this one grew and spread rapidly until the vision was acutely affected and red congested blood vessels could be seen in the pterygium itself. The iris zone covered by it was all of the back and spine. The man had no structural strength at all, had lost his job as a steelworker, and could not stand or even sit for very long without his back 'giving way', as he put it. I advised him to have the pterygium surgically removed as soon as possible. After a successful operation his back problems vanished.

When pterygiums are located only in the sclera (the white of the eyes), no interference with body function can be observed. How delicate is the iris in its recording mechanisms!

GLAUCOMA

Glaucoma can be acute and threatening to vision if not treated immediately. If sub-acute it may need the permanent support of drugs and eye-drops; if milder it may be unrecognised. The fluid pressure in the eye tissues builds up as constriction occurs in tiny vessels and valves. An 'up-tight' person gets glaucoma, just as easily as haemorrhoids and headaches, if the eye structure takes part of the stress load. A tiny pupil may result; but more often it becomes tiny as drugs relieve the fluid pressure and release the tissues from the load. If this cannot be done, it may be necessary to operate through iris tissue and quickly release fluid as well as provide an escape channel for further build-up. A black wedge of iris tissue removal may show under the torch (see photograph 10 in Chapter 9).

215

Whatever iris zone the operation has excised will feel the result as *removal of function*. I have seen the most tired patient ever exhibiting this scar over the vitality zone. Another developed epilepsy right after the operation. Where was the scar? Over the epilepsy segment, left iris. Yet another patient had scars in both irises, one over the anxiety zone, right side; one at the visual zone, left side. She had been on tranquillisers for endogenous depression and anxiety ever since the operation, and her vision in the left eye was deteriorating fast.

CATARACTS

Similar black wedges can be found in the iris after some types of cataract removal. As sure as eggs, the iris zones affected will be down in function and maybe in structure too.

I should like to plead with eye surgeons to consider very carefully where an incision should be made. There is really no 'safe' iris area to use, but consider the person before picking the spot to emasculate! There is a newer, different type of cataract removal or glaucoma operation that leaves no iris scars at all, and therefore does not result in physical trauma or functional loss.

BLINDNESS

What a challenge to iris analysis lies here! Theoretically, a totally blind person cannot 'see' anything, and yet some sensory stimuli *must* get through, because the iris registers them. Here lies the difficulty in trying to explain the recording ability of the iris outside the bounds of anatomy and physiology.

'There is no reason why this should be so,' say the scientific sceptics. 'Nevertheless, it *is* so,' I counter. 'Now start looking for a reason!'

I have seen partially blind eyes in which the iris shape is

distorted abnormally: areas flattened or pulled away from the pupil, whole groups of segments misplaced, stretched, or 'missing' altogether. Without exception, trauma has been experienced in the body zones affected. One woman, blind in one eye from birth, lost the other after a cricket ball hit it. From the kidney segment right round to the spleen in the left iris, and from the kidney zone out to the ovary in the right iris, the iris signs were so pale as to be hardly visible. And why did she come to seek treatment from me? For ovarian cysts, a grumbling appendix, chronic constipation, abdominal pain, an arthritic pair of knees, sore feet, and low energy. Everything else outside these zones felt fine, as her body function and structure confirmed the recordings of her iris.

Impressions still seem to register in the iris though actual sight may be missing. Even after death, the iris still records, at least for several days, conditions just before the event. Some other system, not yet fully understood, has its own method of communication to and from brain cells and body parts.

Any iris of a blind person still showing some structural indications and colours can be read to a certain degree; but, if no signs are recorded in the glazed, opaque iris tissue of some kinds of blindness, diagnosis must be made from the patient's symptoms alone—a clumsy substitute when one is accustomed to the fine accuracy of normal iris recording.

I should like the opportunity to do further research with the eyes of the totally or partially blind. The validity of iris analysis can be seen most clearly in extreme examples when damage to the iris or an abnormal iris shape has produced abnormal function in the affected zone of the body to which it belongs.

Infections, cysts, warts, inflammation of the conjunctiva, or eyes sensitive to glare, touch, and irritants, may all be noticed during an iris examination. Leave these to the professionals; and don't make comments like, 'You've got something growing on your eye', or 'All the white's a funny colour', or 'It looks all bulgy and red!'

If you learn respect for eyes, as I have done over many

years of looking at them, you won't make too many rash statements or ill-considered diagnoses.

9

CASE HISTORIES

When reading the following case histories, please refer to the colour photographs at the end of the chapter.

1. FEMALE, 21 YEARS, RIGHT IRIS

Some aspects of iridology must be explained separately from the *anatomy* of the eye. The normal reaction of a pupil exposed to a sudden bright light is to dilate (widen) then contract (narrow). Such pupil movement is an indication of how speedy the reflexes are, how fast the patient will react to stimuli. When the pupil is dilated all the time, daylight and dark, stimulated or not stimulated (as in photograph 1a) it is recording body patterns of lethargy, poor iron assimilation, slack muscle tone, skin pimples and lumps, bad posture, and a compulsive need to sleep. This young lady could not be woken up in the morning, she sat quietly in a group of people with her eyelids drooping, and produced one or two words with effort. Her skin was dead-white and she couldn't stand for very long without feeling exhausted.

A bad motor-car accident eighteen months previously,

causing fractured pelvis and lower back injuries: Nerve wreath dark brown and doubled in several places; severe, pelvic misplacement (nerve wreath retracted and irregular from 4.00-5.30). Born with right leg badly twisted from the hip (three incompletely healed lesions at 6 o'clock, also causing poor adrenal function in adjacent zone). Muscle tone sluggish and heavy (deep brown nerve rings all over iris). Bad lymphatic congestion especially visible in the iris at thyroid, throat and right lung (heavy smoker); lymphatic congestion around liver (she had an insatiable craving for cheese); upper jaw tight with double nerve wreath to lower jaw (1.20-1.40— would not talk about her problems). Psoric spot diaphragm/ gall-bladder (resentful and odd sudden pains in chest). Intermittent earaches and pains (brown double nerve wreath, pain flares and brown nerve rings at 10.30).

Photograph 1b shows a remarkable change six months later, after naturopathic treatment. The smaller pupil is immediately obvious. At this point the lass was out of bed at 5.30 a.m., and stirring everyone at the squash court by seven. Two hours of squash routines left her feeling great and not even puffing. She was full of energy and drive (adrenalin firing well), and those *white* nerve rings all around the iris show the almost too-good muscle strength. The 'aura' around the iris rim is a much clearer colour, and she related to those around her much more openly. The lymphatic rosary, still there, needs constant work, exercise—and less cheese! A heavy physical programme, completed over a few weeks, put some new signs in the iris: the beginnings of *radii solaris* to the anxiety, fatigue, and mental ability/speech junction. She would not give up and admit ordinary tiredness, fearing it was a return to her former lethargy. The nerve wreath is less double, and beginning to show its real broad whiteness of load-carrying ability underneath.

One doctor at a recent medical symposium I attended told me, 'I have never seen any proof that irises change as health changes.' 'Have you ever really *looked*?' I challenged.

2. FEMALE, 51, YEARS, LEFT IRIS

Another tired lady, complaining of bowel wind, bloating, pain, and lack of drive. The obvious trauma is recorded in the iris (photograph 2a): the brown toxic 'streamers' from the digestive tract flow out over the nerve wreath to target zones of adrenal/kidney, abdominal wall, left ovary and spleen. She drinks very heavily, smokes even more heavily, and lives on a high animal-protein diet. The acidic yellowish haze under brown has obscured *all* fibres, even the nerve wreath. There are a few tiny bowel 'pockets' in the descending colon zone, producing the wind and bloating of mild diverticulitis.

Six months later (photograph 2b), after herbal treatment, plus dietary supplements, the brown has faded remarkably. However, the lady is taking the path of many people who feel that a few vitamin pills will obviate the results of continued dietary and circumstantial sinning. They won't, and the iris will register the fact! She is now drinking even more, and eating more T-bones, and no amount of advice as to what is really happening will change her views.

And, behold; a few fibres have become visible, zig-zagged though they be, at the chest areas! Under all that acidic tissue-yellowing would be a blue iris, if she cared to work at it.

Notice the three white nerve rings which have suddenly appeared! She felt so good with her rather too high vitamin intake that she was positively dangerous! She then came scurrying back to me, her confidence in shreds, with 'heart palpitations'. The iris showed a gap with a dark streak through the nerve wreath at the aorta; the ego area was dark and a developing *radii solaris* to the head showed at the perception zone.

'I thought I was *well*,' she flapped.

'You are, comparatively,' I said. 'How about getting that bowel of yours cleaner?' (The double nerve wreath adjoined the descending colon.)

She agreed to a week's 'being good' about her diet. The

palpitations went. They came back again as her return to heavy protein and alcohol reproduced the same symptoms and the same iris signs.

High supplementary synthetic vitamins may make you *feel* wonderful; but the iris records a much better and more permanent change if the vitamins are obtained from the more whole and balanced sources of foods and herbs.

3. FEMALE, 57 YEARS, LEFT IRIS

Photograph 3 is as near to a Silk iris as you'll ever find. See the overall sheen and the white thin fibres close together— and that tiny pupil with its neurasthenic ring so brown and obvious. A lovely lady, strong and bright. 'Easy-going, I am,' she told me, as she presented with galloping osteo-arthritis in lower spine, knees, elbows, and feet! A little conversation proved her to be a total *absorber* of stresses, large and small, to avoid hurting or upsetting those less able to bear them than herself—a direct route to emotionally based arthritis. She sings happily to her grandchildren, runs the legal office with an unshakeable smile, and wall-papers her ceiling in extreme pain from back, elbows, and knees. Truly a Silk, and now suffering from calcified nodes and spurs as her body registers its mineral imbalance.

See the strong nerve wreath flaring white? This patient is like a jumping-jack, her spine propels her into constant activity.

'I like to be busy,' she said brightly.

'Your body can still be busy if we get those mineral salts out of your joints,' I reassured her; 'but it would help your body to do this if you would stop taking burdens *unnecessarily* from other people's shoulders and loading up your own spine, knees, and feet.'

'Isn't that what life's about?' She looked puzzled.

'Very few people are able to carry *all* the burdens of those around them and escape an overload,' I told her.

After several months of treatment, she saw some sense in

this, but still felt 'guilty' if she sat in the sun for a few hours and read a book. Silks take a lot of convincing that their loads are getting too heavy.

The yellow lymph spot over the back is giving her no physical trauma. I feel some of the 'arthritis' is of a different sort, and that this woman could be quite fiery if she ever lost control of her stress absorption. 'Slow to anger' she may be; but on behalf of someone else I feel she could be quite a tiger. She had a lifelong history of unexplainable 'anaemia' (underfunction of the spleen).

'You never got angry enough to defend yourself,' I told her.

She smiled. 'It might have upset people too much. I can take it all, they can't.'

It can be difficult to remove arthritis from Silks!

The iris is a good clear blue, but the white fibres and flares pale it. No brown or yellowish digestive patterns show at all. She is burning up her fuel in physical use, and excreting food wastes efficiently.

4. MALE, 22 YEARS, LEFT IRIS

This young gentleman has a classic 'hard drugs' iris (photograph 4). He was a heroin addict for three years. Note the totally brown nerve wreath, flaring brown at the head, and with gaps (also at the head), and much doubling, especially over the bronchial tree, and irregularity of the nerve wreath over the spine (7.30-8.30). The greyish, closed-off 'aura' at the iris rim records his physical and emotional detachment from people and circumstances, a usual post-addiction symptom. He *says* he no longer uses the drug. I feel this may not be the truth, since his recent history of liver disorders, spleen enlargement (4.15 white raised fibres), and testes/pelvis inflammation (5.00-5.15), are signs often shown in the iris *during* heroin use. The multiple dark nerve rings are another hard-drug reaction often recorded in the iris.

Don't panic if your iris looks like this and you've never

even had a sip of alcohol, let alone drugs of any description. Certainly don't suspect a friend or one of the family if an iris looks like this, *without asking all those questions* so necessary in using the iris as a diagnostic tool. It may only be spinal arthritis, lots of pain with it, and the heavy medical drugs taken to subdue it, that you are seeing recorded there. It needs an expert to separate the finer details, but you *can* say, 'Your physical nervous system is toxic; your muscles and many organs are in tight spasms and cramps and pain; you are not relating to people too well; and you are easily irritated and angry.' That white-hot spleen! 'You could have a too-fast or too-slow pattern of energy and weight loss or gain, and you never know which speed you are going to be at, hyper-active or dead stopped.' (A psoric spot over thyroid in the 'organ itself' part of the thyroid zone.)

See how the patient's feedback is so necessary to *accurate* iris analysis?

This young man wished his *herpes genitalia* to be treated. An increasing problem is the resistance to treatment of this nerve affliction, involving a viral irritation with blisters, on the genitals of both males and females. The alternating vague brown and then white zones between groin, pelvis, and testes, together with the psoric spot near the nerve wreath in this zone, and the deep fibre lesion beside it, could add up to a need for prolonged treatment, which still might not eradicate the problem completely.

The lesions and distension of the nerve wreath at 3.00-3.30 still record a childhood dogged by bronchitis and pneumonia.

5. FEMALE, 25 YEARS, LEFT IRIS

Of all the pupils I have ever seen, this was the largest! (Photograph 5.) The lady made and broke three appointments, saying she was too exhausted to get there. At the fourth attempt, her husband drove her, and one look at her irises, even without a torch, confirmed her very real exhaustion. Organs and the blood and nerve supply to them were so overshadowed by the pupil size that accurate reading of the iris was very difficult. In such a case, to overcome the physical depletion first, I give herbs high in iron, tonic and stimulant tinctures and extracts mixed together.

This patient had one child, and had haemorrhaged badly after the birth, never 'feeling right' since. That wide yellowish lymphatic fog at the spleen (4.30) and poor circulation to it, have been recording sub-clinical anaemia. The circulation in the lower parts of the body (brown iris rim from 5.00 to 6.30) gave her 'numb legs which collapsed like rubber', she told me. The fuzzy outside rim of the whole iris showed severe circulation slowness and therefore low oxygenation. She was half-way up Mt Everest permanently, trying vainly to get enough from several dozen cups of black coffee daily to keep her feet moving at all!

She demanded a 'miracle' fix: 'I've got to be right within a few weeks,' she said, 'or my husband won't let me come back.' I gave her the most powerful herbs I could for the problem, but explained it would certainly take more than a few weeks. She didn't return. Patients often expect from naturopaths the 'miracles' they haven't received from long medical treatment. Time, and change of the circumstances producing the problem, are both required for naturopathic treatment to produce its very real permanent best effects.

6. MALE, 46 YEARS, RIGHT IRIS

Here is the white calcium ring of a man who has never used common salt in his life! (Photograph 6.) Many iridologists go 'by the book' on such indications, and are puzzled as to how such a sign can appear when 'the book' says its cause is dietary alone. Look always at the iris as a picture of the body. Here is a man with a clinical history of a 'stroke' which later was discovered to be a tumour on the brain-stem, right side. Think of what such pressure has produced in the circulation, and the calcium ring becomes an accurate record of arterial hardening, especially visible at head and chest areas. The brownish patch, not quite a psoric spot, over the 1 o'clock zone, shows the tumour site. Lymph glands were removed from the groin some months before (some scar tissue under psoric spot at groin, 6.15). The misnamed 'stroke' produced eye and upper jaw loss of function (small healing lesions at 1.20-1.30) and visual disturbance (same psoric spot overlaps to eye zone adjacent). Many psoric spots around the iris— especially at neck and shoulder (10.00-10.30), hand and arm to lower ribs (around 8 o'clock), bladder (4.30), and anxiety area (11.35)—are recording inefficient functional recognition in these body areas. The patient does not appear worried by his severe illness patterns.

It is seldom that all psoric spots go into 'trouble' at once; but in this case a massive health attack has come from all sides. Herbalist/naturopaths are by law not allowed to treat cancer. We can only support this patient's body functions to give him greater efficiency and a better fighting chance.

7. MALE, 27 YEARS, RIGHT IRIS

A former rheumatism sufferer (photograph 7). A good example of 'healing lines'. The fibre lesions at 11.00, 1.00, 8.00-9.00 had been 'darned' well after good chiropractic and acupuncture treatment before this photograph was taken. The patient now wanted herbal medicine to clear the 'dull pain' he said afflicted his shoulder still. This photograph shows one undarned lesion at the spine (4 o'clock). I gave him a herbal mixture containing the calcium phosphate and magnesium phosphate and silica that he needed, in natural form, to supplement the physical removal of his symptoms chiropractically.

He has had low blood pressure (small string of faded lesions through nerve wreath at 12.30), which I suspect to have been caused from low-ego causes. The physical frustration shown in the zig-zag fibre pattern came from his being tied to a desk job in advertising when he has a potential

Linen structure underneath (and the desire, unsupported by his wife, to be a farmer). His thick white nerve wreath is cramped into a square, almost, by that hated square desk he sits at all day.

The original fibre lesions were acquired when a trampoline accident as a child tumbled his now very large bones about at the back, shoulder, and right side of the neck and head. The *left* shoulder pain he now had was the last residue of his body's structural re-balancing after the accident.

The fuzzy colour of the iris rim over all the head area confirms his 'slowness' (says his wife) to think, concentrate, and remember. Hard physical exercise would pump the blood up there much more efficiently and remove most of this problem. Good overall colour reflects his equally good diet over many years.

8. FEMALE, 24 YEARS, RIGHT IRIS

This lass was brought along forcibly by one of her friends. Her apathy and total disconnection with circumstances around her was pathologically obvious in the first five seconds. It was recorded in the iris as the total greying, almost to black, of the outer rim and the 'aura' (photograph 8). I asked her her problems. She said, 'Asthma, coughing, and tiredness.' Her friends said she had been hospitalised for a psychiatric disorder, and had been released as OK one week before I saw her. She had done nothing but stare at the wall and sleep ever since.

The iris here records an old inguinal hernia (almost healed), a sore right ankle and a foot which was 'tender' (lymph spot), and a few zig-zag fibres here and there. The frightening *radii solaris* to the head, the almost totally 'toxic' nervous system with deep brown and some white nerve rings all around, recorded a long history of psychiatric disturbances and hospitalisation.

I questioned her about her daily routines—bowels, urine, appetite, sleep. She had few answers until I inquired about her emotional and sexual life.

'I don't believe in all that,' she answered with a martyred smile. 'I'm religious.'

Her left iris (not shown) recorded adrenal stasis, piled-up anger in a white-fogged spleen with a *radii solaris* through it, and more *radii solaris* to every part of the head. In her right iris, her former lack of adrenal function and its slow recovery shows in a darning lesion at 5.40. The only *active* areas are the bronchial tree and lung, and the liver and diaphragm. The liver is trying hard to throw off her drug medication and the lung painfully coping with deep-seated asthma (nerve wreath almost reverse-curved between 8.00 and 9.30). The rest of her body is in toxic stasis.

I gave her a powerful herbal mixture to try to pull her out of it all and back to living; but that grey-black head area in the right iris was too strong. She committed suicide three days later.

Don't panic if your dark-brown eye looks superficially like this one. You may only be suffering from a spastic colon, weight increase, and a bad skin. How necessary the patient is in the *interpretation* of what is recorded in an iris!

9. MALE, 29 YEARS, LEFT IRIS

Here is a 'healthy' iris (photograph 9), except that its owner can't sleep! When you look at all that white head-energy up there, can you wonder? He lies for hours, can't turn his thoughts off, and the slightest noise as he's drifting off will wake him again to more hours of 'trying to get to sleep'. See the faint and irregular dark break through the nerve wreath at 11.45? Not only is his transverse colon sometimes too speedy and sometimes too slow, but his movements are jerky, tight, and awkward (locomotor zone).

He has low blood pressure and low blood supply to the head (faded iris colour); but the blue 'aura' outside this and all around the iris records his clear rosy skin and his good interaction with people and surroundings. The doubling of the otherwise strong nerve wreath tells of long-term marihuana use. I chided him.

'It helps me to *sleep!*' he protested.

'We'll find a better way to do that,' I promised him. 'It's a shame to have to disconnect and scramble that good head of yours as a way of producing sleep.'

He admitted his concentration and drive had dropped as well. The tiny psoric spot on the white solar plexus zone recorded an intermittent hiatal hernia as well as 'bad vibes', he said, about change. When he *did* change the timing was always wrong; when he didn't he missed good opportunities.

A thin dark streak through the upper jaw area recorded his teeth-grinding while asleep.

10. FEMALE, 70 YEARS, LEFT IRIS

A typical glaucoma incision, neatly done and well healed (photograph 10)—*but* this lady has now developed speech difficulties, 'senile' loss of mental faculties, say her doctors, and a blood pressure that fluctuates wildly up and down. None of these symptoms was evident before the operation.

She was formerly a bright perky lady, happy with her children and grandchildren, working hard in her garden and loving all her neighbours and friends with equal kindnesses. Her beautiful near-Silk iris since birth, with its tight but broad and active nerve wreath, records her control of her body under many other pressures until the 'pressure' of glaucoma proved her one structural weak spot. The orange stains, from bladder to kidney and groin, record much aspirin taken for chronic cystitis—which she 'forgot' to mention to anyone; and the larger orange patch at 4 o'clock also records aspirin taken for 'rheumatism' in the hands and arms.

She felt 'a bit stiff', she said, and a few yellowish and white lymphatic spots show her rusting outside armour, due to her unaccustomed and enforced inactivity since her post-operative symptoms of blood pressure variation appeared.

She had come to me, at her family's insistence, for a 'simple' herbal treatment for her blood pressure. I had to tell her it could not be stabilised by me or anyone else now—not with that big black hole there in her iris.

I felt I had let her down. 'There's always a way, dear,' she said pleadingly. 'Not now, unfortunately,' I told her again. I spent more time explaining, but her former keen mind could only vaguely comprehend such a strange hypothesis. I sent her off with tonic herbs to support and balance function and circulation as much as possible within the limits of her new pattern.

11. FEMALE, 25 YEARS, RIGHT IRIS

'What's the problem?' I asked this lady.

'Oh, just a general check,' she answered. 'I feel I could be a lot healthier.'

Where to start on an iris like this one? (Photograph 11.) She couldn't have been more *un*healthy if she had worked hard at it. Answers to my questions were monosyllabic. 'Bowels?' I queried. 'OK.' 'Stress?' 'I guess everyone has that,' she hedged.

I quit being polite and said, 'Lady, you're in one hell of a mess!'

She burst into tears, and out came a story of everything from being raped at eight years of age to wind and sharp abdominal pains for the last four years!

'I need to know all these things before I can get your pattern accurately assessed,' I told her much more gently.

'I'm just out of practice,' she apologised. 'My husband can't stand to hear me complain about *anything*, so I keep it all bottled up' Her iris confirms this!

We started with the head *radii solaris* (sexual area, anxiety area, ego, and speech zones).

'My husband believes sex is for procreation only, so we only have intercourse once a month after my period, when it's safe. 'He doesn't want a child for two years yet.' (I would hate to see her husband's irises!)

We continued with the *radii solaris* to the mental ability zone.

'My husband thinks my job is suitable. We need money for a house.' She was an insurance company clerk.

'Are you trained for anything else?' I wanted to know.

'I was doing commercial art. I loved it. But there's no money in it.'

Her uterus zone showed a psoric spot and *radii solaris* through it. She confessed to having had a pregnancy termination done, without her husband's knowledge, several months before. What a 'doormat' lady!

Her nerve wreath is obscured by brown muck and broken by that 'Crown of Thorns' she has put on. High acid waste levels appear in a yellow fog underneath. Her skin is the best part of her body, and even though the nice blue 'aura' that appears here and there shows she is living as she is for an unselfish reason, her body will soon explode into major illness by sheer pressure from within.

Another psoric spot covers the ovary, and the bronchial tree shows an open lesion of catarrh, and congestion structurally. She breathes shallowly and quickly.

We started in on treatment. She rang me a few days later.

'My husband won't let me take this mixture. He says there's nothing wrong with me, like you say there is.'

I felt very sad. 'It's *your* choice,' I said.

12. FEMALE, 33 YEARS, RIGHT IRIS

Here is another lady with everything against her (photograph 12); but she is beginning her battle to get well, and has made the choice of naturopathic treatment. She has had a tumour removed from the thyroid. She has been on hard drugs of all kinds for years. She has given up a legal career and spent time in psychiatric hospitals. Now she has had enough, and is making positive steps towards regaining health. This photograph was taken on her first visit.

Note the nerve wreath irregularity and the two healing lesions with the white band of scar tissue between them at the thyroid zone. There are also brown lymphatic beads all around, but especially at the thyroid and throat zones.

A *radii solaris* shows in the speech and mental segments. That legal practice is sorely missed! A greyish fog on the kidney area and the inflamed liver with the open fibre lesion are results of the former hard-drug usage. (She had serum hepatitis at one stage.) The highly irregular nerve wreath is physically reflected in her posture (she seems too rigid in some spots and too floppy in others). The medulla zone is brown, but the few white nerve rings appearing generally in the iris record her resolve to regain control and do something positive. The brown rubbish showing still in the bladder which has almost healed its adjacent structural lesion (the sacrum has been posturally corrected with chiropractic treatment) will eventually be drained from the area. The toxic wastes will be eliminated by those hard-working lymph glands, still loaded with the results of past sins but busily clearing the eye from the inside towards the outside. I feel she will recover her health, but much elimination must first be done of that brown residual biochemical rubbish and she will feel quite 'off' for many weeks yet as her body works extremely hard to regain its homoeostasis.

Her closed-off 'aura' has also been productive of pathological withdrawal symptoms. She is to have counselling and gentle supportive boosting. Regular massage over the period of elimination will help to move body fluids around, tone tissues, and hasten the 'undoing', uncomfortable part of treatment, as well as improve the circulation to the skin.

Her iris will gradually clear from the inside to the outside, as will her body, and her final elimination may be lumps, boils, cysts, and itching, plus an increase in perspiration as her 'outside layer' becomes 'clean'.

13. FEMALE, 41 YEARS, LEFT IRIS

This patient is a textbook classic of iridology (photograph 13). Even without her personal confirmation, her story can be read accurately on iris evidence alone. She presented with a history of strange lifelong symptoms of balance-loss (*radii solaris* through the equilibrium zone at 12.45); two lumps on her neck (vague fibre lesion at 1.50 and a brown lymph spot at the end of it); *radii solaris* through the pituitary zone a long the edge of the self-image zone (she doesn't have the energy to 'worry people' with her problems); dark lesion and retracted nerve wreath at the solar plexus (her mother had recently died of a brain tumour and she was now terrified of her 'neck lumps' being diagnosed as malignant).

The red/brown discoloration area covers the aorta and heart zones and the lesions through the nerve wreath at these zones show her 'heart-sick' grief at her beloved mother's death as well as her own recent shortness of breath. Deep brown nerve rings from 2.30 to 4.00 also show chest tightness.

A small fibre lesion confirms that her left ovary is structurally poor (5.00), and another almost healed lesion in the spleen zone—mid-zone and therefore referring to the organ itself—still registers her recent anger at her mother's untimely death (4.15).

Her right iris (not shown) records her inability to conceive in eight years of trying. A psoric spot covers the uterus zone, and chronic cystitis registers with another psoric spot covering the bladder area.

Such an easily read iris seldom presents itself in the day of an iridologist.

Can you see one more *radii solaris* pointing through the speech zone at 11.25? Not only did this lady not want to 'worry' others by talking of her own problems: she found it difficult to explain why she had come to an iridologist at all.

14. FEMALE, 47 YEARS, RIGHT IRIS

Because of its many tiny fibre irregularities, this iris is as difficult to read as the iris in the preceding case was easy (photograph 14). It often helps an iridologist to narrow his or her eyes slightly when viewing an iris, to bring into more obvious contrast the most important *differences* visible—just as an artist, sighting his subject through half-squinting eyes, sees contrasts and tones more quickly and easily. Looking at this iris in this manner brings forward two parallel lesions in the transverse colon (12.30 and 12.45) as being most 'different' from the remainder of the iris with its strong but zig-zagged Linen structure and near-perfect colour. The patient presented with abdominal discomfort and a swollen 'tummy'. She complained of stiffness and chronic clumsiness, more pronounced when she was tired (a half-darned lesion between movement and vitality zones at 11.50), and of anxiety all through a bad marriage in which sexual activity had been absent altogether for four years (multiple tiny lesions on the border of the sexual and anxiety zones at 11.30).

She had had meningitis several months before (disturbed fibres at the neck zone and an exaggerated whitish spot near the iris rim; slight flattening of the iris rim over this zone).

Difficult to see, under the eyelid, which the patient is holding up with a finger, is a vague paler area indicative of her very low blood pressure. The brownish drug accumulations at uterus and vaginal zones record some ten years' usage of the contraceptive pill.

The whiteness of the fibres and the clear overall blue colour show her abounding vitality and very good general health, but the faintly discernible nerve wreath here and there, as well as gaps through it, show she is better advised to use her energy in short, sharp bursts, since sudden tiring may be caused by irregular nerve supply from the spine itself to many body functions.

Photographs to Illustrate the Case Histories

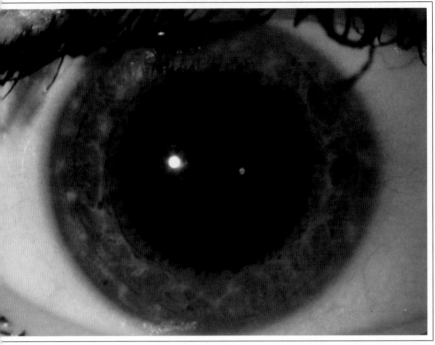

1a. Female, 21 years, right iris (p.219)

1b. Female, 21 years, right iris, six months later (p.220)

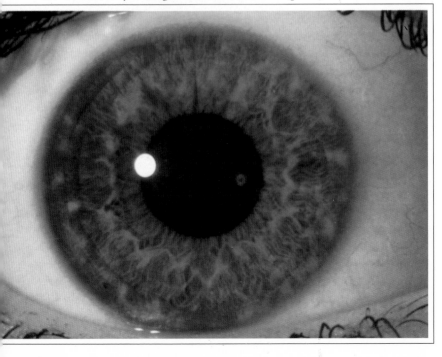

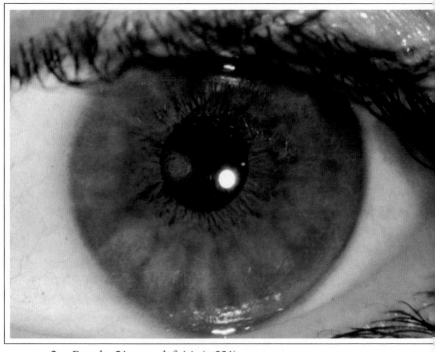

2a. Female, 51 years, left iris (p.221)

2b. Female, 51 years, left iris, six months later (p.221)

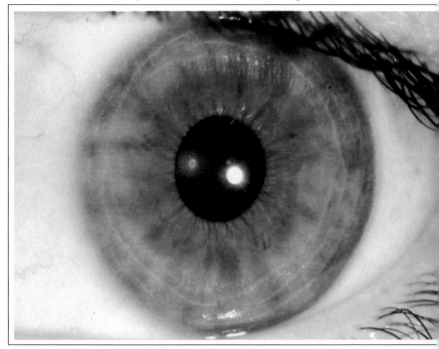

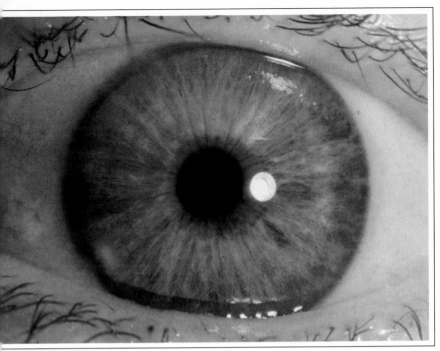

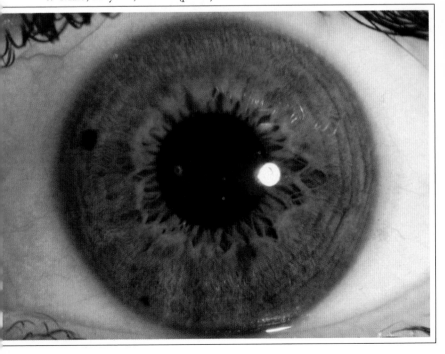

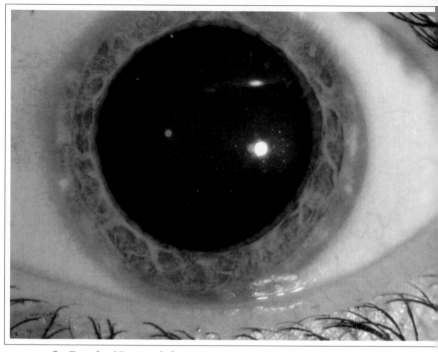

5. Female, 25 years, left iris (p.224)
6. Male, 46 years, right iris (p.225)

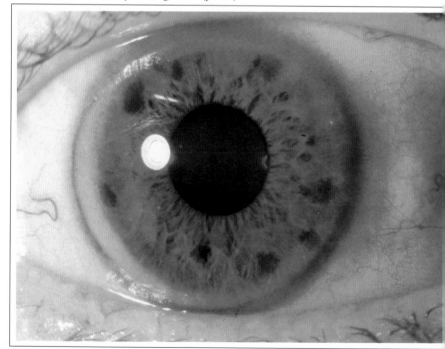

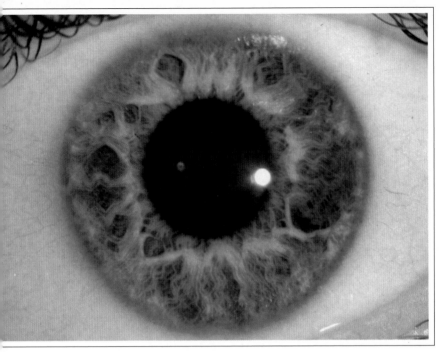

7. Male, 27 years, right iris (p.226)
8. Female, 24 years, right iris (p.227)

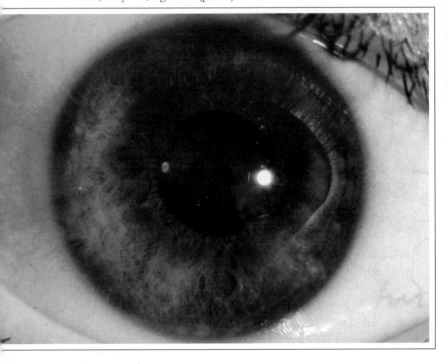

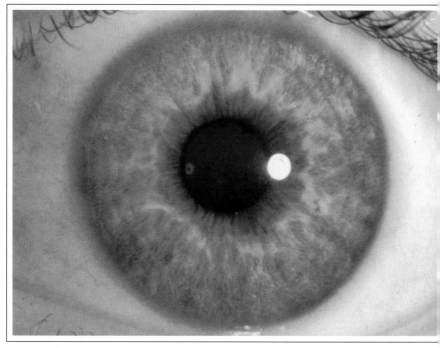

9. Male, 29 years, left iris (p.228)

10. Female, 70 years, left iris (p.229)

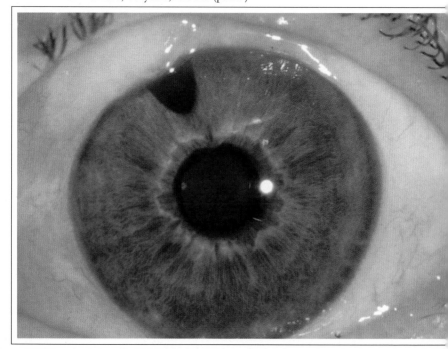

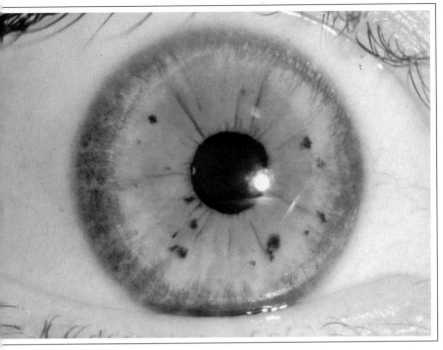

11. Female, 25 years, right iris (p.230)
12. Female, 33 years, right iris (p.231)

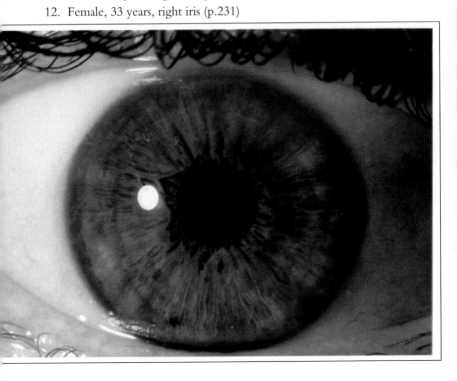

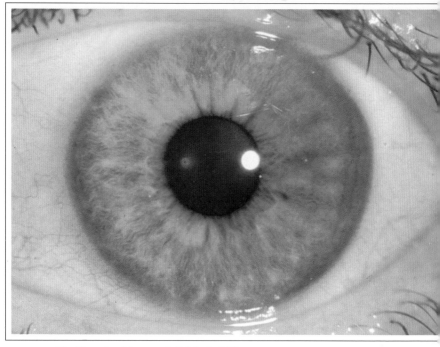

13. Female, 41 years, left iris (p.233)
14. Female, 47 years, right iris (p.234)

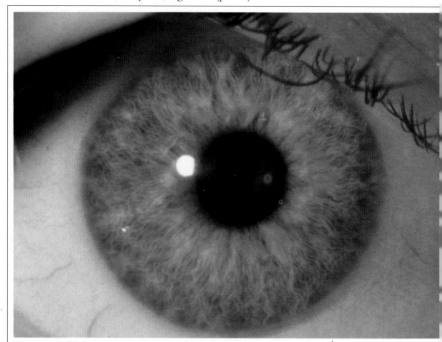

INDEX

INDEX

*Page numbers in **bold** type refer to main entries*

For further information about iridology, including training courses and registered practitioners in the UK, contact:

The British Society of Iridologists
40 Stokewood Road
Bournemouth
Dorset BH3 7NE
Tel: 0202 529793

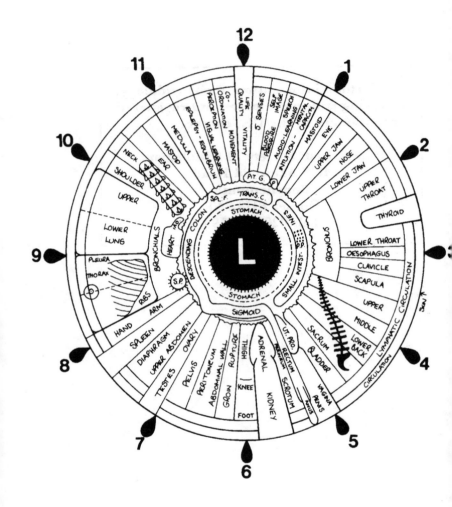

The Iris Map, left eye
(*mirror image of one's own left eye*)

* Iris clock must be transposed,
e.g. 10 o'clock becomes 2 o'clock,
4 o'clock becomes 8 o'clock, and so on.

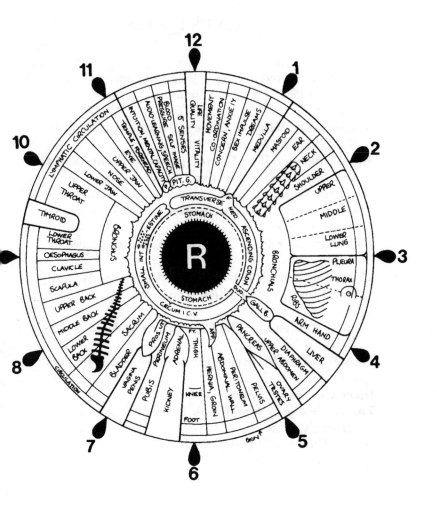

The Iris Map, right eye
(*mirror image of one's own right eye*)

* Iris clock must be transposed, e.g. 10 o'clock becomes 2 o'clock, 4 o'clock becomes 8 o'clock, and so on.

PIATKUS BOOKS

If you have enjoyed reading iridology, you may be interested in other books Piatkus publish on health and healing.

Acupressure: How to Cure Common Ailments the Natural Way Michael Reed Gach

Aromatherapy: The Encyclopedia of Plants and Oils and How They Help You Daniele Ryman

Arthritis Relief at Your Fingertips: How to Use Acupressure Massage to Ease Your Aches and Pains Michael Reed Gach

The Encyclopedia of Alternative Health Care Kristin Olsen

The Good Health Food Guide: Which Foods and Supplements Will Boost Your Health Dr Eric Trimmer

Herbal Remedies: The Complete Guide to Natural Healing Jill Nice

Homeopathic Medicine for Children and Infants Dana Ullman

Increase Your Energy Louis Proto

The Reflexology Handbook Laura Norman and Thomas Cowan

Stress Control Through Self-Hypnosis Dr Arthur Jackson

For a free brochure with further information on our full range of titles, please write to:

Piatkus Books
Freepost 7 (WD 4505)
London W1E 4EZ